I0651976

Hollywood's Image of the South

Recent Titles in
Bibliographies and Indexes in the Performing Arts

Censorship and Hollywood's Hispanic Image: An Interpretive Filmography, 1936–1955
Alfred Charles Richard, Jr.

A Guide to American Silent Crime Films
Larry Langman and Daniel Finn

Contemporary Hollywood's Negative Hispanic Image: An Interpretive Filmography, 1956–1993
Alfred Charles Richard, Jr.

Theatre at Stratford-upon-Avon, First Supplement: A Catalogue-Index to Productions of the Royal Shakespeare Company, 1979–1993
Michael Mullin

A Guide to American Crime Films of the Thirties
Larry Langman and Daniel Finn

An Index to Short and Feature Film Reviews in the Moving Picture World: The Early Years, 1907–1915
Annette M. D'Agostino, compiler

A Guide to American Crime Films of the Forties and Fifties
Larry Langman and Daniel Finn

Theatrical Design in the Twentieth Century: An Index to Photographic Reproductions of Scenic Designs
W. Patrick Atkinson

American Film Cycles: The Silent Era
Larry Langman

A Guide to Charlie Chan Films
Charles P. Mitchell

Productions of the Irish Theatre Movement, 1899–1916: A Checklist
Nelson O'Ceallaigh Ritschel

The Complete H.P. Lovecraft Filmography
Charles P. Mitchell

Hollywood's Image of the South

A Century of Southern Films

Compiled by
Larry Langman and David Ebner

Bibliographies and Indexes in the Performing Arts, Number 25

GREENWOOD PRESS
Westport, Connecticut • London

Library of Congress Cataloging-in-Publication Data

Langman, Larry.

Hollywood's image of the South : a century of southern films / compiled by Larry Langman and David Ebner.

p. cm.—(Bibliographies and indexes in the performing arts, ISSN 0742–6933 : no. 25)

Includes indexes.

ISBN 0–313–31886–7 (alk. paper)

1. Southern States—In motion pictures. I. Ebner, David. II. Title. III. Series.

PN1995.9.S66L36 2001

791.43′6275—dc21 2001033997

British Library Cataloguing in Publication Data is available.

Library of Congress Catalog Card Number: 2001033997
ISBN: 0–313–31886–7
ISSN: 0742–6933

First published in 2001

Greenwood Press, 88 Post Road West, Westport, CT 06881
An imprint of Greenwood Publishing Group, Inc.
www.greenwood.com

Printed in the United States of America

The paper used in this book complies with the Permanent Paper Standard issued by the National Information Standards Organization (Z39.48–1984).

10 9 8 7 6 5 4 3 2

The first time my Mama saw all done up with blond bleached hair all piled up, and my lips, cheeks, and nails as red as I could get them, she screamed to the Lord, 'Why are you testing me this way?' And she told me the Devil must have made me do it. 'Heck no,' I told Mama. 'Let's give credit where it's due. I did this all myself.'

Dolly Parton

Robert De Niro, as a vindictive killer, enlightens his victim: 'You're scared. But that's O.K. I want you to savor that fear. The South was born in fear. Fear of the Indian, fear of the slave, fear of the damn Union. The South has a fine tradition of savoring fear.'

Cape Fear (1991)

'There's a growing number of people in this part of the country that regard us in the South as not only geographically beneath them. They ignore the fact that slavery is so interwoven in the fabric of this society that to destroy it would be to destroy us as a people. It's immoral, that's all they know, so are we – immoral and inferior . . . . We're not as wealthy as our Northern neighbors. We're still struggling. Well, we all know what happens then – North and South. What President wants to be in office when it all comes crashing down around him?'

Senator John C. Calhoun, in *Armistad* (1997)

Contents

Preface

In this book, we seek to establish the "southern" as a legitimate film genre. The South has always held a unique place in the American mind. Just as the West was perceived in a particular way, the South had its own hold on our imagination. To what extent these stereotypes were the product of the movie industry or were arrived at independently, will never be fully answered. Nevertheless, to underestimate the influence of Hollywood in determining these images would be a mistake.

A "western" movie is instantly recognizable. A western has lots of space, Indians and/or outlaws. It usually pits a lonesome individual against a group of bullies or predators. A "southern" is a bit subtler. When we categorize a film as a "southern," we mean to say that it has passed the "Confederate test." The action either takes place *at any time* in one of the states that composed the Confederacy or else it takes place during the Civil War in some other state but Southern troops are involved.

Southern films span the gamut of musicals, dramas, comedies and mysteries and Hollywood has produced them ever since the silent era. In the early days, the movie industry was in a bind. It couldn't very well condemn the South for its institution of slavery and its secession from the Union for fear of losing the large Southern audience. On the other hand, it couldn't approve of these practices for fear of alienating the rest of the country, so the industry had to very carefully weigh its options.

This work cites and describes several hundred films set in the Old South and the New South. The entries are arranged alphabetically, printed in boldface and appear within the framework of the chapter.

Several film entries include historical references or background information. These end with an asterisk to help separate them from the next film entry.

Each entry features the title, the year of release, the distributing company, the director, a brief commentary on the work and, if applicable, the title and author of the original work. A complete Title Index should help the reader locate individual titles discussed in the book.

Several persons have contributed to the final manuscript and deserve recognition. They include Shoshana Kaufmann, Coordinator of Information Services at Queens College, Flushing, New York; Lisa Flanzraich of the Reference Department and Richard Wall of the Theatre and Film Reference Library at Queens College.

To others whose contribution is ongoing – Stuart Ebner, Steven Ebner, Emily Ebner – thank you for your contributions.

We greatly appreciate the efforts of Barbara Blanchard for her many helpful suggestions.

Introduction

Ever since the Civil War, the South has held a particular fascination for the American public. For outsiders, the South was always viewed as a strange and exotic place with its own particular mores and codes. Residents tended to agree and were especially proud of that difference.

Writers and Hollywood studios seized and exploited this attraction and they began producing books and films describing in detail all areas of life in the region. At first, in the nineteenth and early twentieth centuries, these stories and films were highly laudatory. However, as time went on, both books and films became more and more critical. Nevertheless, throughout all of these re-evaluations, we continued to be mesmerized by the South.

Antebellum Southern literature described certain traits and ideals of the culture and society of the Old South. Southern aristocrats looked to the English author Sir Walter Scott for inspiration and they adopted his descriptions of the English court in the Middle Ages and transplanted them to the American South. Their chivalrous code and the romantic idealization of Southern women stemmed directly from Scott. John P. Kennedy, the author of *Swallow Barn* (1832), carried on this tradition and he was the best-known American writer responsible for promoting the myth of the plantation as medieval manor.

Early film directors such as D.W. Griffith, E. Mason Hopper and Paul Sloane appropriated the fiction of the plantation as the embodiment of all things pure and good and portrayed it on the screen. In this version, the master of the plantation was handsome and honorable and his wife was supportive of both him and her family. She was a virgin on her wedding night and remained true to her only love, her husband. In fact, she was the glue that kept her Christian family together. The slaves were benevolently treated and they just loved to "lift that cotton and tote that bale." In fact, they were so happy, they sang while they worked!

The epic Southern film of all time, *Gone With the Wind* (1939), although basically concerned with the Civil War and its effects, tangentially touched upon the plantation system as a veritable Garden of Eden.

Harriet Beecher Stowe's novel *Uncle Tom's Cabin* was adapted for the screen in 1903 and it was one of the very few early films to condemn the institution of slavery and to critically examine the Southern plantation that gave birth to it. At the time, the film was an aberration because, until the 1940s, most Hollywood productions took a very benevolent view of the plantation system.

The Civil War presented both an opportunity and a challenge for the movie industry. On one hand, the entire country was captivated by this period in American history. On the other hand, sectional animosities were still strong and a favorable treatment of Southern conduct during the war would alienate movie audiences in the rest of the country while unfavorable treatment would alienate Southern audiences.

What was Hollywood to do? In general, film studios treated Abraham Lincoln with kid gloves. They decided to depict Lincoln as a tragic figure with the full burden of the war on his shoulders. He was portrayed in numerous silent and sound features and virtually all of these productions portrayed him with compassion and sympathy.

In contrast to this treatment of the Union President, Southern soldiers were usually portrayed more sympathetically than their Northern counterparts. Southern officers were pictured as professional soldiers who were defending their own land against invaders. Northern officers and soldiers were usually pictured as ruffians and invaders. No where is this portrayed more dramatically than in film versions of Lee's surrender to Grant at Appomattox. The contrast between the two generals could not be sharper. Lee, tall, handsome, immaculately groomed, a flashing sword at his side, always appears astride his white charger to meet his victor. Grant appears in his "working clothes," his boots dappled with mud, a private's coat with his stars tacked on thrown over a rumpled shirt and bearing no sword. Nevertheless, by some strange quirk of fate, the plain man from nowhere was able to humble a glamorous representative of a fading aristocracy.

Beginning in the 1930s, a group of indigenous Southern writers began to turn the ideal picture of the South on its head. In place of the happy society described by earlier authors, these new writers portrayed a very dysfunctional world. The studios were quick to film William Faulkner's *The Sound and the Fury* (1959) and *Sanctuary* (1961), Tennesee William's *A Streetcar Named Desire* (1951) and *Baby Doll* (1956), Lillian Hellman's *Toys in the Attic* (1963) and Carson McCullers' *Reflections in a Golden Eye* (1967). All of these films painted a bizarre world of gloom, peopled by demented characters who lived in crumbling mansions.

Once these Southern writers began destroying the myth of an idyllic society, together with the fiction of Southern "family values," a flood of books and movies appeared critically examining all other facets of Southern life. By the mid-1950s, raw realism in Southern literature in the United States largely replaced romantic sentimentality. Whereas earlier writers and films treated the plantation system and slavery lightly and often even favorably, new books and movies were openly critical. Post World War II films such as Raoul Walsh's pre-Civil War drama *Band of Angels* (1957), Michael Curtiz's *Adventure of Huckelberry Finn* (1960) and Julie Dash's historical drama *Daughters of the Dust* (1991) realistically depicted the institution of slavery. Steven Spielberg's *Armistad* (1998) continued the trend of critically examining the horrors of slavery. Other films critically examined racism, white supremacy, the chain gang segregation and discrimination. Unfortunately, these films tended to focus on Southern problems and ignored the same issues in the rest of the country.

Perhaps films about the American Civil War continue to fascinate us because of the continuing social, ethnic and religious conflicts throughout the world. Roland Flamini, in his study, *Scarlett, Rhett, and a Cast of Thousands: The Filming of Gone With the Wind*, emphasizes the film's strange but universal appeal. Flamini notes that 75 years after the American Civil War, Londoners, who were being bombarded by German V-2 rockets in 1939 – the same year the film was released – identified with the Confederacy as portrayed in *Gone With the Wind.* At the same time, conquered peoples in occupied mainland Europe began to empathize with Scarlett O'Hara as a symbol of resistance, so the Nazis banned both the novel and the film.

Abbreviations

AA	Allied Artists
AI	American International Pictures
ARC	American Releasing Company
BV	Buena Vista
Col.	Columbia
DCA	Distributors Corporation of America
EL	Eagle Lion
FC	Film Classics
MGM	Metro-Goldwyn-Mayer
Mon.	Monogram
Par.	Paramount
PRC	Producers Releasing Corporation
Rep.	Republic
RKO	Radio-Keith-Orpheum
TCF	Twentieth Century-Fox
U	Universal
UA	United Artists
UI	Universal-International
WB	Warner Bros.
Dir.	Director
Sc.	Screenwriter
Unc.	Uncredited

Hollywood's Image of the South

1

Plantation Life and the Cotton Fields Back Home

When we think of the antebellum South, we usually conjure up images of vast plantations, with hundreds of slaves working the cotton fields. Films like Victor Fleming's sweeping historical drama *Gone With the Wind* (1939), with its huge cast of thousands and its pictorial Georgian mansions, have contributed immensely to these images.

The reality was that the vast majority of white residents of the South were independent or yeomen farmers while a larger number of blacks lived as slaves on small farms, rather than on large plantations. According to the 1860 U.S. Census, approximately 1,250,000 white families resided in the Southern states. Of these families, about 380,000 owned one or more slaves and only about 45,000 owned 20 or more slaves and were thus able to be classified as "planters."

Once again, contrary to myth, most planters and their wives did not enjoy easy lives. Wives of plantation owners were not ladies of leisure. They spent most of their time supervising the black slaves who served as cooks, weavers or gardeners. Any extra time was devoted to caring for sick family members and slaves or delivering babies. Only the very wealthy aristocrats of the planter class were able to luxuriate in a life of leisure. Although planters as a class were probably better off than the majority of independent farmers, most were constantly in debt and their crops often failed. After a number of years of planting cotton, the fertility of the land often gave out and the planters had to uproot their slaves and their families and move West to more productive areas. In most cases, the majority of planters owned various plots of land in non-contiguous areas, requiring them to travel between these properties.

Besides Sir Walter Scott, John P. Kennedy, one of the privileged members of the Virginia aristocracy, was most responsible for promoting the myth of the plantation as medieval manor. However, whereas the Englishman's work was appropriated and used as propaganda to defend a completely alien social system, Kennedy was an indigenous Southerner who wrote *Swallow Barn* (1832) to specifically defend plantation life. To him, it was the successor to all that was good in medieval times – namely, honesty, good fellowship, family and honor.

In general, plantation aristocrats were hospitable to any visitors. Plantations were usually located in remote areas, and owners welcomed any diversion from the usual farming routines. Since planters' families were essentially removed from the rest of the community, visitors often provided entertainment, news and a link with the outside world. The plantation owners followed the Old Testament guidelines for welcoming strangers as a prescription for their own generous hospitality.

In their portraits of the "Old South," creators of literature and films often "followed the money" and the money led to the wealthy planter class. This offered more fascination and entertainment when compared to the simple, prosaic lives of the numerous poorer planters and independent Southern farmers.

*

Since the earliest days of the silent film, various releases of Harriet Beecher Stowe's famous novel, *Uncle Tom's Cabin,* presented brief views of life on a Southern plantation. The limitations of these one-reel films – approximately ten to fifteen minutes in length – could only offer brief views of impoverished black slaves working in the rich cotton fields of their aristocratic masters. The pioneer director D.W. Griffith, who had grown up in the South and learned about the genteel plantation life of the wealthy whites, turned out a series of silent films. They captured the lives of black and white Southerners, the rich and the poor, culminating in his masterpiece *The Birth of a Nation* (1915). Unfortunately, he carried with him from his colorful past the baggage of bigotry in his depictions of "happy" slaves and painted a heroic picture of the rise of the Ku Klux Klan. Griffith's background in the theater and the strong influence of 19th century romantic literature affected the atmosphere and plots of his early films. Nevertheless, he, along with other early film directors, like E. Mason Hopper and Paul Sloane, underscored the importance of plantation life and its two major crops of cotton and tobacco. Most of these filmmakers focused on the romantic elements of life on the plantation in the Old South, including its gentility, its resistance to change and its firm belief that slaves in general were treated well and, more importantly, were vital to the South's way of life. Joseph Pevney's romantic comedy *Tammy and the Bachelor* (1957) portrays a plantation set in the New South in which at least one character, the bachelor's mother, would like to convert her plantation back to its former glory. In general, few films emphasized the hard, backbreaking work of the slaves who picked the cotton and handled the routine chores of the mansion.

*

Drum (1976), UA. Dir. Steve Carver; Sc. Norman Wexler; Cast includes: Warren Oates, Isela Vega, Ken Norton, Pamela Grier, Yaphet Kotto, John Colicos.

Kyle Onstott wrote a revisionist novel, which was adapted for the screen the following year. A poorly produced exploitation drama directed by Steve Carver, the film concerns the theme of slave breeding in the antebellum South. Warren Oates portrays a slave breeder who purchases Ken Norton and Yaphet Kotto from a bordello queen who is Norton's real mother. When an effete and sadistic New Orleans slave owner dandy (John Colicos), accompanied by his passive lover (Alain Patrick), vindictively orders one of his own slaves to kill Norton, Norton's mother interferes. The slave owner then shoots her in cold blood and flees. At the funeral of the murdered bordello queen, Norton, still unaware that the woman was his real mother, remarks about the killer, "He should have been arrested and jailed." But Paula Kelly, the mother's lesbian lover and maid, and the woman who had raised Norton, reminds him of the reality of his status. "Who would take the word of two black men against a white man? You're a slave."

The boorish Oates marries a prim and proper Southern belle, but also buys Pamela Grier – Ken Norton's girlfriend – as a "bed wench," a sleep-in mistress. His new wife objects, but Oates ignores her. The breeder's teenage daughter (Rainbeaux Smith) shows more than a passing interest in her father's male slaves, especially the two friends – Norton and Kotto – whom she constantly tries to seduce.

When his wife wants to keep the pair as house servants instead of studs, Oates is outraged. "Do you expect me to waste these boys serving the table!" he exclaims. "These are strong boys – they have yearnings. Their sap is arisin'. If I don't give them wenches, they're going to be after the white ladies. Then I gotta castrate them!" Kotto is kept in chains and ready to be sold or killed. But he dreams of escaping. "I got freedom in my heart," he says, "and I'm gonna take it." Norton secretly breaks his chains. Kotto, instead of escaping, arouses a group of male slaves to revolt and kill a gathering of white masters and their women. Following a brutal scene of slaughter and mayhem and the murder of a vicious slaver (Royal Dano), white riders come to the rescue of the remaining whites under siege. During the confusion, Oates, whom Norton has rescued from the rampaging slaves, allows Norton to escape. "They act human sometimes," Oates muses as he watches Norton flee into the darkness of the night, "then all of a sudden, they just go crazy. Once they get human blood in them, they just can't act like proper niggers no more."

*

Historian Kenneth Stampp, who in 1956 wrote *The Peculiar Institution*, a revisionist history of slavery, acknowledges the existence of several such plantations used as breeding farms for slaves – and dramatized by authors like Onstott. However, Stampp suggests that most slave breeding took place in an unorganized manner by masters whose remote plantations were far from slave markets. To increase their supply of workers for the ever-expanding cotton fields, the plantation owners were forced to raise their own labor force.

Gone With the Wind (1939), MGM. Dir. Victor Fleming; Sc. Sidney Howard; Cast includes: Clark Gable, Leslie Howard, Olivia de Havilland, Vivien Leigh, Thomas Mitchell, Hattie McDaniel, Evelyn Keyes, Ann Rutherford, George Reeves, Butterfly McQueen.

Many of the opening sequences in Victor Fleming's drama are set at Tara, the rich and lush plantation of the O'Hara family before the Civil War. Here aristocratic neighbors gather to admire the lifestyle of the owner as well as to gawk at his daughters. An atmosphere of congeniality, gentleness and hospitality pervades the estate as Southern belles flirt with handsome, well-attired admirers while black servants obediently wait upon them. Gerald O'Hara (Thomas Mitchell), an Irish immigrant, owns Tara, the Georgian plantation. On the mansion's veranda sits Scarlett (Vivien Leigh), his headstrong teenage daughter (the oldest of three). The Tarleton twins (Fred Crane and George Reeves), Leigh's suitors, beg to take her to an upcoming barbecue at a nearby plantation, Twelve Oaks. She tries to learn about the man she loves, Ashley Wilkes (Leslie Howard), the oldest son of Twelve Oaks' patriarch. Seeing her father galloping across the meadow, Leigh runs to meet him. She complains about life at Tara – to which Mitchell angrily and firmly responds that Tara is a priceless inheritance, that "land is the only thing worth living for, worth dying for – it's the only thing that lasts."

Hallelujah (1929), MGM. Dir. King Vidor; Sc. Wanda Tuchock; Cast includes: Daniel L. Haynes, Nina Mae McKinney, William Fountaine, Harry Gray, Victoria Spivey.

The introduction of sound to Hollywood films added a new dimension to the plantation film. Director King Vidor attempted to blend comedy, romance and tragedy into this drama, one of the earliest all-black talking features. *Hallelujah* concerns a cotton picker who turns preacher but still retains the weaknesses of an ordinary, flawed human being. Vidor has realistically depicted the cotton fields of the South where hardworking and singing blacks scratch out their meager living as they toil in the fields and bring in the cotton crop to waiting wagons. Today, the film seems dated, stylized and melodramatic.

Hearts in Dixie (1929), Fox. Dir. Paul Sloane; Sc. Walter Weems; Cast includes: Clarence Muse, Eugene Jackson, Stepin Fetchit.

Hollywood's first all-black feature, *Hearts in Dixie* unfolds as a series of sketches of life among American blacks. A plantation party provides some Southern atmosphere to the screen, and Stepin Fetchit contributes his comic antics to the production. The thin plot focuses on Grandfather Nappus, his daughter Chloe, her young son, and her lazy husband, Gummy. To make certain his grandson does not end up like his father or become tainted by the superstitions that dominate the community, the grandfather, an old slave, decides to send the boy away. One particularly tender scene shows Nappus' love for his grandson, whom he sends North for schooling. The film ends with the youngster's departure aboard a riverboat.

Kildare of Storm (1918), Metro. Dir. Harry L. Franklin; Sc. Jere Looney, Jane Mathis; Cast includes: Emily Stevens, King Baggot, Crauford Kent, Florence Short, Edwards Davis.

Early silent dramas presented melodramatic plots, with plantations serving peripherally as background. For example, in the drama *Kildare of Storm*, based on the 1916 novel by Eleanor Kelly, young Emily Stevens is pressured by her mother to marry King Baggot, a wealthy Southern plantation owner. Baggot's servant, Florence Short, the mother of his illegitimate son, protests the marriage. Baggot, in turn, takes away her child. Now the disappointed bride discovers he is both coarse and a brutal alcoholic. She befriends Crauford Kent, a local doctor, and his sympathetic mother. When the plantation owner is found dead, the doctor is charged with murder and imprisoned. Later the dead man's servant confesses to the crime and the doctor is exonerated.

Littlest Rebel, The (1935), TCF. Dir. David Butler; Sc. Edwin Burke; Cast includes: Shirley Temple, John Boles, Jack Holt, Karen Morley, Bill Robinson.

David Butler's Civil War drama, based on the play by Edward Peble, served chiefly as a vehicle for the popular child star Shirley Temple. The movie follows early Hollywood stereotypes of the South as a romantic and wonderful Garden of Eden. It depicts the conflict between the North and the South as a simple misunderstanding among good-natured gentlemen with conspicuously happy slaves.

The film, with its stress on the codes of Southern gentility, opens before the war during a birthday party for young Temple and her little friends at her Virginia plantation. The conflict begins, and the human losses take their toll, including the death of the child's mother. Cute and talented Shirley sings and dances her way through the struggle. In fact, she manages to end up sitting on Abraham Lincoln's knee while sharing an apple with the attentive President.

Mandingo (1975), Par. Dir. Richard Fleischer; Sc. Norman Wexler; Cast includes: James Mason, Susan George, Percy King, Richard Ward, Brenda Sykes, Ken Norton.

Richard Fleischer joined George Marshall in the revisionist approach towards the ante-bellum South. This exploitation drama, based on the novel by Kyle Onstott, depicts the slave-based white society in the pre-Civil War South. James Mason portrays a slave breeder whose son, Percy King, falls in love with slave Brenda Sykes. Meanwhile, his jealous wife (Susan George) seeks to humiliate her husband for his sexual escapades and she has an affair with Ken Norton, a slave stud and friend of King's. Mason is an inveterate gambler who bets on Norton in numerous boxing matches. Most of the incidents sink to banality in this embarrassing production. Onstott's novel was adapted for the stage by Jack Kirkland in 1961, which resulted in a dreary production.

Prodigal, The (1931), MGM. Dir. Harry Pollard; Sc. Bess Meredyth, Wells Root; Cast includes: Lawrence Tibbett, Esther Ralston, Roland Young, Cliff Edwards.

A Southern gentleman (Lawrence Tibbett) returns home to his plantation with two disreputable pals after experiencing life on the road as a hobo in Harry Pollard's 1931 musical. Tibbett gets to sing several songs, including a few numbers at a barbecue surrounded by African-Americans. Scenes of plantation life add slightly to the film, which failed at the box-office. This plantation film shifted its focus from African-Americans to whites as its main characters. In so doing, it lost much of its charm, culture and lifestyle in its depiction of the common folk. These elements – which had previously appeared to better advantage in earlier, similar sound films – were essential for films in this genre.

Sangaree (1953), Par. Dir. Edward Ludwig; Sc. David Duncan, Frank Moss; Cast includes: Fernando Lamas, Arlene Dahl, Patricia Medina, Francis L. Sullivan, Charles Korvin.

Edward Ludwig's historical drama, based on the novel by Frank G. Slaughter, is set in the antebellum South. Fernando Lamas, as the free son of an indentured servant, inherits control of a large Georgia estate when his benefactor dies. Tom Drake, the son of the deceased man, accepts Lamas as the controller. But the dead man's angry spitfire daughter, Arlene Dahl, resents the takeover. Lamas face other problems. As a public health officer for Savannah, which is currently threatened with the plague, he must act to save the community. He also gets involved in a feud with Francis L. Sullivan, an old doctor rigidly set in his backward ways, and his son, lawyer John Sutton. Lamas and Dahl, as many in the audience may have guessed by this time, finally work out their business and personal differences.

Something for the Boys (1944), TCF. Dir. Lewis Seiler; Sc. Robert Ellis, Helen Logan, Frank Gabrielson; Cast includes: Carmen Miranda, Michael O'Shea, Vivian Blaine, Phil Silvers, Sheila Ryan.

Hollywood found a new plot device for the old plantation in this World War II musical based on the play by Cole Porter. Distant cousins Carmen Miranda, Vivian Blaine and Phil Silvers inherit a broken-down plantation and decide to convert the house into a home for army wives. To raise the necessary funds, they put on a big show, featuring singer Perry Como – who makes his screen debut – and Blaine and Miranda. Since the production was basically an entertainment project, there is little mention of any social, political or economic problems in the South.

Curiously, the film, based on the Broadway musical, changed the setting from a Texas ranch to a Georgia plantation. The film includes such numbers as

"80 Miles from Atlanta," "I Wish We Didn't Have to Say Goodnight," "In the Middle of Nowhere," "Wouldn't It Be Nice" and "Samba Boogie."

Tammy and the Bachelor (1957), U. Dir. Joseph Pevney; Sc. Oscar Brodney; Cast includes: Debbie Reynolds, Leslie Nielsen, Walter Brennan, Mala Powers, Sidney Blackmer.

This romantic comedy, based on the novel by Cid Ricketts Sumner, concerns the familiar story of the wide-eyed innocent transported to a sophisticated world. Debbie Reynolds is the teenager Tammy, who hails from the backwoods bayou country of Louisiana. She is invited to visit the estate of bachelor playboy Leslie Nielsen after she and her grandpa (Walter Brennan) rescue him from a plane crash. Tammy ends up helping him and other members of his family to fulfill their wishes. Nielsen would like to make his plantation self-sustaining, and his mother would like to restore conditions to resemble the Old South. Meanwhile, his maiden aunt prefers to develop her art career in New Orleans. On the side, Tammy eventually wins Nielsen away from his shrewish and self-centered girlfriend (Mala Powers).

Tap Roots (1948), UI. Dir. George Marshall; Sc. Alan LeMay; Cast includes: Van Heflin, Susan Hayward, Boris Karloff, Julie London.

George Marshall's Civil War drama is one of the earliest Hollywood productions to break the mold of the idealized plantation of the ante-bellum South. In this movie, the Dabney clan of Mississippi's Lebanon Valley and a group of neighboring farmers have prospered on their plantations and abolished slavery in their corner of the state. Determined to secede from the rest of the state as well as from the Confederacy, they raise their own army. Ward Bond as Dabney, the acknowledged leader of the valley, entreats his neighbors to avoid the impending civil war. When the state secedes from the Union, the valley withdraws from the state.

Newspaper publisher Van Heflin, who believes in the farmers' cause, falls in love with the strong-willed daughter (Susan Hayward) of the Dabneys. Family members are willing to take on the Confederate Army to protect their plantation and remain neutral during the conflict between the North and South. Julie London plays Hayward's younger passionate sister. Boris Karloff, as an Indian, is a loyal friend to the family. The superior Southern troops decimate the brave but ill-equipped force in a pathetic battle. However, Heflin rescues the wounded Bond and they seek shelter in a cabin, where Hayward joins her father and the man she has grown to love. The farmers reorganize and finally drive the invading army from the once-peaceful valley.

*

The film was adapted from the novel by James Street, which, in turn, was based on an actual incident during the war. Southern troops were forced to crush a seditious Mississippi community that announced its independence and neutrality. The lopsided battle occurred at Lebanon Valley where the defenders were slaughtered.

Tar Heel Warrior, The (1917), Triangle. Dir. Mason Hopper; Sc. J. G. Hawks; Cast includes: Walt Whitman, Ann Kroman, William Shaw, George West.

This silent drama, a crude tale with a contrived ending, tells the story of an old Southern colonel (Walt Whitman), whose granddaughter is married to a New York stockbroker. The colonel is desperate for money and is on the verge of selling his old plantation. As a last resort, he travels to Wall Street to the broker who informs him that his own money is all tied up. Whitman borrows $5,000 from another man and then loses it in the stock market. Broken emotionally and financially, he returns to his plantation and prepares to take his own life. But his granddaughter and her husband rush to the colonel's home and save him in the nick of time. The broker has just made a killing in the stock market and he comes through with a large infusion of cash at the last minute.

Virginia (1941), Par. Dir. Edward H. Griffith; Sc. Virginia Van Upp; Cast includes: Madeleine Carroll, Fred MacMurray, Sterling Hayden, Helen Broderick.

In this romantic drama, showgirl Madeleine Carroll, in need of money, returns to her small town in Virginia to claim her inheritance, an old plantation. Possibly the most intriguing element of the film is its emphasis on the old Southern values of the past in contrast to the moneyed contemporary Northern standards. She is forced to sell her estate to raise much-needed cash. Meanwhile, she meets a neighbor, Virginian Fred MacMurray, an upstanding resident who was forced to sell his property to wealthy Eastern newcomer Sterling Hayden. She likes both men and is torn between the former, with his sincerity and old-fashioned ideals of Southern gentility and honor and the latter, with his materialistic world and offer of financial security. The rest is obvious. Character player Leigh Whipper portrays an old slave who returns home to die.

Way Down South (1939), RKO. Dir. Bernard Vorhaus; Sc. Clarence Muse, Langston Hughes; Cast includes: Bobby Breen, Alan Mowbray, Ralph Morgan, Clarence Muse.

Shirley Temple was not the only child star to appear in a plantation film. Young Bobby Breen inherits his family's plantation after his father dies in this romanticized drama set in the 1850s before the Civil War. He is highly sympathetic to the slaves. The boy battles the harsh taskmasters in an effort to treat his plantation slaves humanely. The slaves and the young master enjoy themselves singing spirituals together. Although the Old South was idealized in this picture, some of the evils of slavery were touched upon. However, the film skirts the basic issue of freedom by laying the blame on a handful of misguided taskmasters and exonerates the slave owners of any responsibilities.

2

Slaves and Slavery

With the confluence of the coastal exploration of Africa, the discovery of North and South America by Europeans in the 15th century and the subsequent colonization of the Americas during the next three centuries, the modern slave trade came to fruition. England entered the slave trade late in the 16th century. The American colonies themselves subsequently joined the practice as competitors.

In 1619, the first blacks were kidnapped to North America and landed at Jamestown. Brought by early English privateers, they were subjected to limited servitude, a status given to Indian, white, and black servants preceding slavery in most of the English colonies in the New World. The number of slaves imported was small at first, and it did not seem necessary to define their legal status. In 1713 the exclusive right to supply the Spanish colonies with slaves was granted to the British South Sea Company.

The development of the plantation system in the Southern colonies in the latter half of the 17th century increased the demand for black slaves. The North shared in the profits as a few northern coastal cities became the ports of entry for the slave traffic. Generally, in the Northern colonies, slaves were used as domestics and in trade; in the Middle Atlantic colonies they were used more in agriculture; and in the Southern colonies, where plantation agriculture was the primary occupation, the majority of slaves worked the plantations.

As the number of blacks increased and they became important for the English colonies in America, but critical for the economy of the South, the laws affecting them were modified. By the time of the American Revolution, they were no longer indentured servants but slaves in the fullest sense of the term. Specific laws defined their legal, political, and social status with respect to their masters.

Slaves had no legal rights, such as support in old age or sickness or a right to limited religious instruction. Custom gave slaves numerous rights such as private property, marriage, free time, contractual ability, and, for females, domestic or lighter plantation labor which, however, the master was not bound to respect. Barbarities such as mutilation, branding, chaining and murder were regulated or prohibited by law, but instances of cruelty were common before the 19th century.

Denmark, in 1792, was the first Western country to abolish the slave trade. Great Britain followed in 1807, and the U.S. prohibited trading in slaves in 1808. At the Congress of Vienna in 1814, Great Britain exerted its influence to induce other foreign powers to adopt a similar policy, and eventually nearly all the states of Europe passed laws or entered into treaties prohibiting the traffic in slaves.

Although eminent American statesmen from the earliest period, including George Washington, Benjamin Franklin, Thomas Jefferson, James Madison, John Jay, and Alexander Hamilton, regarded slavery as evil and inconsistent with the principles of the Declaration of Independence, many owned slaves. The Society of Friends opposed slavery and argued against it. The Presbyterian Church made formal declarations against it between 1787 and 1836. The Methodist Episcopal Church held strong antislavery views, but in 1844, when one of its bishops was suspended for refusing to emancipate slaves he had inherited through his wife, secession took place and the Methodist Episcopal Church, South was formed. Individuals and almost all religious persuasions defended the institution. Nevertheless, little by little, antislavery views grew steadily. Many who personally held strong antislavery opinions were reluctant to join any abolitionist movement and were unwilling to dispute what many citizens believed to be within their rights.

In spite of being torn from their native African culture, black slaves managed to maintain large parts of their native religions by blending their indigenous practices with Christianity – particularly the evangelical branch. By concealing their own religion under that of their slavemaster's, blacks preserved some of their African rituals and customs for future generations. Slaves used the plantation structure and environment to create their own black family and community. Plantation owners preferred male blacks for manual labor while they purchased black women for sex and housekeeping work. The presence of black females also deterred their men from escaping.

John P. Kennedy, one of the privileged members of the Virginia aristocracy, was most responsible for promoting the myth of the plantation as medieval manor. He wrote *Swallow Barn* (1832) in an effort to portray Southern plantation life as the reincarnation of all good things in medieval times. Despite Kennedy's personal opposition to slavery, in his writing he softened the institution's abuses. The master, he advocated, should never be cruel, only paternal, and the slave never resentful, only docile and devoted to the master and his family. Director D. W. Griffith accepted many of Kennedy's principles regarding the behavior of master and slave. *His Trust* (1911) and *His Trust Fulfilled* (1911), two of Griffith's silent films set during the Civil War propagated this point of view.

*

Film studios were caught on the horns of a dilemma when faced by the moral dilemma of slavery. They were unwilling to estrange their Southern audiences and, at the same time, they were afraid of alienating the rest of the country. Hollywood was surprised by the box office success of the movie version of Harriet Beecher Stowe's anti-slavery novel *Uncle Tom's Cabin*. However, very few early films condemned the practice of slavery or discrimination outright. On the contrary, short early silent comedies such as *The Nigger in the Woodpile*, which were popular during the pioneer years of the industry, poked fun at and were insulting to, blacks. The film versions of Mark Twain's works *Pudd'nhead Wilson* (1916) and *Huckleberry Finn* (1920) were rare exceptions. Major changes in Hollywood's presentation of the institution of slavery did not occur until after World War II, in such films as Raoul Walsh's pre-Civil War drama *Band of Angels* (1957) and Julie Dash's historical drama *Daughters of the Dust* (1991). Hollywood, in its twisted wisdom, even tried to depict a comedic view of slavery in several films, including Sydney Pollack's comedy drama *The Scalphunters* (1968) and Paul Bogart's comedy *Skin Game* (1971), set in pre-Civil War days. Steven Spielberg's well-meaning historical drama *Amistad* (1998), about the evils of the slave trade and its ramifications, stands out as a sincere, if flawed, effort to explore the topic.

Adventures of Huckleberry Finn (1960), MGM. Dir. Michael Curtiz; Sc. J. Lee; Cast includes: Tony Randall, Eddie Hodges, Archie Moore, Patty McCormack.

Michael Curtiz's historical drama is based on Mark Twain's classic novel. Young Eddie Hodges portrays the author's title character, an adventurous boy fascinated by the riverboats and the hustle and bustle along the Mississippi River. To avoid his strict aunt, Huck builds a raft and joins up with his African-American friend Jim (Archie Moore) who, afraid of being caught as an escaped slave, is seeking the safety of free territory. Both have a series of adventures before Huck returns home. An earlier black-and-white version, one of several, appeared in 1939, with Mickey Rooney in the lead role.

Amistad (1997), Dreamworks. Dir. Steven Spielberg; Sc. David Franzoni; Cast includes: Morgan Freeman, Nigel Hawthorne, Anthony Hopkins, Djimon Hounsou, Matthew McConaughey, David Paymer.

Steven Spielberg's epic drama, about a mutiny aboard a slave-ship and its ensuing trial, reminds its audience about an ignominious episode in American history. The somber and stark events depict the Atlantic crossing of Africans who have been captured by slavers, put into chains and compelled to suffer untold horrors on their journey to the New World as slaves. But a bloody mutiny occurs aboard the ironically named *La Amistad* (Friendship). Two Spanish captives trick the slaves into sailing to New England instead of returning to Africa. The Africans are arrested and held for trial. They have innocently become embroiled in America's controversy over slavery and are forced to undergo several trials before they are finally freed by the Supreme Court. During their months of captivity, various voices address the issues. Northern abolitionists pray for them and support their cause. The cautious President Martin Van Buren, fearing rebellion from Southern states, refuses to set the captives free. South Carolina's Senator John Calhoun, at a Washington Presidential dinner party, eloquently presents the Southern cause to the guests: "There's a growing number of people in this part of the country that regard us in the South as not only geographically beneath them," he argues. "They ignore the fact that slavery is so interwoven in the fabric of this society that to destroy it would be to destroy us as a people. It's immoral, that's all they know, so are we – immoral and inferior. . . . We're not as wealthy as our Northern neighbors. We're still struggling. Well, we all know what happens then – North and South. What President wants to be in office when it comes crashing down around him?" President Van Buren grimaces uncomfortably at Calhoun's threatening remarks.

Later, an elderly John Quincy Adams (Anthony Hopkins), now retired, takes up the cause of the African prisoners, led by Cinque (Djimon Hounsou), and argues their case before the U.S. Supreme Court. He begins by quoting Calhoun's written remarks: "Slavery has always been with us. It is neither sinful nor immoral. Rather, slavery is natural as it is inevitable." In contrast, Adams argues that "the natural state of man is freedom." The Court agrees with Adams and orders the immediate release of the Africans, who are jubilant at the decision. Morgan Freeman portrays a black abolitionist working to help free the Africans, and Matthew McConaughey plays their New England lawyer who has struggled through several trials to win the release of the captives.

Band of Angels (1957), WB. Dir. Raoul Walsh; Sc. John Twist, Ivan Goff, Ben Roberts; Cast includes: Clark Gable, Yvonne De Carlo, Sidney Poitier, Efrem Zimbalist Jr., Rex Reason.

Band of Angels is based upon the novel by Robert Penn Warren. When Yvonne De Carlo's father dies, she is forced to leave an exclusive girls' school only to discover that she is part African-American. Raoul Walsh's pre-Civil War drama is based on the novel by Robert Penn Warren. In New Orleans, she is sold as a slave to powerful landowner and enlightened former slaver Clark Gable. He rescues her from the clutches of a villainous plantation owner and installs her in his luxurious mansion as his mistress. When war erupts and the Union army advances through the South to New Orleans, Gable's black overseer, Sidney Poitier, seizes his opportunity for freedom, abandons his master and joins the Northern army.

Gable intends to burn his cotton crops in protest against the Southern institution of slavery and, although threatened with execution by Southern troops for his plans, he goes through with his strategy and retreats to one of his more remote plantations. Poitier, hating his former white master, pursues him but lets him live when he realizes that Gable had raised him as his own son. Gable and De Carlo sail away to safety with a sea captain, a former slaver.

Warren's novel *Band of Angels* tells a story about sex and slavery in the South during the Civil War. It was adapted for the screen and directed by Raoul Walsh. The film abounds in stereotyped images of happy, singing slaves, cruel slave owners who flogged their human property as well as kindly, sympathetic slave owners who treated their charges well. This simplistic formula worked against any effort to make the film a serious study or depiction of the slavery problem.

*

The author of the book *Band of Angels*, Robert Penn Warren (1905-1989), was first and foremost an English professor. Unlike many Southern writers who started as newspaper reporters and then later evolved into literary figures, Robert Penn Warren was an academic. He began teaching English in 1930 at Southwestern College, moved to Vanderbilt University for three years and, in 1934, was appointed associate professor in the English department of Louisiana State University. Warren was always troubled by the problem of good versus evil and he felt strongly that the pre-Civil War system of slavery was evil institutionalized.

Warren wrote fiction for several years, switched to poetry for a while and then returned to fiction. It was after he wrote *Selected Poems* (1944) that he produced the semi-historical "biography" of Huey Long, *All the King's Men* (1946), for which he is best known. Long was governor of Louisiana, a U.S. Senator, a very serious demagogue and a threat to democratic institutions. In *All the King's Men*, Warren once again returns to the problem of good versus evil but, realistically, offers no solution. Only after Huey Long is killed is everything resolved. It seems that this "happy ending" was only added after the novel was completed and is not an integral part of the work. In Robert Rossen's 1949 screen version, Broderick Crawford portrays the crafty and brutal Willie Stark, a figure closely resembling Huey Long. The hypocritical and aspiring politician rises from the backwoods of a Southern state to governor. Stark cleverly exploits the gullibility of the populace after his early defeat as an idealistic candidate for a minor office. Newsman John Ireland, following Stark's political career from the beginning, falls for his charm and charisma.

Dan (1914), Par. Dir. George Irving, John H. Pratt, Sc. Hal Reid; Cast includes: Lew Dockstader, Lois Meredith, Gale Kane, Beatrice Clevener.

This silent Civil War drama tells the tale of Dan, a black slave who sacrifices his own life to save that of his master's son. The young man, a Confederate officer, is captured by Union troops and sentenced to death as a spy. Dan gains access to the tent where the prisoner is being held and persuades him to blacken his face to facilitate his escape. In the morning the black servant is executed in place of his white master.

Lew Dockstader, the famous minstrel entertainer, was especially selected for the title role, and he blends the appropriate mixture of drama and comedy in his portrayal. Although the theme of the servant's overzealous loyalty to his master is unbelievable and disagreeable, the film, released in the early days of World War I, was timely for its war background and battle scenes.

Guerrilla, The (1908), Biograph. Dir. D. W. Griffith; Sc. D. W. Griffith; Cast includes: Arthur Johnson, Mack Sennett, Harry Solter, George Gebhardt.

This was D.W. Griffith's first of a series of one-and two-reel Civil War dramas that he turned out for Biograph Studios and it marked his initiation as a film director. The story deals with a loyal black servant who, during the Civil War, rides to the rescue of his master. Even after his horse is shot, the rider gets through with the message entrusted to him. Although a simple and crude film by later standards, it whetted the director's appetite to return to the war and use it as background for ten more short films and, finally, for his 1915 masterpiece, *The Birth of a Nation*. Griffith repeated the theme of the faithful black servant in two other short Civil War dramas – *His Trust* (1911) and *His Trust Fulfilled* (1911).

His Trust (1911), Biograph. Dir. D.W. Griffith; Cast includes: Wilfred Lucas, Dell Henderson, Clare McDowell, Edith Haldeman.

In this short silent Civil War drama a faithful black servant is assigned to protect the wife and little daughter of the Southern master who leaves for the war. When the master is killed in action, friends return with their fallen comrade's saber and present it to the widow. The servant then mounts it over the mantel. Later, Union troops raid the village and set fire to the widow's home, but the servant rescues the child and rushes back into the flames to retrieve his former master's sword. He takes the widow and child to his own humble cabin.

It was a more of a comment on white audiences in the early twentieth century than it was on the psyche of black slaves that the former found nothing strange in the theme of black slaves sacrificing for their white masters in a number of films. The hardly-believable tale of the faithful black servant adheres to the stereotype and continues in the sequel. The few battle scenes are effective, considering the year the drama was made.

The film was the first of two parts, both of which Griffith planned to have released as two-reelers. The movie executives at Biograph saw more profit in two separate releases and rejected his Griffith's plans. Each film was released separately and each contained a complete story. The second part is titled *His Trust Fulfilled.*

His Trust Fulfilled (1911), Biograph. Dir. D.W. Griffith; Cast includes: Wilfred Lucas, Claire McDowell, Gladys Egan, Dorothy West, Harry Hyde.

Griffith's second half of a two-part drama (the first was titled *His Trust*) begins four years later. The Civil War has ended. The servant, still loyal to his deceased master, has been paying the bills for the education of his master's daughter. When he runs out of funds, he considers stealing but soon rejects the temptation. Fortunately, an English relative arrives in time to make the payments and he falls in love with the girl. As the newly married couple leaves for England, the servant tearfully looks on and is content in the knowledge that he has fulfilled his master's wishes.

As repulsive as the theme may be to today's audiences, Griffith innocently attempted to ennoble his main character, the black slave, by bestowing upon him two favorite Southern traits, the qualities of trust and loyalty. Little did he realize he was stereotyping blacks (white actors made up in blackface). Nor was he the first. As early as 1900, short comedies such as *A Bucket of Cream Ale* and *A Nigger in the Wood Pile* had already established blacks as abject servants and the victims of white pranks.

Scalphunters, The (1968), UA. Dir. Sydney Pollack; Sc. William Norton; Cast includes: Burt Lancaster, Shelley Winters, Ossie Davis, Telly Savalas, Nick Cravat.

In this boisterous comedy drama Burt Lancaster portrays a stubborn-minded fur trapper and Ossie Davis is a runaway, educated slave who is captured by Indians. Somehow Lancaster takes possession of Davis. Telly Savalas plays the head of a crew of Indian scalp hunters and Shelley Winters, his mistress, chews on a cigar and studies astrology in their covered wagon. Lancaster and Davis decide to follow Savalas. Following a series of comical complications, including brawls, chases and an avalanche, Davis and Lancaster, who by now are buddies, quarrel and end up fighting each other in a mud pond. They finally emerge – both the same color!

Seven Angry Men (1955), AA. Dir. Charles Marquis Warren; Sc. Daniel R. Ullman; Cast includes: Raymond Massey, Debra Paget, Jeffrey Hunter, Larry Pennell.

John Brown's crusade to liberate the slaves provides the subject of Charles Marquis Warren's Civil War drama. Raymond Massey portrays Brown as a ruthless murderer, a religious fanatic who cares little about the number of lives that are lost as he tries to get Kansas to join the Union as a free state. His son (Jeffrey Hunter) falls in love with Debra Paget and marries her. Leo Gordon plays Reverend White, a minister who resists Brown's preaching. The film climaxes with the famous battle at Harpers Ferry, Virginia, in which Colonel Robert E. Lee captures John Brown. Massey had played the religious crusader in an earlier film, *Santa Fe Trail* (1940), starring Errol Flynn as "Jeb" Stuart.

Skin Game (1971), WB. Dir. Paul Bogart; Sc. David Giller, Peter Stone; Cast includes: James Garner, Lou Gossett, Susan Clark, Brenda Sykes, Edward Asner, Andrew Duggan.

James Garner portrays a con artist and Lou Gossett is his partner in this clever comedy set in pre-Civil War days. Garner repeatedly sells Gossett, as a slave, to unwary white landowners, and then helps his partner to escape. They then plan for their next sale. Following several successful capers, complications arise involving Andrew Duggan, a mean-spirited plantation owner, and Edward Asner, a villainous slave trader. All hell breaks loose at a slave auction when an intruder, resembling the fanatical John Brown, bursts in to raid the sale. At times, the film approaches a social consciousness.

Slave Ship (1937), TCF. Dir. Tay Garnett; Sc. Sam Hellman, Lamar Trotti, Gladys Lehman; Cast includes: Warner Baxter, Wallace Beery, Elizabeth Allan, Mickey Rooney, George Sanders.

Warner Baxter is the captain of a slave ship. He decides to end his career as a slaver in this action drama, based on a novel by George S. King. Baxter orders Wallace Beery, his first mate, to dismiss the crew and hire other seamen. Now a respectable merchant mariner, Baxter brings his bride aboard and discovers that Beery and his old crew have taken over and are still in the slave trade. With the help of a few loyal crewmembers, he overpowers the mutineers and regains control of the slave-free vessel.

Slaves (1969), Continental. Dir. Herbert J. Biberman; Sc. Herbert J. Biberman, John O. Killens, Alida Sherman; Cast includes: Stephen Boyd, Dionne Warwick, Ossie Davis, Robert Kya-Hill, Barbara Ann Teer, Gale Sondergaard.

The plight of slaves in the pre-Civil War South serves as the subject of this drama. A fair-minded Kentucky horse-breeder sells his Christian slave (Ossie Davis) to a brutal Mississippi slave owner (Stephen Boyd). The slave owner has a black mistress (Dionne Warwick) who proves to be an attractive but quick-tempered, emotional young woman. Boyd's father is a minister in Boston, but he himself is philosophical about slavery. He describes the economic and social eruption that would result if the slaves were set free and flooded the North.

Warwick and Davis decide to escape together. Davis, an idealistic and heroic Christian, discovers that he must struggle for his freedom and salvation before he can solely trust in God. Although their plan ends in failure, Davis demonstrates his moral superiority over Boyd by turning down the master's offer of freedom in return for killing another slave. The film only peripherally shows sympathetic slave owners who cared about their charges and tried to keep slave families together. They stand in stark contrast to other slave owners who exploited their slaves and even bred slaves for sale.

Tom and Huck (1995), BV. Dir. Peter Hewitt; Sc. Ron Koslow, David Loughery; Cast includes: Jonathan Taylor Thomas, Brad Renfro, Eric Schweig, Charles Rocket, Amy Wright.

This version of Mark Twain's mischievous famous youngsters features the popular TV child star Jonathan Taylor Thomas as Tom Sawyer and Brad Renfro as Huck Finn. Both boys witness a midnight killing in a graveyard and take an oath of secrecy. When a wrong man is accused and tried for the murder, Tom breaks the oath and names the real criminal as Injun Joe, who flees from the courtroom and swears revenge. In the climactic sequence, Tom, Huck, Becky and the villain chase each other around a cave with an endlessly deep pit. Excepts for such scenes in which Tom cons neighborhood boys into whitewashing his Aunt's picket fence, very little of the author's original writings are salvaged in this flawed production.

*

Mark Twain's stories presented a Norman Rockwell version of America. Although Twain (1835-1910) – real name Samuel Langhorne Clemens – wasn't born in the South, his stories of life along the Mississippi as described in *Tom Sawyer* (1876) and *The Adventures of Huckleberry Finn* (1884) earn him a well-deserved place in Southern and American literature. He grew up in a slaveholding community, served in the Confederate Army and is important historically for helping to describe the period between the frontier days and the Civil War.

Clemens, in real life, was at least as adventurous as the characters in his novels, for in 1857 he decided to leave the printing and newspaper business and become a river pilot. He served his apprenticeship on a Mississippi steamer and then worked as a river pilot for four years – until the Civil War made it impossible to navigate the river. Clemens so loved his life on the Mississippi that he changed his name to "Mark Twain," a navigational signal, and later made good use of his adventures in *Life on the Mississippi* (1883).

Tom Sawyer was a humorous depiction of adolescent adventure on the Mississippi and captured a young person's fantasies as well as an adult's nostalgia. The book remains an idylic picture of America's golden age, a time that had already vanished when Twain recreated part of his own boyhood. *The Adventures of Huckleberry Finn* included critical social commentary and contrasted Christian principles with the practice of slavery. Although Twain made lots of money from his books and lectures in the U.S. and abroad, he lost most of it in publishing investments. He became despondent after the death of his daughter in 1896 and his wife in 1904 and couldn't write for many years. *The Mysterious Stranger,* his last book, was published posthumously in 1916 and reflects the change in outlook from his optimistic earlier works. It describes Satan's visit to 16th century Eseldorf and Twain's own pessimistic view of life. Considering all of his publications – especially *The Adventures of Huckleberry Finn* – many critics regard Mark Twain as the greatest American novelist.

A number of Twain's earlier works have been transformed into entertaining films. *The Adventures of Huckleberry Finn* came to the screen as *Huckleberry Finn* in 1920, 1921 and 1974, and in its full title in 1939, 1960 and again in 1993. Ernest Hemingway once commented that all American literature began with Twain's novel about Huck Finn. Two good reasons may be that this was the first great novel to be told in the American vernacular and it was also the first great novel to deal honestly and forthrightly with the subject of race relations.

Adventures of Tom Sawyer was filmed in 1917, 1930, 1938 and 1973. *A Connecticut Yankee in King Arthur's Court* came to the screen in 1921, 1931 (as *A Connecticut Yankee*) and in 1949, as a musical tale with Bing Crosby. *The Further Adventures of Tom Sawyer* was filmed in 1918 with the title *Huck and Tom.* This abbreviated title was repeated in Peter Hewitt's 1995 film, which does not have even one Aftrican-American appearing on screen! Twain's novel *The Tragedy of Pudd'nhead Wilson,* a highly acclaimed production directed by a young Cecil B. DeMille, came to the silent screen in 1916. Critics commended the author for his original use of fingerprint identification in the story, set in the South between 1830 and 1850, as well as his courageous treatment of the race relations.

Uncle Tom's Cabin (1903).

This silent drama, one of the earliest screen versions of Harriet Beecher Stowe's famous novel about slavery in the antebellum South, unfortunately establishes the stereotypes of African Americans. It does so while telling the sensitive and provocative story about the "good" slave Tom and his family and the brutality of their masters such as Simon Legree. Several other silent adaptations of Stowe's novel were released in 1913, 1914, 1918, 1927 and 1958.

Uncle Tom's Cabin (1918), Famous Players. Dir. J. Searle Dawley; Cast includes: Marguerite Clark, Jack W. Johnston, Florence Carpenter, Frank Losee, Walter P. Lewis.

Still another version of Stowe's novel, this drama stars Marguerite Clark. This production diverged from the book so much as to make it almost unrecognizable. This 1918 release is perhaps the classical showpiece of what we imagine the slave plantation to have been. Scenes include old plantations along the Mississippi, riverboats loaded with cotton and singing black slaves hauling cotton.

Different versions of Stowe's classic American novel about the good religious slave have appeared since 1903. Early adaptations often cast a white player in blackface for the Tom character. But in 1914, Sam Lucas, a black actor, played Tom, followed by another black actor, James B. Lowe, in 1927. The film included a spectacular baptismal scene not seen in earlier versions.

Writers such as Harriet Beecher Stowe, William Wells, Henry Bibb and ex-slave Frederick Douglas disabused the public of popular myths about "happy" slaves working on plantations and brought their readers face-to-face with the harsh reality of slavery. Stowe's work, *Uncle Tom's Cabin* (1852), sold four hundred thousand copies within its first year of publication and became a major tool of the abolitionists. Its powerful themes and poignant story frustrated Southern writers from replying with any comparable work of stature.

3

Southern Aristocrats

Scottish and English immigrants formed the nucleus of European immigration to the early South. These new immigrants considered themselves more British than American and they looked to Great Britain for cultural leadership and social standards. Sir Walter Scott's medieval novels, which romanticized the English court, captured the early Southern imagination and the medieval knight rather than the rough American pioneer was the Southern ideal. In real life, these early Southern settlers couldn't really be knights, so they modeled themselves after the closest contemporary archetype of the medieval knight – the British nobleman.

Chivalry, especially the code of knightly behavior that was a feature of the High and later Middle Ages in Western Europe, eventually declined in the 14th and 15th centuries, and merged into the Renaissance idea of the gentleman in the 16th century. The ideals of knighthood and chivalry acquired a charm and fascination that combined aristocratic qualities, Christian virtues, and courtly love of women. The ideal knight was a man of prowess, loyalty and generosity.

The newer foreign ideologies of materialism, feminism and pacifism – the very values of the North – exemplified the antitheses of honor and chivalry. To counter these alien ideas, the South developed its own scaled-down version of the medieval court – the Southern gentleman and his belle. The belle was supposed to be demure and fragile while the ideal gentleman had a code of honor, which he was sworn to defend with his life.

Southern aristocracy reached its pinnacle of power in the late antebellum period in the Old South. Although aristocrats owned a majority of the wealth and land, it was their slaves who turned the plantations into successful enterprises. The large plantations became autonomous states, with their own rules and strictly enforced regulations. The aristocrats encouraged their slaves to embrace Christianity, or at least combine their own African culture with that of Christianity. The whites believed that Christianity served as a means of justifying slavery – that turning slaves into Christians was a religious and moral duty.

The ideal Southern aristocrat was quick to take offense and perhaps just as quick to suggest a duel. The duel, historically, was a prearranged combat with deadly weapons between two persons. It usually took place under formal arrangements and in the presence of witnesses – seconds – for each side. The sword and the pistol were the traditional weapons throughout history, and duels were usually fought early in the morning at relatively secluded places. The slighted party normally sent a written note challenging his slanderer to a duel. Each of the combatants nominated a second and elaborate rules of etiquette had to be followed. Gentlemen only dueled with members of their own class and avoided duels with members of the lower classes. Not to be outdone in retaliatory violence at every imagined slight, the lower classes aped the aristocrats and fought their own duels with any weapon at hand, including knives, rocks, clubs, boots or fists. Whereas the aristocrats emerged from a duel either with their honor satisfied or else dead, the members of the lower classes often remained alive but severely maimed.

The duel, in the modern sense, did not occur in the ancient world. Modern dueling arose in Teutonic countries during the early Middle Ages. Dueling to avenge one's honor was never legal. In most cases, the law prohibited its practice.

Early American settlers took to dueling like bees took to honey. Duels were common from the time of the first settlement at Plymouth in 1621. Such combats, under all conditions and with every variety of weapons, were frequent during the 18th and early 19th centuries and were usually fatal. In 1777, the American patriot Button Gwinnett was killed in a duel. Alexander Hamilton was killed by his political rival Aaron Burr in 1804 and became the most famous American victim of a duel. The District of Columbia outlawed dueling in 1839, and since the American Civil War all states have legislated against dueling, with punishments ranging from disqualification from public office to death.

It has been estimated that there were some 3,950 duels between gentlemen in the South during the two decades preceding the Civil War. At one time or another, most of the important political figures in the region – including Andrew Jackson and Cassius Clay – were participants in a duel. Dueling reached such staggering figures that a number of Southern states enacted statutes prohibiting the practice and anti-dueling groups were established to mediate between the aggrieved parties.

By the beginning of the 20th century, dueling was almost universally prohibited by law and treated as a criminal offense. The major forces in the suppression of dueling, however, were social changes and social disapproval. The greatest of these social changes was the decline of the Southern aristocracy that was the bastion of the culture of the duel. The British Anti-Dueling Association, founded in 1843, and its aristocratic European counterpart, founded in 1900, were formed to organize a public relations campaign intended to take the glamour out of the practice of dueling and to further its social disapproval.

*

American studios occasionally released silent dramas in which the leading characters participated in duels. More often than not, these dramas were set in the Old South and involved the honor of the heroine. Sometimes the film story line was taken from a literary source, such as Booth Tarkington's play *Magnolia*, which gave rise to three screen versions, or Paul Wellman's novel *The Iron Mistress*, a fictional account of the adventures of James Bowie. In Rudolph Maté's drama *The Mississippi Gambler* (1953), two duels take on added importance. When the son of a wealthy New Orleans aristocrat shames the family name by backing out of a duel, his father bans him from returning home. Later, the father is killed when he is forced to fight a duel with another club member who has insulted Tyrone Power, a gambler in love with the aristocrat's daughter. In virtually all cases, the duel certainly heightened the sense of danger for the participants and the suspense level for those in the audience.

Hollywood often portrayed Southern aristocrats as refined gentlemen, usually adhering to the codes of Southern gentility, valor and honor. But the very same pride of the aristocrats led them into a false anticipation of victory. For example, in *Gone With the Wind* (1939), some of these younger aristocrats boast that if war erupts between the North and South, the South will certainly defeat the Yankees within months. The lone dissenter from this proud contention is Rhett Butler (Clark Gable), who explains to them a more realistic view. The war, he states, will be a prolonged struggle, one the North will win in the long run, since it is equipped with heavy industry to produce unlimited war supplies and a vast population from which to draw soldiers.

On the other hand, sometimes the Southern aristocrat can sometimes play the role of a cad, as in Frank Lloyd's *The Sins of Her Parent* (1916) and Walter Edwards's *The Bride of Hate* (1917). In Michael Gordon's drama *Another Part of the Forest* (1948), Fredric March, the tyrannical head of the Hubbard family, castigates his son (Dan Duryea), a whining coward. "Try to remember," March says, "that though ignorance becomes a Southern gentleman, cowardice does not." Some films pointed out the darker side of the Southern aristocrat. In Walter Edwards's *The Bride of Hate* (1917), a drama of revenge, an aristocrat has seduced a doctor's grand niece.

Most startling of all in the various portrayals of the Southern aristocrat are those depicted in the later works (and their film adaptations) of several Southern writers (William Faulkner, Tennessee Williams, Lillian Hellman, Truman Capote and others). They set their plots and characters chiefly in the post-Civil War years. These writers focused on the poverty, depression and lassitude of their aristocrats. The men have turned into unfaithful husbands, family tyrants, abusers or women and sexual deviates. The lightheaded Southern belles, in turn, have been transmogrified into "faded Southern belles." These highly atmospheric Southern gothic tales are filled with crumbling mansions, lost souls and neglected agricultural fields – all symbolic of a defeated South.

*

Battle, The (1911), Biograph. Dir. D. W. Griffith; Sc. D. W. Griffith; Cast includes: Blanche Sweet, Robert Harron, Charles West, Donald Crisp.

Another in Griffith's early series of short Civil War dramas, this entry describes a young coward who is inspired by his sweetheart to perform acts of heroism. As a battle rages near the home of the young woman (Blanche Sweet), the young soldier (Robert Harron) recoils in fear and darts into Sweet's quarters and seeks shelter. Her mocking laughter at his spineless behavior gives him the necessary impetus not only to rejoin his unit but also to volunteer and reconnoiter for needed supplies. Although the journey is perilous, he manages to accomplish his mission.

Griffith directed dozens of one and two-reel films during his stay with Biograph, eleven of which had Civil War backgrounds. Made between 1908 and 1912, the films were shot chiefly in New Jersey. Characters and incidents from several of these films reappear in his 1915 epic masterpiece, *The Birth of a Nation.*

Bride of Hate, The (1917), Triangle. Dir. Walter Edwards; Sc. John Lynch; Cast includes: Frank Keenan, Margery Wilson, Jerome Story, David M. Hartford.

Frank Keenan, a Southern doctor, is determined to seek revenge upon an aristocrat who has seduced the doctor's grand niece in this drama of revenge. Kennan encourages a romance between the seducer and a slave and finally succeeds in promoting a marriage between the pair. Later, when the seducer marries another woman, a popular Southern belle in town, the doctor exposes the bridegroom's earlier secret marriage to a black woman. The seducer, in disgrace, wanders into a section of town that is under quarantine against yellow fever. When he tries to leave, a guard shoots him.

Cameo Kirby (1914), Par. Dir. Oscar Apfel; Sc. William C. de Mille; Cast includes: Dustin Farnum, Winifred Kingston, Dick La Reno.

Dustin Farnum portrays the title character, a gentleman gambler, in this silent action drama set in the days of Southern chivalry in the antebellum South. Falsely accused of murder, Kirby flees from the law and ends up dueling in the woods with the real killer, an unscrupulous gambler. Kirby is eventually exonerated of all charges. The film contains an exciting riverboat race.

Carolina (1934), TCF. Dir. Henry King; Sc. Reginald Berkeley; Cast includes: Janet Gaynor, Lionel Barrymore, Robert Young, Richard Cromwell.

The Connelly clan, a proud Southern family, has fallen on hard times after the Civil War in Henry King's drama, a portrayal of a fading South. The members of the family, including Lionel Barrymore, try to live up to the glories of an aristocratically proud past. A veteran of the war who has become a heavy drinker, he dwells upon better days in the past and laments the South's defeat. He and his wife (Henrietta Crosman) resent the present and fear the future. When a neighbor, an expatriate Pennsylvania farmer, dies, Barrymore, the owner of the farmer's land, ejects the man's daughter (Janet Gaynor) in an attempt to gain the entire property. On the side, Barrymore tries to marry her into his family by arranging a match between her and Robert Young, another Connelly family member. The film includes scenes of tobacco fields and the harvesting and manufacture of cigarettes. It ends after the couple marries and the plantation is restored to its former glory – obvious symbols of the reconciliation of the North and South.

City of Illusion, The (1916), Ivan. Dir. Ivan Abramson; Sc. Ivan Abramson; Cast includes: Mignon Anderson, Joseph Burke, Blanche Craig, Carleton Macy.

The bright, romantic city lights lure a young wife in this trite drama. Carleton Macy, a wealthy Southerner, marries his caretaker's daughter, Mignon Anderson. But the young bride proves unsophisticated and out of place in her husband's family home. She meets a New York lawyer, Macy's cousin, who paints a rosy picture of city life and hypnotizes Anderson. She insists on a divorce, heads for the city and expects to marry the lawyer. Instead, he marries a wealthy woman and plans to run for district attorney.

Coward, The (1915), Triangle. Dir. Reginald Barker; Sc. Thomas Ince, C. Gardner Sullivan; Cast includes: Charles Ray, Frank Keenan, Gertrude Claire, Margaret Gibson.

When the Civil War breaks out, the cowardly son of a proud Virginia colonel refuses to enlist. His father has to force him to join the Confederate army at the point of a gun. The boy (Charles Ray) deserts on his first night of picket duty, and his father substitutes for him. Back at his home, the son overhears Union plans for an attack and captures the plans. He rides furiously to his own lines with the information but is shot down by his own father who mistakes him for the enemy. Although seriously wounded, the boy succeeds in delivering the important documents.

Honor of His Family, The (1910), Biograph. Dir. D. W. Griffith; Sc. Frank Woods; Cast includes Henry B. Walthall, James Kirkwood, William J. Butler.

In D. W. Griffith's silent Civil War drama, a young Southerner answers the call to arms. His father, too old to enlist, fights the war vicariously through his son, who is an officer. But during a major battle, the boy turns coward and flees back home. The patriotic father, disgusted with his son's behavior and the ensuing dishonor he has brought upon the family, shoots the boy and returns the body to the battlefield. He positions the corpse with sword in hand, facing the enemy.

House With Closed Shutters, The (1910), Biograph. Dir. D. W. Griffith; Sc. Emmett Campbell Hall; Cast includes: Dorothy West, Henry B. Walthall, Charles West, Edwin August.

Another in the series of D. W. Griffith's early one-reel films with a Civil War background, this drama details the tragedy that befalls a Southern family due to a son's cowardice and his drinking problem. When the war erupts, the young alcoholic son wins a commission and is assigned to General Lee's staff. His sister sews a flag for his regiment before the troops march to the front. The son is stricken with fear when he is sent on an important mission and begins to drink heavily. He goes awol, returns home and continues to hit the bottle. His sister poses as a soldier and carries out his mission for him. But she is fatally wounded, protecting the flag. News reaches his mother that her son was killed in action. To avoid shaming the proud family name by telling the truth, she closes the house's shutters and keeps her cowardly son locked in. He remains locked in his home until death.

Iron Mistress, The (1952), WB. Dir. Gordon Douglas; Sc. James R. Webb; Cast include: Alan Ladd, Virginia Mayo, Joseph Calleia, Phyllis Kirk.

This biography of Jim Bowie, the frontier adventurer and inventor of the legendary Bowie knife, mixes truth and fiction. Gordon Douglas' drama is based on the novel by Paul I. Wellman and stars Alan Ladd. The action takes place in picturesque New Orleans in the early 1800s. Bowie's brawling adventures begin when he travels to New Orleans to sell lumber. He falls in love with self-centered Creole belle Virginia Mayo. He wants to make lots of money to impress and then marry her, so he speculates in land and cotton. Unfortunately for Bowie, she marries someone else. He fights several duels with local dandies and eventually meets Phyllis Kirk, the daughter of Texas's vice-governor. This new romance helps him to forget his earlier obsession with Mayo.

Jezebel (1938), WB. Dir. William Wyler; Sc. Clements Ripley, Abem Finkel, John Huston; Cast includes: Bette Davis, Henry Fonda, George Brent, Margaret Lindsay, Fay Bainter.

In William Wellman's drama, Bette Davis plays a tempestuous Southern belle. She loses her fiancé, Henry Fonda, who marries a Northerner. Davis is angry at this rejection and influences George Brent, who loves her, to believe Fonda offended her honor. Brent now challenges Fonda to a duel, but Fonda must leave suddenly. His younger brother (Richard Cromwell) takes his place on the field of honor and kills Brent.

Kennedy Square (1916), Vitagraph. Dir. S. Rankin Drew; Cast includes: Antonio Moreno.

S. Rankin Drew's delightful romantic drama is set in Baltimore, circa 1850, and it just oozes Southern charm. Antonio Moreno portrays a young Southerner who has a slight drinking problem. His sweetheart (Muriel Ostriche) rejects him because of his drinking. However, an elderly friend patches things up between the couple, and an engagement party is held. When a slightly inebriated young man who is also in love with Ostriche insists on dancing with the young woman, Moreno challenges him to a duel. When Moreno severely wounds the interloper in the chest, Moreno's father disowns him for breaking every rule of Southern hospitality and dishonoring the family. Moreno first moves to New York City, to Kennedy Square, a fashionable section of the city. After that, he tries his fortune in South America. He returns wealthy, buys the Southern estate of his elderly friend, who is now bankrupt, and restores it to him. All ends well as Moreno and his father make up and he renews his romance with his old sweetheart.

Mice and Men (1916), Par. Dir. J. Searle Dawley; Sc. Hugh Ford; Cast includes: Marguerite Clark, Marshall Neilan, Charles Waldron, Clarence Handyside, Maggie Halloway.

Charles Waldron, a gentleman from Virginia is unsuccessful in finding an ideal wife, and decides to raise his own. He adopts young Marguerite Clark, in this drama based on the play by Madeleine Lucette Ryley. Although grateful for his treatment and the education he has given her, the young woman falls in love with Marshall Neilan, Waldron's nephew. When she suspects Neilan of having a romantic affair with another woman, she drifts back to her benefactor and says she will marry him although she loves another. For some unexplained reason, Waldron reassures her that Neilan is faithful to her and the young lovers are married. Waldron resigns himself to bachelorhood with the knowledge that he has raised the ideal wife – for someone else.

Mississippi Gambler, The (1953), U. Dir. Rudolph Maté, Sc. Seton I. Miller; Cast includes: Tyrone Power, Piper Laurie, Julia Adams, John McIntire, Paul Cavanagh, John Baer.

In this romantic drama set in pre-Civil War days, Mike Fallon (Tyrone Power) meets Southern belle Piper Laurie and her brother (John Baer) before they all board a riverboat for New Orleans. Power and Baer have an honest card game but Power breaks Baer. Later in town, Power meets Laurie again. In the meantime, Baer is insulted but refuses a gun duel. His father intervenes as a second in order to salvage the family honor and dies for his efforts. The film represents New Orleans as the epicenter of dueling and voodoo.

President's Lady, The (1953), TCF. Dir. Henry Levin; Sc. John Patrick; Cast includes: Susan Hayward, Charlton Heston, John McIntire, Fay Bainter, Whitfield Connor.

Henry Levin's biographical drama is based on a novel by Irving Stone. It focuses on Andrew Jackson's marital problems. Charlton Heston portrays Jackson. Susan Hayward portrays his future wife, Rachel, who leaves her current philandering husband when she first meets Jackson. She obtains a divorce and marries Jackson, only to learn two years later that her divorce was never finalized and they are forced to remarry. The humiliating circumstances almost kill Jackson, who is compelled to defend her honor in a duel. His wife dies before his election to the White House. The focus of events in Jackson's life is more personal than historical. However, the dueling incident emphasizes the significant hold that that practice had on the society of the Old South.

Pride of the South, The (1913), Mutual. Dir. Burton King; Sc. Burton King; Cast includes: Mildred Bracken.

In this silent domestic tragedy, which takes place during the Civil War, a Confederate colonel disowns his daughter when she marries a Union officer. The family is not reunited until the proud colonel's little granddaughter convinces him to visit his daughter on her deathbed. The film includes several battle scenes.

River of Romance, The (1929), Par. Dir. Richard Wallace; Sc. Ethel Doherty, Dan Totheroe, John V. A. Weaver; Cast includes: Charles "Buddy" Rogers, Wallace Beery, Mary Brian, June Collyer.

Buddy Rogers, a son of the Old South, believes in nonviolence and refuses to fight any duel. Wallace Beery's romantic drama is based on the stage play *Magnolia* by Booth Tarkington. Rejected by Southern society, Rogers decides to join the crew of a riverboat and he soon rises to the challenge of a villain, thereby reestablishing his soiled reputation. A musical remake appeared in 1935 entitled *Mississippi*, with Bing Crosby in the lead and W. C. Fields.

Sins of Her Parent, The (1916), Dir. Frank Lloyd; Sc. Thomas Forman; Cast includes: Gladys Brockwell, William Clifford, George Webb.

Gladys Brockwell portrays a dual role – as mother and daughter – in Frank Lloyd's cautionary drama concerning a young woman's transgression. The son of an aristocratic family ruins Brockwell, whom he considers as "poor white trash." When he refuses to marry her, she forces him at gunpoint into a marriage union. Brockwell eventually leaves her husband and settles in Alaska as a dance-hall girl. She sends her money back home to raise her daughter who believes her to be dead. Years later, when she learns that the same man who had ruined her is about to take advantage of her daughter, she kills him. The mother and daughter are eventually reunited.

Stand Up and Fight (1939), MGM. Dir. W. S. Van Dyke; Sc. James M. Cain, Jane Murfin; Cast includes: Wallace Beery, Robert Taylor, Florence Rice, Helen Broderick, Charles Bickford.

Some films cleverly integrated several Southern themes into one drama. W. S. Van Dyke's action drama includes a mix of railroad building, a lost plantation, slave stealing, a feud, Southern chivalry and a Southern belle. Robert Taylor is an alcoholic, but reforms and becomes a captain of industry. However, when he loses his Maryland plantation to Wallace Beery, a bitter feud results between the two rivals. Taylor discovers that Beery, who operates a stagecoach line owned by Florence Rice, is helping thieves steal slaves. Taylor then starts building a new railroad line and tries to force Rice to sell him a right of way. He eventually gets the right of way and hires Rice and Berry as employees of the railroad.

Sun Shines Bright, The (1953), Dir. John Ford; Sc. Laurence Stallings; Cast includes: Charles Winninger, Arleen Whelan, John Russell, Stepin Fetchit, Francis Ford.

Based on the short stories of Irvin S. Cobb, John Ford's comedy drama focuses on Bill Priest (Charles Winninger), the mayor and judge of a small Kentucky town during the turn of the century. The film explores some of the town's beautiful traditions of the past as well as the some of its more shameful practices. Priest reveres his Confederate heritage and does not accept the defeat and shame of the South. General Woodford, a lonely figure, mourns the death of the Old South and the loss of his son, who was killed over a scandal involving his bride. Woodford refuses to recognize his daughter-in-law, now an ill and destitute widow who lives all alone. When she dies, Priest is one of the few locals willing to provide the widow a funeral. Finally, Woodford and the other townspeople are embarrassed and join the funeral procession. The large turnout symbolizes the town's acknowledgment of its dark past and serves as a good portent for the future.

Tol'able David (1921), FN. Dir. Henry King; Cast includes: Richard Barthelmess, Gladys Hulett, Walter P. Lewis, Ernest Torrence. Ralph Yearsley.

Honor and chivalry are found even in rural dramas such as this silent entry set in hillbilly country. Richard Barthelmess is the title character, the youngest son of the Kinemons. He wants to follow in his brother's footsteps as a postal driver. In the meantime, a neighbor receives visits from three relatives – escaped convicts who have been pursued across the state line. The visitors soon create problems for the family. They injure his older brother and steal his mailbag. Barthelmess fills in for his brother and eventually gets into a terrible fight with the fugitives, but he beats them and saves the mail. A local posse arrives in time to round up the escaped convicts.

Toy Wife, The (1938), MGM. Dir. Richard Thorpe; Sc. Zoe Akins; Cast includes: Luise Rainer, Robert Young, Melvyn Douglas, Barbara O'Neal.

Sometimes a devoted Southern belle and an honorable Southern gentleman succumb to the temptations of the heart and betray their code of honor. Luise Rainer, as a Southern belle in this old-fashioned historical drama, has just returned home to Louisiana after a trip to France. Her sister (Barbara O'Neil) is engaged to Melvyn Douglas. Robert Young, another aristocrat, wants to marry Rainer. However, she grows more interested in Douglas and lures him into marriage. They soon have a son, but Rainer finds it too difficult to manage the plantation, the slaves and her family. Douglas asks his sister-in-law, O'Neil, to move to the plantation and to assume his wife's chores. Rainer now has lots of time on her hands, so she decides to rekindle her romance with Young and runs off to New York with him. When Rainer and Young return to New Orleans, Douglas kills Young in a duel. Rainer becomes ill and dies, but her son, her husband and her sister forgive her for her sins. Rainer already won two Academy Awards prior to appearing in this film. The producer, Merian C. Cooper, had already made *King Kong* (1933).

Uncle Sam of Freedom Ridge (1920), Levey. Dir. George A. Beranger; Sc. Margaret Prescott Montague; Cast includes: George McQuarrie, William D. Corbett, Paul Kelly, Helen Flint.

A strong antiwar drama, George A. Beranger's silent film tells the story of a West Virginia mountain man and true patriot who sends his son to answer his nation's call to arms when World War I erupts. The father accepts the authority of the federal government, heeds the nation's call to arms and agrees with President Wilson's idealism. He personifies the New South. Convinced that his boy is fighting for Wilson's cause – to make the world safe for democracy – the father accepts the news of his son's death with a sense of comfort and resignation. Later, when he realizes that the "war to end wars" was but an illusion and nationalism is more important than democracy, he somewhat unrealistically commits suicide. He wraps himself in his cherished American flag that has always flown over his cabin and shoots himself in protest.

White Rose, The (1923), UA. Dir. D. W. Griffith; Sc. D. W. Griffith; Cast includes: Mae Marsh, Carol Dempster, Ivor Novello, Neil Hamilton.

In a change of pace from his usual historical pieces, D. W. Griffith presents an absorbing romantic drama. Mae Marsh leaves an orphan asylum and secures a job at a Southern resort, where she meets theology student Ivor Novello, the son of an important aristocratic Virginia family. Novello, traveling under a pseudonym, is engaged to Carol Dempster, a member of the social set. After having an affair with Marsh, Novello decides that she is too promiscuous and abandons her to return to his studies. Marsh, meanwhile, has his child and loses her job and apartment. On her own and destitute, she seeks a job elsewhere. Ironically, she inquires at the home of her seducer's fiancée, but is unsuccessful in obtaining a position. However, an African-American servant helps Marsh and offers her shelter in a cabin belonging to Dempster's family. When she becomes severely ill, the servant notifies Novello, who is now an ordained minister. He visits Marsh and decides to marry her. His former fiancée marries another society figure. Although the aristocratic Novello behaves abominably early in the story, he eventually redeems himself.

4

Southern Belles

Sir Walter Scott probably had a more influential role in shaping aristocratic myths in the antebellum South than he did in his native England. For some still unexplained reasons, Scott's idealization of the medieval courts and their knights and ladies fed into the Southern psyche of the time and led to the creation of the myth of the Southern belle. The wealthiest of the planters who could afford to live in a make-believe world adopted the fictional image of the medieval "lady" and fitted her into a Southern milieu. The Southern gentleman, in turn, was always quick to protect the honor of his woman. Following in the tradition of the medieval knight, the gentleman insulated his belle against the vulgar remarks and sexual innuendoes of the outside world and heaven help those who crossed the line.

The prevalent picture of the ideal Southern woman depicted her as an air-head with no political or economic ideas of her own. She couldn't vote and she was completely dependent upon her husband for everything – until the day he died. In all probability, the myth was not intended to restrict Southern women and to limit their possibilities. However, in a convoluted way it served just that purpose.

The Southern belle provided a counterpoint for the Southern "gentleman." She was a white woman, a virgin prior to her marriage and a self-indulgent free spirit without any obligations whatsoever. The belle always dressed in white, wore elaborately coiffured hairdos and spent most of her time drinking mint juleps and discussing Sir Walter Scott's novels. After marriage, she completely devoted herself to her husband and her family and was always virtuous and faithful to her husband. She was the glue that kept her Christian family together. Although this ideal Southern woman was catered to, the bottom line was that her life was one of severe restrictions.

A second minority view of the Southern *woman* (not belle), more powerful than the first, portrayed her as the backbone of the South; she was well bred with a power and fire beneath her composed exterior. The early Civil War dramas gave writers and directors a chance to expand the role of this strong Southern woman. Now she became useful and important as an added weapon to be employed against the Northern enemy. Several books, such as Seale Ballenger's 1997 entertaining and informative study, *Hell's Belles*, described some of the more famous and infamous of these strong Southern women. Ballenger's subjects ranged from the fictional Scarlett O'Hara and Blanche Dubois to the former Texas governor Ann Richards and Congresswoman Barbara Jordan, and from the refined to the hell-raisers.

Several Southern writers, including William Faulkner, Tennessee Williams and Lillian Hellman, in their post-Civil War works, offered a third portrait of the Southern woman – one less attractive than the ideal Southern belle while still at odds with the picture of the strong hell-raiser. This third view offered a portrait of pathetic fading belles who were relics of the Old South. They often sought escape from their shameful past and their uncertain future by indulging in alcohol, drugs and sordid sexual affairs with younger men.

*

Almost a Husband (1919), Goldwyn. Dir. Clarence G. Badger; Cast includes: Will Rogers, Peggy Wood, Herbert Standing, Cullen Landis, Clara Horton, Ed Brady.

Ziegfeld Follies star Will Rogers portrays a New Englander who moves to a small Southern village and becomes a schoolteacher. This silent romantic comedy is based on Ople Read's novel *Old Ebenezer*. Rogers becomes immediately popular with the local Southern belles who want to marry him. They trick him into a mock marriage with local Peggy Wood, who plays a proud but shy young belle of the town. The hoax, however, is transformed into a real problem when all discover that the alleged fraudulent minister was a real member of the clergy. Since no license is required in the state, the marriage is deemed legal. Peggy tries to avoid marrying an objectionable suitor who is being forced upon her by her father and asks her new husband to remain married to her. Meanwhile, the rejected suitor sends some nightriders against Rogers to force him out of town. Instead, the unintimidated bridegroom starts a run on the bank, whose president is Wood's father. Rogers finally bails out the bank and remains married to his new bride.

Girl Spy Before Vicksburg, The (1911), Kalem. Dir. Sidney Olcott.

Numerous films set in the South converted the sweet and innocent Southern belle into a dangerous foe. In Olcott's silent Civil War drama the heroine disguises herself as a member of a munitions convoy and destroys an ammunition wagon. Aside from some minor fictional elements in this short film, Vicksburg, Mississippi, was indeed a hub for a particularly active band of Confederate agents. Captain Henry B. Shaw organized and commanded a team of about 50 spies who provided intelligence reports for Confederate generals in the region. Known as Coleman's Scouts – after Shaw's nom de guerre – the group constantly engaged in perilous missions, which eventually took their toll. Ten were captured and several were hanged – including Sam Davis, the most famous. A few died of wounds and others were court-martialed before Vicksburg finally fell into Union hands. Southern patriots, including several young women, worked closely with Shaw's spies. Kate Patterson, one such daring belle, placed secret messages in a hollow tree. These local women were probably the source of inspiration for the heroines who appeared in Civil War silent and sound films.

Glass Menagerie, The (1950), WB. Dir. Irving Rapper; Sc. Tennessee Williams, Peter Berneis; Cast includes: Jane Wyman, Kirk Douglas, Gertrude Lawrence, Arthur Kennedy.

Gertrude Lawrence, as Amanda, a faded Southern belle, lives in the past. This drama is based on Tennessee Williams's play, which is set in New Orleans. Arthur Kennedy portrays Tom, the son, who narrates events in the life of the unhappy family. He is a poetic idealist trapped in a dead-end job in a shoe factory. His crippled sister Laura (Jane Wyman), an overly shy young woman, escapes into her own world of small animal figures, her "glass menagerie." She is brought out of her shell by a Gentleman Caller (Kirk Douglas), whom Tom invites to dinner to meet Laura. Just as she starts liking the guest, he reveals that he is engaged to be married. Laura is devastated and withdraws back to her glass menagerie. An argument ensues between the mother and Tom after the caller leaves, and Tom abandons his family to join the Merchant Marines.

Heart of Maryland, The (1915), Tiffany. Dir. Herbert Brenon; Sc. Herbert Brenon; Cast includes: Mrs. Leslie Carter, William E. Shay, Matt Snyder, Herbert Brenon, J. Farrell MacDonald.

The popular stage actress Leslie Carter, who starred as Maryland Calvert in the original stage production of David Belasco's play, repeated her role in this Civil War drama. The war stands between her and the man she loves. She is a Southern belle and he is from the North. Following a series of obstacles, they are finally reunited after the armistice. Carter initially played the role on stage for twenty years before starring in this silent film.

Heart of Maryland, The (1927), WB. Dir. Lloyd Bacon; Sc. C. Graham Baker; Cast includes: Dolores Costello, Jason Robards, Myrna Loy, Warner Richmond, Charles Bull.

Dolores Costello portrays a Southerner who falls in love with a young soldier (Jason Robards) from the North. This romantic Civil War drama is the second film version of Belasco's play. After several coincidental plot complications and the eventual armistice, the lovers get together. Charles Bull portrays Abraham Lincoln in this film, which has, among its few virtues, a rousing climax in a bell tower. This film projected Myrna Loy into stardom in the later sound era and she enjoyed a career that lasted for several decades.

Her Father's Son (1916), Par. Dir. William Desmond Taylor; Sc. Anne Fielder Brand; Cast includes: Vivian Martin, Alfred Vosburgh, Herbert Standing, Helen Jerome Eddy, Joe Massey.

Vivian Martin is a young Southerner who goes to live with her uncle after her father's death. Her uncle had promised her father to accept a nephew as his heir, so she poses as a man. Dressed in men's attire, she is able to fool her uncle (Herbert Standing) and her cousin (Helen Jerome Eddy). When war erupts and a handsome young lieutenant visits the uncle's home, complications arise for the heroine. She eventually reveals her true identity and a romance blossoms. The young officer fights in several battle sequences.

Horse Soldiers, The (1959), UA. Dir. John Ford; Sc. Lee Mahin, Martin Rackin; Cast includes: John Wayne, William Holden, Constance Towers, Althea Gibson, Hoot Gibson.

Constance Towers is a Southern belle who parries with John Wayne, a battle-hardened Union colonel. John Ford's Civil War drama is based on an actual incident. Wayne leads his Northern troop of cavalry on a raid behind enemy lines. A humane army surgeon (William Holden) accompanies the troops. When Towers overhears Wayne's plans for the raid, she is taken along as a prisoner and provides the romantic interest for both Wayne and Holden. By the end of the film Towers and Wayne fall in love with each other.

Director Ford's cynical view of war breaks through several times. In one scene, an elderly headmaster of a Southern military academy proudly but foolishly leads his eager young boys in a march against the Union cavalry. Wayne, surprised at the advance of the eager boys and averse to massacring them, quickly retreats with his men. In another scene, Holden makes repeated sarcastic comments about Wayne's apparent impatience to risk his life and the lives of his troops in order to challenge the enemy.

Two major battle sequences add to the excitement of this outdoor action drama. In an early portion, Wayne's troops surprise a trainload of rebel soldiers who have come to rescue a town under siege by his cavalry. In the ensuing battle the brave but foolhardy Southerners are slaughtered in their head-on attack. The film ends with another engagement between Wayne and the enemy. With a column of Southern soldiers approaching from the rear and an enemy force before him on the other side of a creek, he leads a desperate but heroic charge across a wooden bridge and wipes out the rebel resistance. Holden acts as Wayne's foil and volunteers to remain behind to care for the wounded as the advancing Confederate column approaches. Meanwhile, Wayne blows up the bridge and leads his troops to safety.

In the Fall of '64 (1914), U. Dir. Francis Ford; Sc. Grace Cunard; Cast includes: Francis Ford, Grace Cunard.

Director-actor Francis Ford portrays a Confederate captain arrested for spying behind Union lines in his silent two-reel Civil War drama. Grace Cunard plays Ford's sweetheart, a Southern belle whose estate is captured by Northern troops. When Ford is captured, Cunard poses as a slow-witted boy to gain access to Union quarters, where he is being held. She manages to extinguish a candle, allowing her lover to escape in the ensuing darkness. Cunard later steals the enemy's battle plans and crosses into Confederate territory. The information permits Ford and his troops to score a victory over the Union troops.

The melodramatics of the plot are no doubt fictitious, but a similar incident actually occurred during the conflict in Nashville. Ann Patterson, daughter of a Southern physician whose family members were all spies for the Confederacy, helped free Thomas Joplin after his capture by Union troops. Joplin was a guerrilla spy in Coleman's Scouts, a force of about 50 agents operating in Tennessee.

Jezebel (1938), WB. Dir. William Wyler; Sc. Clements Ripley, Abem Finkel, John Huston; Cast includes: Bette Davis, Henry Fonda, George Brent, Margaret Lindsay, Fay Bainter.

Obstinate Southern belle Bette Davis provokes her fiancé (Henry Fonda) into jealousy but reforms when he is stricken with the plague. This romantic drama is set in 1852 New Orleans and is based on a play by Owen Davis. When Fonda is ordered to a bayou island with the other stricken souls, the self-centered Davis suddenly redeems herself and volunteers to accompany him. The conventional Southern ingredients are present – Southern chivalry, honor and hospitality, formal balls with Southern belles and well-mannered gentlemen and pistol duels.

Jitterbugs (1943), TCF. Dir. Malcolm St. Clair; Sc. Scott Darling; Cast includes: Stan Laurel, Oliver Hardy, Vivian Blaine, Bob Bailey, Douglas Fowley, Noel Madison.

Stan Laurel and Oliver Hardy are on the road but run out of gas. A con artist rescues the boys and hires them to perform in a jitterbug band in his carnival. The trio meets a young woman whose mother has been cheated out of her land and they decide to help the family by searching for the crooks in New Orleans. The young woman is hired as a singer aboard a showboat, Laurel poses as her aunt from the East and Hardy dresses as a Southern millionaire. They manage to get back her money and the con artist calls the police in time to capture the thieves – just as Laurel and Hardy plop into the river.

Madam Who? (1918), W. W. Hodkinson. Dir. Reginald Barker; Sc. Monte M. Katterjohn; Cast includes: Bessie Barriscale, Edward Coxen, Howard Hickman, Joseph J. Dowling, David M. Hartford, Fanny Midgley.

A young Confederate is willing to sacrifice her life for the South and engages in espionage in this Civil War spy drama. Bessie Barriscale portrays the brave Southerner who, when accused of being a traitor to the South, determines to find the real spies. She succeeds in her mission after cleverly outmaneuvering several Union officers. In one particularly dramatic scene, she struggles with a drunken villain (Howard Hickman). Although chiefly a spy drama, there are a few battle scenes near the conclusion.

Raintree County (1957), MGM. Dir. Edward Dmytryk; Sc. Millard Kaufman; Cast includes: Montgomery Clift, Elizabeth Taylor, Eva Marie Saint, Nigel Patrick, Lee Marvin.

Spoiled Southern belle Elizabeth Taylor steals Montgomery Clift away from his girlfriend Eve Marie Saint. This historical drama is based on Ross Lockridge Jr.'s novel. Taylor's romantic maneuver occurs while she is visiting Raintree County in Indiana, just before the Civil War breaks out. The young couple settles in the Deep South. Her husband, Clift, was raised in a slave state and opposes the institution. They then return to Raintree County. Taylor has a nervous breakdown and takes her young son back to the South. Meanwhile, Clift joins the Union army. After the war Clift locates his son in Atlanta and discovers that his wife is in an asylum. She temporarily regains her sanity but regresses and eventually drowns. All ends well when Clift goes back to Saint.

Scarlet Drop, The (1918), U. Dir. John Ford; Sc. George Hively; Cast includes: Harry Carey, Vester Pegg, Molly Malone, Betty Schade, Martha Mattox.

Harry Carey, as "Kaintuck" Ridge, joins a band of guerrillas during the Civil War but escapes to the West to avoid capture. He carves out a new life, but finds himself in difficulty when he rescues a Southern belle from the clutches of the villainous Graham Lyons, played by M. K. Wilson. Lyons wants the young woman, but "Kaintuck" interferes and is shot for his trouble. After recovering and overcoming other complications, he reunites with the heroine in the final scene. The title refers to a drop of blood that falls from a loft where the woman has hidden the wounded hero. The "scarlet drop" lands in a sheriff's whiskey glass, thereby alerting him to "Kaintuck's" whereabouts. The same device appears in the musical drama *The Girl of the Golden West* (1938), starring Jeanette MacDonald and Nelson Eddy.

So Red the Rose (1935), Par. Dir. King Vidor; Sc. Laurence Stallings, Maxwell Anderson, Edwin Justus Mayer; Cast includes: Margaret Sullavan, Walter Connolly, Janet Beecher, Robert Cummings, Randolph Scott, Elizabeth Patterson.

King Vidor's Civil War drama is based on Stark Young's novel and centers on the romantic and domestic problems of a Southern family. Walter Connolly portrays a patriarchal plantation owner who is called to fight against the Union when his only son and heir is killed in battle. Margaret Sullavan, now the mistress of the large Southern plantation, sees her sheltered lifestyle turned upside down by the conflict. She is sustained only by her love for Randolph Scott. But she is able to hold her family together even after her mansion is burned down. Scott plays a Southerner who sympathizes with Lincoln and the Union's cause. The film depicts the Confederate women as strong Southern women and the men as gallant officers while painting the invading Union soldiers as brutish louts who burn and pillage.

This 1935 production sympathizes with the South and with the institution of slavery. In fact, when their masters ride off to do battle against the Union liberators bent on freeing the blacks, the slaves eagerly cheer them. We have no records on audience reaction, so we'll never know how many viewers were bothered by this pro-Southern bias. Laurence Stallings, Maxwell Anderson and Edwin Justus Mayer collaborated on the screenplay. The film failed at the box office – perhaps because of the built-in pro-Southern bias – and effected the production of other Civil War movies for the next several years. Civil War films became anathema to most of the studios who, recalling the expensive disaster of *So Red the Rose*, later rejected such works as *Gone With the Wind*, much to the later dismay of some moguls.

Steel Magnolias (1989), Tri-Star. Dir. Herbert Ross; Sc. Robert Harling; Cast includes: Sally Field, Dolly Parton, Shirley MacLaine, Olympia Dukakis, Daryl Hannah, Tom Skerritt, Sam Shepard.

Herbert Ross' comedy drama, based on a play by Robert Harling, takes place in Louisiana during the 1980s and involves a group of women who are close friends with plenty of time for gossip. "If you have something bad to say about somebody," one character chortles, "sit down right here beside me." Their meeting place is a beauty shop operated by Dolly Parton. She has just hired a new worker (Daryl Hannah), who works hard with Sally Field, the mother of a young bride. Shirley MacLaine is a wealthy and mean local citizen who occasionally drops in, as does Olympia Dukakis, who has lost her husband but is presently entertaining a prospective potbellied suitor. These characters are all strong Southern women who are batty but able to overcome most crises.

The comic chatter ("What separates us from the animals is our ability to accessorize," Dukakis quips) suggests little of the impending tragedy. When tragedy does strike and there is a death in their little group, these women, who are the "steel magnolias" of the title, have the capacity to grieve and the mettle to smile through their tears.

Streetcar Named Desire, A (1951), WB. Dir. Elia Kazan; Sc. Oscar Saul; Cast includes: Vivien Leigh, Marlon Brando, Kim Hunter, Karl Malden.

Vivien Leigh, as Blanche Du Bois, a fading Southern belle, tries to salvage the last vestiges of her world of gentility from the incessant battering of Stanley, her brutal brother-in-law (Marlon Brando). This drama is based on the play by Tennessee Williams. Dismissed from her teaching position for having an affair with one of her 17-year-old pupils, Blanche joins her pregnant sister Stella (Kim

Hunter) and her husband Stanley in New Orleans. Stella is earthier and deeply in love with her crude husband, in contrast to her sister, who is more flighty, sensitive, ethereal and neurotic. Blanche meets Mitch (Karl Malden), a simple bachelor friend of Stanley's. He takes a liking to Blanche's genteel ways and considers marrying her. Blanche is desperate for a little kindness and sees in Mitch a chance for a new life. But Stanley destroys her romantic illusions when he learns of her promiscuous past and informs Mitch. Somewhat distraught and disillusioned at the news, Mitch rejects the delicate Blanche.

Somewhat later, Stanley is alone with Blanche and a battle of wits ensues. Her delicate, genteel and affected mannerisms exasperate Stanley, who has not made love to his wife in weeks because of her pregnancy. He goes after Blanche, who tries to escape, but she is too weak to resist his strength and passion. Stanley then rapes Blanche, who has provoked him. This final indignity, the destruction of her last lingering traces of pride and self-respect, is more than Blanche can withstand and she suffers a mental breakdown. Later, a doctor and a matron come to take her away to a mental hospital. Believing they are escorting her to a liaison, she takes the doctor's arm and leaves with him, saying, "Whoever you are, I have always depended on the kindness of strangers." Some suggest that Blanche, on an allegorical level, may represent a decaying society in a brutal world. Several changes from play to film were made to accommodate studio chiefs. In the play Blanche's first husband was homosexual, but in the screen version he was described as mentally unstable.

Those Without Sin (1917), Par. Dir. Marshall Neilan; Sc. George D. Price; Cast includes: Blanche Sweet, Tom Forman, C. H. Geldert, Guy Oliver.

Blanche Sweet portrays a Southerner in this Civil War drama set in the South. Entrusted on a secret mission, she is captured by Union troops. When an unsavory Northern colonel threatens harm to her family unless she gives herself to him, she reluctantly consents. The colonel then allows her family to escape.

Vanishing Virginian, The (1941), MGM. Dir. Frank Borzage; Sc. Jan Fortune; Cast includes: Frank Morgan, Kathryn Grayson, Spring Byington, Natalie Thompson, Douglass Newland.

Kathryn Grayson stars in this autobiographical drama. The film is based on Rebecca Yancey Williams's bestseller about a strong-willed Southern belle growing up in the early 20th century. Grayson, as Rebecca Williams, upsets her conservative family when she joins the women's suffrage movement – over the objections of her father, Frank Morgan, a civil servant. Despite his headstrong views and his eccentricities, Morgan's love for his family overcomes his distaste for his daughter's views and behavior.

5

Economic Conditions

The invention of the cotton gin in 1793 changed the creaking economy of the South almost overnight by increasing the production of the short-staple, cotton which brought a premium price for growers. The burgeoning plantations quickly developed into massive agricultural factories and the search for quick profits led the planters into the virgin bottomlands of the Gulf States. They bought more slaves and land to grow more cotton. By 1850, the South resembled more of an oligarchy rather than a democracy. The 1860 census indicated a population within the fifteen Southern states of about 1,000,000 million whites owning five or more slaves, more than 6,000,000 non-slave-holding whites, 250,000 free blacks and almost 4,000,000 slaves. Within the slave-owning class, slightly over 1,700 families each owned over 100 slaves. These families represented the economic and political power in the South. Most of the romantic antebellum Southern literature focused on these wealthy planters. And, it was precisely these people who drove the Southern military machine into the war.

*

The South was deeply affected by import tariffs which the industrialized North used to protect manufacturers. The North demanded high tariffs to safeguard their manufactured products from foreign competition. The agrarian South, on the other hand, opposed tariffs since its people imported many manufactured goods. In addition to the attraction of British and Northern imports, the plantation economy in itself essentially made the South a colony of Britain and of New England. The plantation system thus hampered the development of cities in the South.

During the 1850s the North was quick to take advantage of the new industrial advances. Modern textile factories, smelting works, blast furnaces and rolling mills were built in the cities of the North, which benefited from the fresh European immigration. These new inductees into the burgeoning labor class proved eager to embrace the virtues and promise of democracy. The agricultural South, on the other hand, preferred to plow their profits back into the land and increase the number of slaves instead of dotting their landscape with unsightly mills and factories with their billowing smokestacks.

*

As railroads expanded, they began to unite the West and North, and both regions found more in common with each other than with the South. The new immigrant farmers and laborers in the West found little in common with Southern landowners and slaves. The new transportation, including the steamship, proved faster and more efficient than the riverboat. New York replaced New Orleans as the major eastern outlet to international trade, and Chicago surpassed St. Louis as the active marketing hub of the interior. Eastern money poured into the West for further expansion and growth, resulting in the shipment of agricultural products from the West to the East in exchange for the latter's finished manufactured goods.

*

The Mississippi River carried various riverboats, most of which were used to transport products, crops and passengers. Some of these boats were "showboats" which were actually floating theaters and presented present popular plays, vaudeville, concerts and other attractions. Gambling took place on board in separate casinos. Propelled by steam or transported by steam tug, the showboats journeyed up and down rivers – especially the Mississippi – from early in the 19th century until the late 1920s. They ranged from rafts with an improvised auditorium and stage to large elaborate steamships with well-equipped theaters. Performers and other crewmembers often included the owner's family. Hollywood was quick to romanticize the boats and their passengers' adventures.

*

Edna Ferber memorialized the showboat in her novel, *Show Boat* (1926). The book was later made into a successful musical play by Jerome Kern and Oscar Hammerstein II and was then followed by at least three film versions (1929, 1936, 1951). The showboat increased in importance in films, especially during the sound era, since it expanded the opportunities of adding music, singing, dancing and comedy to the plot. Films with a showboat setting include Christy Cabanne's musical *Dixie Jamboree* (1945), Jean Yarbrough's comedy

The Naughty Nineties (1945), with Bud Abbott and Lou Costello, and Frederick de Cordova's musical *Frankie and Johnny* (1966), with Elvis Presley.

Another Part of the Forest (1948), Dir. Michael Gordon; Sc. Vladimir Pozner; Cast includes: Fredric March, Ann Blyth, Edmond O'Brien, Florence Eldridge, Dan Duryea, John Dall.

A prequel to Lillian Hellman's play and film *The Little Foxes*, *Another Part of the Forest* shows the Hubbard family twenty years earlier. Fredric March, the tyrannical head of the family, flaunts his wealth to his Southern neighbors – a wealth built upon the backs of Confederate troops during the Civil War. March humiliates Edmond O'Brien and Dan Duryea, his sons, especially Duryea whom he characterizes as a whining coward. "Try to remember," March enlightens Duryea, "that though ignorance becomes a Southern gentleman, cowardice does not." When the greedy March banishes O'Brien for opposing him, the son digs up the truth about his father's past. He discovers that his father made black-market money during the Civil War and was indirectly responsible for the death of Confederate troops. The son blackmails his father into relinquishing his wealth to him and the mother (Florence Eldridge) completely disowns her greedy children.

*

The author of *Another Part of the Forest*, Lillian Hellman (1905-1984) was the daughter of an Alabama mother and a New Orleans father. She was born in New Orleans at the turn of the century and became one of the leading members of the group of writers of the "Southern Renaissance" movement. She attended schools both in New Orleans and New York.

Hellman constantly portrays life as a struggle between good and evil, with the latter often victorious. Although she could define evil in her writings, in real life she stood truth on its head and became a leading apologist for Stalin throughout his purges and murders. Her defense of the Soviet leader was so biased that it led Mary McCarthy to comment: "Every word that Lillian Hellman writes is a lie – including 'and' and 'the.' " Despite these very considerable shortcomings, her devotees still consider Hellman the "leading woman dramatist of the twentieth century."

*

Cameo Kirby (1914), Par. Dir. Oscar Apfel; Sc. William C. de Mille; Cast includes: Dustin Farnum, Winifred Kingston, Dick La Reno.

Dustin Farnum portrays the title character, Kirby, a gentleman gambler in the days of Southern chivalry. The film takes place aboard a Mississippi riverboat in the antebellum South. Falsely accused of murder, Kirby is forced to flee, with a posse in full pursuit. A duel in the woods between Kirby and the real killer, an unscrupulous gambler, resolves the tale and the hero is exonerated. An exciting riverboat race adds to the suspense of the story.

*

Carolina Moon (1940), Rep. Dir. Frank McDonald; Sc. Winston Miller; Cast includes: Gene Autry, Smiley Burnette, June Storey, Mary Lee.

Singing cowboy Gene Autry and his sidekick Smiley Burnette journey to the Carolinas to help old-time plantation owners hold on to their property when a scheming neighbor (Hardie Albright) threatens them. Autry and his sidekick fight the villain and return the plantation title to the true owners.

Corner in Cotton, A (1916), Metro. Dir. Fred J. Balshofer. Cast includes: Marguerite Snow.

Wealthy Marguerite Snow, an independent-minded young woman, in this silent drama, rescues a Southern businessman and his son from her own father's attempt to corner the cotton market. She hires a private investigator to check her father's business and ends up falling in love with the investigator's son.

Daughter of Maryland, A (1917), Mutual. Dir. John O'Brien; Cast includes: Edna Goodrich, William T. Carlton, Helen Strickland, Carl Brickett.

Following the Civil War, a wealthy major agrees to his daughter's engagement to an unscrupulous young lawyer. The major then hires a Northern landscape artist to upgrade the grounds of his estate. The daughter (Edna Goodrich) initially dislikes the stranger because he's a Northerner. However, when the lawyer is caught robbing the major's safe, he shoots the father. He pays for his crime when he is killed in a fight. The daughter now realizes how mistaken she was about the Northerner and eventually marries him.

*

Dixie Jamboree (1945), PRC. Dir. Christy Cabanne; Sc. Sam Neuman; Cast includes: Frances Langford, Guy Kibbee, Eddie Quillan, Charles Butterworth.

Captain Jack (Guy Kibbee) is at the helm of The *Ellabella,* the last of the showboats. The boat plods along the river, putting on shows at various ports along the Mississippi, in this weak musical. Two fugitive con artists posing as vacationers, Lyle Talbot and Frank Jenks, are on board during one of its trips Frances Langford joins the troupe while Kibbee goes about selling his patent medicine. The con men think he's a moonshiner and scheme to hijack the showboat. Langford and Eddie Quillan, a tramp trumpeter, disrupt their plans. The production treats us to some of Langford's songs and we get to meet some quirky characters along the way.

End of the Road, The (1915), Mutual. Dir. Thomas Ricketts; Cast includes: Harold Lockwood, May Allison.

Harold Lockwood portrays the hero in this romantic drama, which includes moonshining. The story is set in the Carolina Pines and on Southern estates. Lockwood is falsely accused of betraying May Allison, his girlfriend. However, the real villain, a moonshiner and a counterfeiter, is finally exposed. Lockwood manages to prevent Allison's farm from being sold after foreclosure.

Foxes of Harrow, The (1947), TCF. Dir. John M. Stahl; Sc. Wanda Tuchock; Cast include: Rex Harrison, Maureen O'Hara, Richard Haydn, Victor McLaglen.

Rex Harrison portrays Stephen Fox, an adventurer who rises to fame and fortune in nineteenth century New Orleans. The film is based on the novel by Frank Yerby. In one scene, Fox is thrown off a Mississippi riverboat for cheating at cards. His skill at cards and his charm with women soon catapult him to wealth. He persuades Maureen O'Hara, the daughter of an aristocratic family to marry him, but a wedding night quarrel strains their marriage for the next several years. The couple finally resolve their bitter differences. The film explores the South's aristocratic traditions as well as life on the Mississippi showboats and also touches upon voodoo practices.

Frankie and Johnny (1966), UA. Dir. Frederick de Cordova; Sc. Alex Gottlieb; Cast includes: Elvis Presley, Donna Douglas, Harry Morgan, Sue Anne Langdon, Nancy Kovack.

Based on the famous folk song, the plot of this musical, set in the nineteenth century, revolves about two Mississippi riverboat entertainers. Elvis Presley portrays Johnny and Donna Douglas plays Frankie. Although they are lovers, complications set in when Johnny's excessive gambling gets him involved with redhead Nancy Kovack, who, supposedly, will bring him luck.

Hell's Highway (1932), RKO. Dir. Rowland Brown; Sc. Samuel Ornitz; Cast includes: Richard Dix, Tom Brown, Louise Carter, Rochelle Hudson, C. Henry Gordon.

A local contractor hires convicts from a Southern prison camp to help build a new road. For the contractor to make a profit, the prisoners must work twice as hard as usual. To force the recalcitrant convicts to work longer and harder, the guards use the dreaded "sweat box," a corrugated iron box that barely holds one man. One prisoner who faints is strangled to death from the leather collar around his neck.

Iron Mistress, The (1952), WB. Dir. Gordon Douglas; Sc. James R. Webb; Cast include: Alan Ladd, Virginia Mayo, Joseph Calleia, Phyllis Kirk, Douglas Dick.

Gordon Douglas's biographical drama concerns adventurer Jim Bowie, who decides to make his fortune by speculating in land and cotton. He meets Virginia Mayo, the daughter of a wealthy New Orleans aristocrat and tries to win her hand. After all of his business shenanigans, he learns that she has already married someone else. Alan Ladd portrays the legendary Bowie.

*

The hero of the film, James Bowie (1796-1836), was born in Kentucky and was already a famous frontiersman in Louisiana before moving to Texas in 1828, where he became a leading figure in the resistance against Mexico. There, he joined other Americans who had settled in Texas under the leadership of Stephen Austin. Austin received Mexican government approval for bringing in American colonists to help populate the country's sparsely settled northern region.

Bowie married the daughter of the Mexican Vice-Governor of Texas. His Mexican marriage and the problems it engendered are covered in John Wayne's *The Alamo* (1960). The film was a large-scale production featuring Richard Widmark as Bowie, one of the principal characters in the film. *The Last Command* (1955), a film in which Bowie, played by Sterling Hayden, is the main character, takes liberties with his real-life role in Texas politics. It portrays him as a personal friend of the Mexican dictator-general Santa Anna. Contrary to the historical record, the film claims that Bowie sought to negotiate a peaceful settlement in the growing dispute between the American colonists and the Mexican government.

Bowie accepted a colonel's commission in the army of Texas when war broke out and, together with William B. Travis, organized the defense of the Alamo, a fortified former mission building in San Antonio. Bowie was killed, along with all the other defenders, in Santa Anna's attack on the Alamo. He was reportedly shot while he lay sick on his cot. (This is depicted in *The Last Command*). His reputed invention of the Bowie knife – often the center of action in several of his film biographies – is an unverified legend. He also appears at the Alamo in *Man of Conquest* (1939), based on the life of Samuel Houston.

*

Little Foxes, The (1941), WB. Dir. William Wyler; Sc. Lillian Hellman, Dorothy Parker; Cast includes: Bette Davis, Herbert Marshall, Charles Dingle, Carl Benton Reid.

William Wyler's drama is based on Lillian Hellman's biting play. The film focuses on Regina Hubbard (Bette Davis), the central figure of the Hubbard clan, a rapacious and unscrupulous Southern family. Davis schemes against her ailing husband to raise the $75,000 her brother Ben needs to build a local cotton mill. Her husband (Herbert Marshall), discovers this attempt to exploit the cheap labor of a Southern town and determines to stop her. "There must be better ways of getting rich than from building sweatshops," he says angrily. "You'll wreck the town, you and your brothers, you'll wreck the country, you and your kind, if they let you." In another scene, their African-American maid comments: "There's people who eat up the whole earth and all the people in it, like in the *Bible* with the locusts. Then there is people who stand around and watch them do it. Sometimes I think it ain't right to just stand and watch them do it."

*

Mississippi (1935), Par. Dir. Edward Sutherland; Sc. Claude Binyon, Herbert Fields, Jack Cunningham, Francis Martin; Cast includes: Bing Crosby, W. C. Fields, Joan Bennett, Gail Patrick.

After avoiding several duels, Bing Crosby is marked as a social outcast in the Old South and joins a showboat captained by W. C. Fields in this musical romance based on Booth Tarkington's play *Magnolia.* Crosby soon recovers his reputation and wins the love of Joan Bennett, after he sings a few songs from a Rodgers and Hart score. The story had been filmed earlier as a silent film titled *The Fighting Coward* (1924) and an early sound version, *River of Romance* (1929), with Buddy Rogers.

Mississippi Gambler, The (1953), U. Dir. Rudolph Maté, Sc. Seton I. Miller; Cast includes: Tyrone Power, Piper Laurie, Julia Adams, John McIntire, Paul Cavanagh, John Baer.

The riverboat plays a central role in this romantic drama set in pre-Civil War days. As Mike Fallon, the title character, Tyrone Power meets Southern belle Piper Laurie and her brother (John Baer) before they all board a riverboat for New Orleans. Besides the colorful riverboat, this romantic drama includes elements of New Orleans local color as well as fencing, gun duels and a voodoo dance. Over all, *The Mississippi Gambler* emphasizes the importance of river transportation in the antebellum South.

Naughty Nineties, The (1945), U. Dir. Jean Yarbrough; Sc. Edmund L. Hartmann, John Grant; Cast includes: Bud Abbott, Lou Costello, Alan Curtis, Rita Johnson, Henry Travers.

The comedy team of Bud Abbott and Lou Costello gets mixed up with a showboat and some tough gamblers in this mediocre comedy set in the Gay Nineties. The pals soon struggle to free the captain from the schemes of a gambling trio intent on taking control of the boat. The one-liners range from bad to worse. Bud and Lou, in tuxedos, enter a plush nightclub. "It don't look nice chewing gum in that suit," Bud says, criticizing his pal. "I'm chewing in my mouth," Lou corrects Bud. In another scene they play at a crooked roulette wheel. They watch as the ball hops off their winning number and moves to another one. "What kind of ball is that?" Bud complains. "It's got the hiccups," Lou suggests. Nevertheless, the film is saved by the comedy team's perennially funny performance of their classic routine, "Who's on First."

Reap the Wild Wind (1942), Par. Dir. Cecil B. DeMille; Sc. Alan LeMay, Charles Bennett, Jesse Lasky; Cast includes: Ray Milland, John Wayne, Paulette Goddard, Raymond Massey, Robert Preston, Susan Hayward, Lynne Overman.

Cecil B. DeMille's brawling historical drama is set chiefly in Key West in the 1840s and it describes the deliberate sabotage of ships by several scheming salvage operators. These schemers deliberately cause merchant ships to smash into the reefs during their Key West passage to the West Indies and South America. The unscrupulous men then grab the cargoes of the shipwrecked vessels. Paulette Goddard, portrays a wild daughter of the captain of one of these salvage ships. She inherits the ship and falls in love both with John Wayne, a shipwrecked captain, and Ray Milland, a lawyer and son of a wealthy shipping magnate. Milland is trying to gain evidence against the crooked mastermind (Raymond Massey) and his stooges who have wrecked many of the ships. In one scene Massey tries to entice naïve Wayne to join him in the slave trade. "They need ten thousand blacks in Mississippi," he explains. "Black men bring a dollar a pound. I'll put you back on the ship. You take it to the Gold Coast, load it with black ivory. In two years you'll own your own ship." The film includes scenes of old Charleston and the interiors of impressive mansions. One of Cecil B. DeMille's trademarks is his architectural scenes.

Show Boat (1936), U.. Dir. James Whale; Sc. Oscar Hammerstein II; Cast includes: Irene Dunne, Allan Jones, Helen Morgan, Paul Robeson, Charles Winninger.

Helen Morgan portrays the leading lady of a Mississippi showboat in Whale's musical. This film is the second screen version of the landmark stage play by Jerome Kern and Oscar Hammerstein II which was itself based on the novel by Edna Ferber. When it is learned that Julie (Morgan) is a mulatto, she is forced to quit the show because of local legal codes. "You wouldn't call a man a white man that had Negro blood in him, would you?" someone asks the sheriff. "No, I wouldn't, not in Mississippi," the lawman replies. "One drop of Negro blood makes you a Negro in these parts!" Irene Dunne, as Magnolia, a singer on her father's showboat, meets Allan Jones, the gambler Gaylord Ravenal, and they marry and have a baby. Jones wanders off for years but finally returns and finds that his daughter is about to become a singing star. Dunne and Jones are finally happily reunited. Charles Winninger plays Captain Jack, and Paul Robeson, as Joe, gives a stirring rendition of "Ole Man River." The story was previously filmed in 1929 and again, in color, in 1951, directed by George Sidney and starring Kathryn Grayson, Ava Gardner, Howard Keel and Joe E. Brown.

*

Harry Pollard directed the first screen version (1929) of Edna Ferber's novel. The film was based on the successful stage production and, since technology was still in its infancy, was made half in sound and half silent. The film is fairly faithful to the book as it follows a showboat up and down the Mississippi River. Joseph Schildkraut portrays Gaylord Ravenal, the villainous gambler, Otis Harlan plays Captain Andy, and Alma Rubens is the tragic Julie. The songs include "Ol' Man River," "Bill," "Can't Help Lovin' Dat Man," "Look Down That Lonesome Road," "Here Comes the Show Boat," "Down South," and the spirituals "Deep River" and "I've Got Shoes." In real life, Rubens died of drug addiction at an insane asylum at age 33, two years after the release of the film. The production failed at the box-office, but the next version in 1936 corrected most of the shortcomings by avoiding a lengthy prologue while adhering more to the basic plot.

Show Boat (1951), MGM. Dir. George Sidney; Sc. John Lee Mahin (uncredited), George Wells, Jack McGowan; Cast includes: Kathryn Grayson, Ava Gardner, Howard Keel, Joe E. Brown, Marge Champion, Gower Champion, William Warfield.

George Sidney's third film version of Edna Ferber's popular novel and play was much better than the 1929 version and almost equaled the quality of the second 1936 adaptation starring Irene Dunne, Allan Jones, Paul Robeson and Helen Morgan. This production boasted lush Technicolor and offered Kathryn Grayson as Magnolia, Ava Gardner as Julie, Howard Keel as the gambler Gaylord Ravenal, and Joe E. Brown as Captain Andy. At a cost of more than $2 million, it earned more than four times that sum after its initial release. When Gardner, the star singer aboard Brown's showboat, rejects the advances of a deckhand, he informs the sheriff that the entertainer, who is part black, is married to a white man, which is illegal in Mississippi. The sheriff does his duty and attempts to arrest Gardner, but she escapes his clutches by jumping boat. Meanwhile, Grayson falls in love with gambler Keel and they marry. He stops gambling and becomes part of the show. However, he soon reverts to his old habits and the couple separate. Gardner finally brings them back together. Large pieces of the plot were changed from the 1936 version. Gardner's voice proved ineffective, so she was forced to mouth the songs while Annette Warren provided the singing, much to the chagrin of the actress.

Steamboat 'Round the Bend (1935), TCF. Dir. John Ford; Sc. Dudley Nichols, Lamar Trotti; Cast includes: Will Rogers, Anne Shirley, Irvin S. Cobb, Eugene Pallette, John McGuire, Stepin Fetchit.

Will Rogers, as a dealer in patent medicine, becomes involved in a riverboat race on the Mississippi against Irvin S. Cobb, the owner of the competing riverboat. John Ford's comedy drama is based on Ben Lucien Burman's novel. Rogers's nephew kills a man in self-defense and his uncle makes him surrender to the authorities while he searches for half-crazed evangelist Berton Churchill, a witness who can clear the young man. Popular character player Stepin Fetchit adds a lot to the comedy. Ben Lucien Burman wrote the novel and Dudley Nichols and Lamar Trotti were the screenwriters.

6

Political Conditions

The framers of the U.S. Constitution made no provision for political parties. They believed that parties bred corruption and impeded people from freely judging issues on their merits alone. Men like George Washington, and his fellow Founding Fathers included in his cabinet persons with diverse political philosophies and policies. However, political parties soon emerged based on local or temporary issues and controversies. One faction, commonly identified with Secretary of the Treasury Alexander Hamilton and Vice-President John Adams, became known as the Federalist Party. It promoted an active federal government, a Treasury that supported the nation's economic life and a pro-British foreign policy. Another faction, whose central figures were Secretary of State Thomas Jefferson and fellow Virginian James Madison, became known as the Republican Party, which advocated a limited federal government, little government interference in economic affairs, and a pro-French foreign policy. It was this faction that came to dominate Southern politics.

Later changes in the U.S. economy and social structure brought about the gradual formation of new political alignments within the two-party system. One change included the country's westward expansion, with an accompanying development of a large class of pioneer farmers. Their frontier communities represented a type of democratic society never before witnessed in any country. Another change was the agricultural revolution in the Southern states, following the invention of both the cotton gin and textile machinery. These resulted in the dynamic growth of slavery in the South and in a considerable growth in the wealth and influence of manufacturers, merchants, bondholders, and land speculators of the Northern states. The ideas of limited government – from Jeffersonian democracy – appealed to the sectional and class interests of the western frontier and the South. The policies once advocated by the defunct Federalists, however, were still popular with the minority of Americans who favored a more active economic role for the federal government.

The Old South, chiefly in the years immediately preceding the Civil War, moved to the Democratic Party, which became more and more, the voice of the slaveholders. The Whigs, the Liberty Party – which was the political arm of the abolitionists – and the Free Soil Party opposed the Democrats.

*

Not all Southerners were *ipso facto* states' rights advocates. Andrew Jackson (1767-1845), although born in the Waxhaw settlement on the border of South and North Carolina, was a strong advocate of federalism.

Jackson was already the Old West's leading military hero when, as a major general of militia, he arrived in New Orleans early in December 1814 and was charged with the biggest responsibility of his career in the War of 1812. He immediately declared martial law in order to control New Orleans's predominantly anti-American Creole population.

On January 8, 1815, British Major General Sir Edward Pakenham personally led his full force of 7,500 battle-seasoned veterans, fresh from fighting Napoleon in Europe, in three assaults against the 5,000 Americans, about half of whom were poorly armed and untrained militia. Pakenham, two of his senior generals and more than 2,000 of his troops were killed. Another 500 British soldiers were captured. Jackson had lost seven killed and six wounded in the Americans' greatest victory of the war. The battle reinforced Jackson's reputation as a general but had no impact on the war. Peace had already been signed two weeks earlier in Europe, but news had not yet reached the U.S. by ship. Jackson's stand at New Orleans, coming after his victories in the Creek War (1813-1814) and his seizure of a British-Indian base at Pensacola in Spanish Florida (November 7, 1814), projected him into the presidency for two terms (1829-1837). Farmers, backwoodsmen and city workers liked him because, besides his military prowess, he was the first President with a commoner's background.

A man of action, accomplishment and with the common touch, he was a perfect subject for the screen. Hollywood missed the boat and only portrayed Jackson as the main character in two films. Allan Dwan's *Andrew Jackson* (1913), is a film biography – more in the style of a documentary. *The President's Lady* (1953) is a biographical drama about Jackson's marriage prior to becoming president and focuses upon personal, not historical, incidents in his life. Jackson is only pictured briefly in *My Own United States* (1918), a World War I patriotic compilation of highlights in American history. Director Cecil B. DeMille, in *The Buccaneer* (1938), treated General Andrew Jackson, a minor character, with more depth as he enlists the aid of the pirate Jean Lafitte to help fight the British in the Battle of New Orleans.

He is seen as crusty, shrewd and beloved by civilian and soldier alike. In *Man of Conquest* (1939), Jackson (Edward Ellis) is depicted as mentor to Sam Houston, whose rise in Tennessee politics is attributed to Jackson's guiding hand. Cecil B. DeMille eulogizes Jackson and praises his victory at the Battle of New Orleans, in *Land of Liberty* (1939), a patriotic documentary about the history of the United States. In *The Buccaneer* (1958), a remake of the 1938 film, Charlton Heston plays Jackson as a shrewd and tough-minded negotiator who accepts Lafitte's help out of a sense of expediency.

*

Whereas Jackson, a Southerner, was a strong supporter of the federal government, John C. Calhoun (1782-1850) developed into the leading Southern advocate of states' rights. Calhoun was born to a poor frontier family in Abbeville County, South Carolina and his father died at an early age. He managed to enter Yale and graduate with honors in 1804. Calhoun passed the bar three years later and, after a short stint in the South Carolina legislature, was elected to Congress in 1811. He served as vice-president (1825-29) under John Quincy Adams, and again (1829-32) under Andrew Jackson. Perhaps as a reaction to Jackson's strong federalism, a strange metamorphosis now occurred as Calhoun completely rejected his earlier views and became the leading American advocate of states' rights.

The South strongly opposed the tariff of 1828, claiming that it was passed to benefit the Northern textile manufacturers at the expense of the cotton-growing states. Calhoun wrote the "South Carolina Exposition," in which he argued that each state had the right to nullify any federal law it deemed unconstitutional. He resigned as vice-president to better lead the fight in the Senate against Jackson and the protectionist tariffs. Senator Clay intervened and was instrumental in fashioning a compromise tariff, which reduced duties on imported items to a flat 20% rate over a nine-year period. Calhoun supported the Compromise of 1850, which provided for noninterference with slavery in the District of Columbia. He also supported the strengthening of the Fugitive Slave Law; the adjustment of the Texas-New Mexico boundary; the organization of the new territory wrested from Mexico as a territory without mention of slavery; and the assumption of the debts of Texas. In his last appearance in a public debate, he was carried into the Senate to vote for the Compromise of 1850. The Clay Compromise, although supported by many Southerners, was but a Band-Aid on a festering boil which ultimately broke open into armed conflict between the states and the federal government.

States' rights were inextricably tied in with slavery, and the defenders of one system felt that they were compelled to support the other. Thus once Calhoun defended the institution of slavery, he had to look for support from the states.

In the antebellum South, loyalty to the state government took priority over loyalty to the federal government. The Missouri Compromise of 1820 and the Compromise Measures of 1850 tried to resolve the issue of slavery by providing for the admission of free and slave states. Tension mounted in 1857 when the Supreme Court, in the Dred Scott case, ruled that Congress did not have the power to exclude slavery from the territories. In 1859, abolitionist John Brown shocked the South when he seized the federal armory at Harpers Ferry in the hope of initiating a slave resurrection. When the newly formed antislavery Republican Party nominated Abraham Lincoln for president in 1860, the election proved crucial for the nation. The Democratic Party split into Northern and Southern factions and lost its usual unifying effect. Lincoln won and South Carolina seceded from the union in December of that year. Other Southern states soon followed and set up the Confederate States of America in Montgomery, Alabama, with Jefferson Davis elected provisional president.

Gorgeous Hussy, The (1936), MGM. Dir. Clarence Brown; Sc. Ainsworth Morgan, Stephen Morehouse Avery; Cast includes: Joan Crawford, Robert Taylor, Lionel Barrymore, Franchot Tone, Melvyn Douglas, James Stewart, Alison Skipworth, Louis Calhern.

Andrew Jackson's spirited campaign for the presidency, his opening address to Congress and his bitter clash with his cabinet are all included in this historical drama, based on the novel by Samuel Hopkins Adams. Lionel Barrymore portrays the feisty President. Joan Crawford, as Peggy O'Neal, a tavern keeper's daughter, promises her friend, Jackson's wife, that she will remain at his side after the wife's death. O'Neal goes through five love affairs and four husbands in this drama. Robert Taylor portrays her first love. She then marries Melvyn Douglas and then Virginia's states' rights Senator John Randolph, who is eventually shot and killed. Young James Stewart is husband number three. Finally, Franchot Tone, the Secretary of War, becomes love number five and then marries her.

Jackson's two political crises revolve about his dissolution of his cabinet and his attack on John C. Calhoun (Frank Conroy), a fellow Southerner, for Calhoun's anti-federalist speeches. Jackson dissolves his cabinet because of the cabinet members' wives' personal attacks upon the character of Peggy O'Neal.

Howards of Virginia, The (1940), Col. Dir. Frank Lloyd; Sc. Sidney Buchman; Cast includes: Cary Grant, Martha Scott, Sir Cedric Hardwicke, Alan Marshall, Richard Carlson.

This historical drama is set during the American Revolution. Cary Grant portrays a rugged backwoodsman who, with the help of his city-bred wife (Martha Scott), carves out a home in the wilderness. Years pass, and the family prospers. When conflict erupts between the colonists and the British, Grant, over the objection of his wife, sides with the patriots and his sons join the revolt. Several historical incidents are reenacted, including the Stamp Act riots, the Boston Tea Party and the rebels' winter at Valley Forge. Some of the major figures who helped to give birth to the fledgling nation – Patrick Henry, George Washington and Thomas Jefferson – are also shown.

Because of the searing impact of the Civil War on the American consciousness, we sometimes tend to forget that, in colonial times, the State of Virginia was a center of opposition to British imperial rule. Patrick Henry (1736-1799) and Thomas Jefferson were the leaders of the radicals in Virginia and, from there, rose to national prominence. Henry first achieved prominence when, as a member of Virginia's House of Burgesses, he spoke out against the Stamp Act in 1765. Presaging the later states' rights advocates, he contended that Virginia had legislative autonomy and the right to nullify acts by the British parliament. This phase of his career is faithfully recreated in *The Howards of Virginia,* with Richard Gaines portraying Henry.

Hollywood films have unfortunately transformed this passionate orator into a secondary player in which he appears in cameo roles rather than as a leading character. This is especially true in such historical dramas as *Cardigan* (1922), *America* (1924), *Janice Meredith* (1924) and *The Howards of Virginia* (1940). In John Farrow's historical biographical drama *John Paul Jones* (1959), however, Henry, played by Macdonald Carey, is given a little more prominence and allowed to make his famous speech in Virginia.

Hollywood studios have tended to overlook the rather colorful life of Thomas Jefferson (1743-1826) and relegated him to minor roles.

When the colonies were involved in the serious business of obstructing colonial law in America, Jefferson threw in his lot with the opponents of British rule. In 1775, the Virginia legislature appointed Jefferson as a delegate to the Second Continental Congress in Philadelphia. By June of 1776, Congress had tentatively decided upon independence and, in an effort at public relations, charged Jefferson with writing a justification for that decision. Jefferson's document, the *Declaration of Independence*, was as much a reflection of Congress as it was of his own beliefs in personal freedom, republican government and the rights of man. Peter H. Hunt's historical musical *1776* (1972) describes Jefferson's struggle to write this significant document. In a later work, *Notes on Virginia,* written in 1782, Jefferson somehow tried to reconcile his democratic beliefs with the institution of slavery.

Jefferson was at the nucleus of the Democratic-Republican Party and Hamilton occupied a similar position in the Federalist Party. The Democratic-Republican Party championed states' rights and individual liberties while the Federalists were strong supporters of the Federal Government. The same sort of divisions still run through American politics today. Today's Democratic Party supports the Federalist position while today's Republican Party resembles the Democratic-Republican Party of old.

Jefferson was elected President in 1800, reversed his position and quickly adopted some of the Federalist positions. Although he doubted his constitutional authority to do so, he seized the opportunity to purchase the Louisiana Territory from Napoleon in 1803 and effectively doubled the area of the United States. After serving as President for two terms, Jefferson retired in 1809 and, once again, returned to his home in Monticello.

Man Behind the Gun, The (1952), WB. Dir. Felix Feist; Sc. John Twist; Cast includes: Randolph Scott, Patrice Wymore, Dick Wesson, Phillip Carey, Lina Romay.

Randolph Scott portrays an undercover U.S. Army officer assigned to smash a plot designed to make southern California a separate state. Set in pre-Civil War Los Angeles and its environs, the film has several interesting characters, including an overly ambitious and corrupt senator (Roy Roberts) who hopes to carve out his own empire in California and a fiery Southern revolutionary (Morris Ankrum) who tries to tie southern California to the Confederacy. Revolution, he proclaims, will be quick and clean, devoid of politicians' tricks. "California," he protests, "was admitted into the Union with the understanding it would be a slave state." The senator, a fellow stagecoach passenger, mocks the hot-headed revolutionary, and states that he "believes everyone born south of St. Louis is born of a separate and distinct race – and is no longer a part of America."

Philip Carey, who plays a naïve U.S. Army captain, eventually helps Scott defeat the plotters. In the middle of this conflict, both men compete for the affections of schoolmarm Patrice Wymore. The army raised Scott, the most complex character in the film, after Native Americans killed his parents. When he learns that the captain plans to marry Wymore, Scott is torn between his duty, his honor and his personal feelings. "Duty is the religion of the army," he explains to her. "Forget it for a minute and the top sergeant beats it back into you with the flat of the saber. Duty is a god – a jealous god. It makes demands that can tear you to pieces. But you kneel down."

Man of Conquest (1939), Rep. Dir. George Nicholls Jr.; Sc. Wells Root, E. E. Paramore; Cast includes: Richard Dix, Gail Patrick, Edward Ellis, Joan Fontaine, Victor Jory.

Richard Dix portrays Sam Houston in this historical drama about the creation of the state of Texas. The story begins with Houston's rise in Tennessee politics under the guiding hand of Andrew Jackson (Edward Ellis) and continues with his governorship, his unsuccessful marriage and his participation in the Texas War of Independence. Vivid sequences include the battles of the Alamo and San Jacinto, both of which adhere fairly closely to historical truth. Joan Fontaine portrays Houston's indifferent first wife. Gail Patrick plays the second love interest in his life. The major figures at the Alamo, Davy Crockett, Stephen Austin and Jim Bowie, are played by Robert Barrat, Ralph Morgan and Robert Armstrong, respectively. C. Henry Gordon treats us to another of his villainous portraits, this time as Santa Anna.

*

A writer of fiction would be hard-pressed to generate a story that matched the life of Sam Houston (1793-1863). Films on Houston certainly had a rich trove from which to draw. Although most focused on his accomplishments, his personal tragedies were usually overlooked. Houston served under Andrew

Jackson in the Creek War of 1814, part of the War of 1812, and was seriously wounded in the Battle of Horseshoe Bend. He won election as Governor of Tennessee in 1827 but resigned the office in 1829 after his wife left him. Facing a serious drinking problem at this time, he left the state and drifted for the next few years. He briefly rejoined the Cherokee in their new home in Oklahoma, to which most of the tribe had been forcibly resettled from their eastern lands, then moved to Arkansas and, in 1833, went to Texas to join the rapidly growing colony of Americans there.

While attending the 1836 convention that declared Texas independent from Mexico, Houston was appointed General of the Army of Texas. At the San Jacinto River, near the present site of Houston, the Texans mounted a surprise attack in which they soundly defeated a Mexican force of 1,200 troops and captured Mexico's President and commanding general, Santa Anna. Houston's victory at San Jacinto (April 21, 1836) successfully ended the war for Texas, and he was subsequently elected the first president of the new republic.

Although honored as a military hero in two wars and considered the savior of Texas independence, the "Hero of San Jacinto" died a sad and politically scorned man in the state for which he did so much.

Two films showed Houston's early rise to political power in Tennessee before his military and political triumphs in Texas – *Man of Conquest* (1939) and *The Conqueror* (1917). The former has a wealth of historical personal detail, including his close relationship with the Cherokee, his rise to political prominence in Tennessee, his broken first marriage and, ultimately, his successful role as leader in the Texas rebellion. *The Conqueror* covers much of the same ground in a more limited version but distorts events in his failed first marriage by having him leave his wife. In reality, she left him. *The First Texan* (1956) is an effective biography of Houston's life beginning with the time he left Tennessee through his military success in the war against Mexico up to his election as first president of Texas.

As far as the studios are concerned, Houston's career ends on a note of triumph and popularity. There is no mention of his loss of two public offices for his principled stand against secession. No films describe his unsuccessful efforts to preserve the Union and prevent the coming wave of fratricidal warfare.

Santa Fe Trail (1940), WB. Dir. Michael Curtiz; Sc. Robert Buckner; Cast includes: Errol Flynn, Olivia de Havilland, Raymond Massey, Ronald Reagan, Alan Hale, William Lundigan.

Errol Flynn portrays J.E.B. "Jeb" Stuart, a recent West Point graduate, in this pre-Civil War historical drama about the exploits of the radical abolitionist John Brown and his followers. Stuart and George Custer (Ronald Reagan), two young cavalry officers recently sent to Fort Leavenworth to help maintain order in Kansas, are assigned to guard a freight caravan. They quickly clash with Brown and his followers over a shipment of rifles. The officers are reassigned, together with a cavalry troop, to capture the fanatic Brown and his small ragtag army. They manage to locate the armed group and, during a night skirmish, drive them into the hills. Stuart comments that this is the end of Brown's force. But Custer senses the impending storm over slavery that will drench the nation in blood and tears. "Nothing will break the force of John Brown," he says to his friend, "not even death."

Some time later Brown solicits funds from Boston abolitionists who support his plans to raise an army. Brown's trail of bloodshed and devastation ends in a violent battle at the U.S. arsenal at Harpers Ferry. Brown intends to arm more than a thousand followers with his newly acquired weapons, but he is surrounded and overwhelmed by government troops. John Brown (Raymond Massey) is presented as a religious zealot who leads bloody raids through Kansas while simultaneously shipping slaves through the famed "underground railroad." Brown is captured and goes to the gallows unrepentant, convinced that he is right. "I, John Brown, am now quite certain that the crimes of this guilty land can never be purged away but with blood," he announces to the solemn spectators. "Aye, let them hang me. I forgive them, and may God forgive them, for they know not what they do."

Van Heflin plays one of Brown's followers and is expelled from West Point for distributing political leaflets supporting abolition. In a quarrel with Stuart, a Southerner who criticizes Heflin for beating his horse, Heflin says scathingly: "You know how to harness Negroes – with a whip across their back!" Alan Hale and Guinn "Big Boy" Williams, as Flynn's sidekicks, provide the comic relief. Aside from a handful of brief scenes, the film skirts the controversial issue of slavery and emphasizes instead the melodramatics of the plot. In an incident aboard a train, two proslavers try to regain custody of a family of blacks from one of John Brown's sons (Alan Baxter), who is transporting them to a free state. In a later sequence during a battle between Brown's troops and the U.S. Army, a black couple, caught in the middle, voice their confusion. One of them remarks: "If this is freedom, I don't want no part of it."

Historical inaccuracies abound. Only one authentic event is dramatized in the film – the capture of John Brown, but the script tampers even with this event. The film shows Brown's capture by Captain Stuart. Historically, Col. Robert E. Lee was credited with the capture. According to the screenplay, Custer, Stuart, Sheridan and Longstreet all graduated from West Point in the same class – that of 1854. James Longstreet, born in 1821 and who later proved to be a brilliant Confederate general, would have graduated at age 34. Custer, born in 1839, would have had to be a child prodigy to finish at age 15. (Actually, he graduated in 1861 at the bottom of his class.) The film probably has and refers to more historical figures than any other Hollywood work. These include, aside from those already mentioned, Phil Sheridan, Jefferson Davis and Kit Carson. History buffs should recognize the various places and events, such as "bloody Kansas," the underground railroad, Harpers Ferry and West Point.

7

Social Conditions

Society in the Old South was divided approximately into five social classes. The large planters who owned over one hundred slaves were the acknowledged leaders. Most planters owned about twenty to thirty slaves while the smallest planters owned ten to twenty slaves. Yeoman farmers were independent individuals and represented approximately sixty percent of the population. They worked their own piece of land and might have owned one to three slaves. They worked the hardest and were the least racist. The hillbillies were next down the social ladder and were probably descendents of the indentured servants of the colonial period. These poor whites were quite backward as a result of poor diet and heredity. Their land was the poorest, and they were forced to eat whatever their crops provided. The fourth social class, the black freedmen, numbered approximately 250,000 by 1860. They worked as artisans, unskilled laborers or servants in towns throughout the South. With their lives in constant danger, they survived only at the whim of their white neighbors. The fifth and last group were the African-American slaves, which numbered almost four million in 1860. They comprised about one third of the entire population of the South.

Mexicans and Indians worked as indentured servants in the territories of New Mexico and Arizona, and in the South. Prior to the Civil War, both poor blacks and whites suffered abuses of this system. Following the war, the adoption of the 13th Amendment to the U.S. Constitution prohibited involuntary servitude except as punishment. However, several Southern states passed their own individual laws, which permitted prisoners to be leased to independent contractors. This gave rise to the dreaded chain gangs. Convicts had their legs shackled to prevent escape, and they were connected to one another by a continuous chain and forced to work in the fields and mines and to build roads. In 1910, the U.S. Supreme Court declared state laws permitting such practices unconstitutional.

As early as 1910, Hollywood was quick to exploit the chain gangs in a series of dramas and comedies. In particular, scenes of men chained together under a hot sun as they swung their sledgehammers against stubborn rocks and boulders seemed a popular subject for dramas. With the advent of sound, studios were quick to portray these prisoners singing soulful work songs and spirituals in chorus as unsympathetic guards looked on. Some films simplistically focused on the melodrama of the plot elements while others suggested social and racial themes. Many condemned abuses of the system, the brutality of the guards and conveyed sympathy for the shackled prisoners.

*

Bar Sinister, The (1917), Abrams-Werner. Dir. Edgar Lewis; Sc. Anthony Paul Kelly; Cast includes: Preston Rollow, Mary Doyle, William Anderson, Hedda Nova, Mitchell Lewis.

A black man dies as the result of the cruelty of his employer, a colonel. His bereaved wife becomes vindictive and kidnaps the white employer's daughter. In this social drama, the woman, her own daughter and the kidnapped child run away to another part of the South. The colonel's daughter Belle is now an adult and lives in a small Southern town with her alleged mother, but she refuses to believe that she is black. Although a mulatto falls in love with her, Belle instead loves a young white gentleman who shuns blacks. She tries to hide her background from him, but when he discovers the truth about her supposed "mother," he rejects Belle. The widow finally confesses that Belle is the daughter of a distinguished white gentleman.

Birth of a Nation, The (1915), Mutual. Dir. D. W. Griffith; Sc. D. W. Griffith, Frank Woods; Cast includes: Lillian Gish, Mae Marsh, Henry Walthall, Miriam Cooper, Mary Alden, Ralph Lewis, George Siegmann, Walter Long.

In *The Clansman,* D. W. Griffith traces the fortunes of two intertwined families (the Northern Stonemans and the Southern Camerons) from the antebellum period through the war and beyond. This historical drama is based on Thomas Dixon Jr.'s play and brings to life the story of America's most tragic period. Henry B. Walthall portrays Ben Cameron, a son of the South, who invites his fellow classman from the North, Phil Stoneman (Elmer Clifton), to visit his family in Piedmont, South Carolina. Stoneman shows a small picture of his sister Elsie (Lillian Gish) to his friend, who immediately falls in love with her and keeps the photo. Stoneman is welcomed by the aristocratic Dr. Cameron (Spottiswoode Aitken), the head of the family, and Flora (Mae Marsh), Ben's little sister. When war erupts between the states, Cameron's sons are quick to enlist and fight for the South.

Meanwhile, the Stonemans enlist in the Union cause. Both families soon suffer losses in the battles that follow. Griffith introduces important historical events, including the early battles, the rise of the "Invisible Empire" of the Ku

Klux Klan, the Reconstruction era and the assassination of President Lincoln. On a more personal level, Elsie Stoneman visits the military hospital and falls in love with the wounded Ben, who still carries her photo. Ben, the "Little Colonel," returns to his beloved Piedmont, where he witnesses the abuses of the Northern occupation troops. Flora Cameron commits suicide rather than submit to rape by a black renegade (Walter Long). Griffith justifies the rise of the Klan as a righteous reaction to the abuses of Northern politicians, troops and carpetbaggers who invaded the beaten South. Klan members ride to the rescue of white Southern citizens and they rout the occupation forces in a thundering conclusion.

Griffith's portrayal of the Klan made its members heroic figures and incited riots in the streets of several cities. The movie provoked African-Americans to organize the National Association for the Advancement of Colored People (NAACP) and spurred litigation in the courts. Despite its racism and anti-Northern bias, critics and others acclaimed the film as a work of art, one in which virtually every cinematic convention was used so skillfully that millions were moved and manipulated as never before.

Blackmail (1939), MGM. Dir. H. C. Potter; Sc. David Hertz, William Ludwig; Cast includes: Edward G. Robinson, Gene Lockhart, Ruth Hussey, Esther Dale.

Edward G. Robinson is arrested and imprisoned for a crime he did not commit. Sentenced to serve time on a Southern chain gang, he escapes and begins a new life. He marries, becomes a devoted family man and stars a business fighting fires at oil wells. Gene Lockhart, who is actually the guilty party, arrives in town and confides to Robinson that he is responsible for the fires. Following some complications, Lockhart turns Robinson in to the authorities who return him to the chain gang, where conditions grow worse. To exacerbate matters, Robinson learns that Lockhart has taken over his business and has left his wife and child in poverty. He escapes once again, starts an oil-well fire to which Lockhart responds, and forces the guilty man to confess in front of witnesses. Now satisfied with the public admission, Robinson extinguishes the raging fire and returns to his family.

Broken Chains (1916), World. Dir. Robert Thornby; Sc. E. M. Ingleton; Cast includes: John Taney, Carlyle Blackwell, Herbert Barrington, Stanhope Wheatcroft.

Robert Thornby's silent drama is set in the South during a period of racial tension. Captain Harry Ford (Carlyle Blackwell) and a troop of cavalry are in the area as some blacks steal a ballot box from a polling station. When a white man refuses to pay a black to return a stolen box, the black man kills the white and frames Captain Ford. The trooper is sentenced to life on a chain gang, but he manages to escape. A young Southern woman who loves the captain helps him prove his innocence.

Chain Gang (1950), Col. Dir. Lew Landers; Sc. Howard J. Green; Cast includes: Douglas Kennedy, Marjorie Lord, Emory Parnell, William Phillips.

Newspaper reporter Douglas Kennedy goes under cover to expose the brutality and exploitation of chain gang prisoners in this humdrum action drama. For all his noble efforts, Kennedy is almost gunned down by a hail of bullets when the corrupt camp authorities discover his real identity. The reporter discovers that the father of his girlfriend (Marjorie Lord) is the chief villain – a plot cliché.

Chain Gang Killings, The (1985), VCL. Dir. Clive Harding; Cast includes: Ian Yule, Ken Gampu.

Two hate-filled, shackled convicts escape from a brutal chain gang in an action drama, which is reminiscent of *The Defiant Ones,* with Sidney Poitier and Tony Curtis. One prisoner is black and the other white. They experience a series of uninteresting but rather violent adventures. Like Poitier and Curtis in *The Defiant Ones,* the two escapees realize they must put aside their prejudices and help each other if they are to survive.

Chain Gang Women (1972), Acorn Vid. Dir. Lee Frost; Sc. Lee Frost; Cast includes: Robert Lott, Barbara Mills, Michael Steams, Linda York.

A killer who escapes from a chain gang is still shackled to a fellow prisoner. The two commit a series of rapes and robberies and end up being pursued by the husband of one of their innocent victims.

Color Purple, The (1985), WB. Dir. Steven Spielberg; Sc. Menno Meyjes; Cast includes: Whoopie Goldberg, Danny Glover, Margaret Avery, Adolph Caesar, Rae Dawn Chong.

This historical drama, based on Alice Walker's popular novel, describes the bonding of Southern black women in early twentieth-century Georgia. The women are portrayed as unselfish, overworked and patient while their men are brutish, lazy and lecherous. Director Steven Spielberg captured many of these characteristics in his 1985 screen version and enhanced the work with splendid visual depictions of their surroundings. Whoopie Goldberg portrays the heroine Celie, whose father impregnates her and then gives away her child, just as he had done with their first child. He then turns her over to a cruel and brutish farmer (Danny Glover), who marries her chiefly to clean, cook and care for his brood of children from his first wife. When Celie's sister leaves their lecherous father and comes to live with her and Glover, he tries to rape her. When the sister physically resists his advances, Glover evicts her from his house. The sister later writes to Celie, but Glover hides all her letters.

Glover occasionally beats Celie, offers little affection and finally ignores her completely after he invites the sensual Shug (Margaret Avery), a former girlfriend to live with them. "You as ugly as sin!" she exclaims upon first seeing Celie. Shug later appreciates Celie's gentleness, her character and her kindness and she falls in love with her and both become close friends. Sophia (Oprah Winfrey), a powerful black woman, marries Harpo, Glover's son from his previous marriage. She indiscreetly dares to tell the white mayor and his wife to "go to hell." For this, the local sheriff knocks her down, arrests her and locks her up for several years. As a foil character to Celie, Sophia is damaged by life while Celie is regenerated. The film ends as a paean to the human spirit, as Celie not only endures but also prevails.

Cumberland Romance, A (1920), Realart. Dir. Charles Maigne; Cast includes: Mary Miles Minter, Monte Blue, John Bowers, Guy Oliver, Martha Mattox, Robert Brower.

John Bowers plays an Eastern engineer who journeys to the Cumberland Mountains where he meets Easter Hicks (Mary Miles Minter) and soon falls in love with her. However, a local young man (Monte Blue), who is studying for the ministry, also loves Hicks. Following several complications, the engineer's aristocratic parents arrive from the East for the wedding. But another problem arises when Hicks' father instigates a shooting. During the fray, she steps in to save Blue's life. She is wounded in the shooting but she now realizes she really loves Blue.

Devil's 8, The (1969), AIP. Dir. Burt Topper; Sc. Willard Huyck, John Milius, James G. White; Cast includes: Fabian, Christopher George, Ralph Meeker, Leslie Parrish, Ross Hagen.

Christopher George, as a federal agent, arranges for the escape of six convicts from a chain gang. This weak action crime drama is based on a story by Larry Gordon. The agent proposes to use the convicts to help him smash a moonshine ring controlled by Ralph Meeker. To accomplish this, he trains them to drive and to simultaneously toss lighted bombs at designated targets.

Girl on a Chain Gang (1966), Gross. Dir. Jerry Gross; Sc. Jerry Gross; Cast includes: Julie Ange, R. K. Charles, William Watson.

Jerry Gross's drama is an obscure exploitation exercise that combines civil rights with life on a Southern chain gang.

Grip of Jealousy, The (1916), U. Dir. Joseph De Grasse; Sc. Ida May Park; Cast includes: Louise Lovely, Grace Thompson, J. Belasco, Hayward Mack, Colin Chase, Lon Chaney.

A young white woman has been raised as a slave because she is believed to be the daughter of a black woman and a plantation owner (Lon Chaney). This historical drama is set in the pre-Civil War South. Louise Lovely knows the truth – that the young slave is really the child of her own sister Beth and a gentleman, Jack. Louise believes the couple was never married, so she decides to keep quiet in order to protect her sister's reputation. In the meantime, Louise falls in love with Jack's brother. Chaney has enslaved the so-called "black" woman and now promises Louise that he will free this woman if Louise marries his son. Jack returns in time to resolve the issues and brings proof of his marriage to Beth. This releases Louise from her promise to marry Chaney's son. During the silent era Lon Chaney, the father of Lon Chaney Jr., a popular character actor in many horror films, became famous for his disguises and his interpretations of a string of offbeat characters.

Hill Billy, The (1924), Allied. Dir. George Hill; Sc. Marion Jackson; Cast includes: Jack Pickford, Lucille Ricksen, Frank Leigh, Ralph Yearsley, Jane Keckley.

To gain possession of land rich in coal, Frank Leigh kills Jack Pickford's father and marries the widow. This silent drama about mountain life is based on John Fox Jr.'s story *Valley of the Wolf.* Pickford loves Lucille Ricksen, Leigh's niece, who has been teaching him to read but Leigh forces her to marry his son. Several complications ensue. Pickford is falsely accused of killing the prospective bridegroom and pursues Leigh in order to learn the truth. Fortunately, Leigh drowns during the pursuit and this allows Pickford to marry the young woman he loves.

I Am a Fugitive From a Chain Gang (1932), WB. Dir. Mervyn LeRoy; Sc. Sheridan Gibney, Brown Holmes; Cast includes: Paul Muni, Glenda Farrell, Helen Vinson, Preston Foster, Edward J. McNamara, Sheila Terry, Allen Jenkins.

Mervyn LeRoy's powerful and memorable production tells how James Allen is buffeted by forces outside of his control. The film is more of a social documentary than a crime film. The drama, based on the novel by Robert E. Burns, is so grim that it remains imbedded in moviegoers' thoughts long after they have left the theatre. Allen experiences the most degrading and brutal conditions as a prisoner in the notorious chain gang. He escapes and, as the result of hard work, becomes an outstanding engineer, but the police persist and keep trying to find him. Allen voluntary surrenders in return for a nominal sentence. However, the authorities break their promise of leniency and give him a stiff sentence. It seems that Allen has no trouble breaking out of prison because, once again, he escapes, but this time he fades into total obscurity. On a secretive nocturnal visit to his one-time girlfriend, she asks how he has been surviving. The edgy fugitive replies, "I steal," as he fades into the blackness of the night. Paul Muni does a wonderful job of playing James Allen.

In the Heat of the Night (1967), UA. Dir. Norman Jewison; Sc. Stirling Silliphant; Cast include: Sidney Poitier, Rod Steiger, Warren Oates, Lee Grant, James Patterson.

In this racially charged crime drama, set in a Southern city, a local sheriff (Rod Steiger) arrests an African-American (Sidney Poitier) at a railroad station and charges him with murder. The sheriff then learns that his prisoner is a top homicide detective from Philadelphia who was visiting his family.

This film raises sensitive issues about race and it follows such classics as *Crossfire* and *Gentleman's Agreement* (1947), which focused on anti-Semitism, and *Pinky* and *Home of the Brave* (1949), which dealt with anti-black attitudes.

Leadbelly (1976), Par. Dir. Gordon Parks; Sc. Ernest Kinoy; Cast includes: Roger E. Mosley, Paul Benjamin, John Henry Faulk, Loretta Greene, Lynn Hamilton.

In Gordon Parks's biographical drama Roger E. Mosley portrays the title character, a blues singer and accomplished guitar player. The film explores highlights from his life on the road and his experiences as a convict on the Texas and Louisiana chain gangs. The sometimes brutal and often realistic drama features several songs, including "Rock Island Line" and "Goodnight Irene," but this is far from the typical light musical that audiences have been accustomed to over the years.

*

Leadbelly (Huddie Ledbetter) (1888-1949), the real-life model for the lead character, was actually born and raised in Louisiana and roamed the Southeast in his younger years. During one of his sojourns, he learned to play the blues from Blind Lemon Jefferson. He had a violent temper and, in 1930, was sentenced for 30 years to Angola Prison in Louisiana for two murders. While in Angola, Leadbelly entertained the guards and other prisoners with his renditions of popular songs, blues and folk ballads.

Alan Lomax, the famous musicologist, discovered Leadbelly during one of his trips to Angola. At the time, the musicologist was recording black folk music and was so impressed with Leadbelly's musical talents that he petitioned Louisiana Governor O. K. Allen to pardon the prisoner for no other reason than for his musical ability and his knowledge of black folk music. Surprisingly enough, the governor pardoned Leadbelly into Lomax's custody.

Leadbelly worked for Lomax for one year, but then, in 1935, moved to New York City where he met a group of left-wing folk singers, including Woodie Guthrie and Pete Seeger. They became close friends and eventually Leadbelly left his roots in the blues and developed into a folk singer. He wrote some of the most famous left-wing songs of the day, such as "Bourgeois Blues" and the "Scottsboro Boys," which carried strong political messages. One year after Leadbelly's death in 1949, Pete Seeger and the Weavers recorded his song, "Goodnight Irene," and it immediately rocketed to number one on the charts.

Hollywood produced some similar folk music films such as *Sullivan's Travels* (1941), *Desire in the Dust* (1960), *Take the Money and Run* (1969), *Sweet Sugar* (1972) and *Mean Dog Blues* (1978).

*

Little Shepherd of Kingdom Come, The (1920), Goldwyn. Cast includes: Jack Pickford, Clara Horton, Pauline Starke, J. Park Jones.

Jack Pickford portrays the title character in this rural drama about feuds and the Old South. The film is based on the famous novel by John Fox. Pickford is a mountain lad who is introduced to Southern culture after he walks down from the Blue Grass Mountains of Kentucky. *The Little Shepherd of Kingdom Come* was remade in two sound versions, one in 1933 and the other in 1938. A contemporary critic found both the book and the early film dated and possibly of little interest to film audiences. *The Little Shepherd* returned to the screen in 1928 as *Kentucky Courage*. Andrew V. McLaglen's 1961 color and sound version was released with Fox's original title.

McMasters, The (1970), Chevron. Dir. Alf Kjellin; Sc. Harold Jacob Smith; Cast includes: Burl Ives, Brock Peters, David Carradine, Nancy Kwan, Jack Palance.

In this drama, Brock Peters, a former slave of rancher McMasters (Burl Ives), leaves to join the Union troops during the Civil War. After the conflict he returns to the ranch. When Ives, now old and generally weak, learns that Peters signed up to fight under the name "McMasters," he is impressed that Peters had taken the name of his master and decides to make him his partner in the ranch. However, his other hands refuse to take orders from a black man and quit. Peters befriends some Native Americans, who agree to work for him during a cattle drive. Later, the Indian leader, David Carradine, allows Peters to marry his sister (Nancy Kwan). But this incites the local whites. Ex-Confederate soldier Jack Palance and other local bigots try to buy the ranch from Ives, but they are physically evicted. They return and besiege the ranch house. A gunfight ensues in which Ives is killed and Peters is wounded. The Indians rescue Peters and chase off the attackers. Peters is invited to join the tribe, but he decides to remain on the ranch, which he now owns.

Mourning Becomes Electra (1947), RKO. Dir. Dudley Nichols; Sc. Dudley Nichols; Cast includes: Rosalind Russell, Michael Redgrave, Raymond Massey, Kirk Douglas.

Incest, greed, love, murder and hate are all part of everyday life with the Mannon family. This period drama is based on the play by Eugene O'Neill and set in 1865 at the close of the Civil War. The matriarch of the family (Katina Paxinou) kills her husband (Raymond Massey), who has returned from the war. Their revengeful daughter (Rosalind Russell) encourages her brother (Michael Redgrave) to kill the mother's secret lover. The mother, distraught over the murder, takes her own life. Based on the Greek tragedy *Oresteia*, O'Neill uses strong dark Freudian influences and sexual tensions to motivate his characters.

My Fighting Gentleman (1917), Dir. Edward Sloman; Sc. Edward Sloman; Cast includes: William Russell, Francilia Billington, Jack Vosburgh, Clarence Burton.

Director Edward Sloman investigates a different type of prejudice in this historical drama. William Russell, the son of a Southern colonel, returns home at the end of the Civil War to his damaged Virginia plantation and is shunned by his neighbors because he had fought for the North. Even his former girlfriend, Francilia Billington, rejects him. Instead, she shows an interest in a licentious Southern aristocrat (Jack Vosburgh), who has formed a close friendship with a carpetbagger (Clarence Burton). When Russell competes with Vosburgh for a political office, the latter and Burton frame Russell for murder. But their scheme goes awry, and Vosburgh kidnaps Billington. Several complications ensue, including an attempted lynching. Russell gets a confession from the carpetbagger, exposes his rival and wins back his girlfriend.

Naked Hearts (1916), Bluebird. Dir. Rupert Julian; Sc. Rupert Julian; Cast includes: Rupert Julian, Zoe Bech, Francelia Billington, Gordon Griffith, Jack Holt, Douglas Gerrard.

Although Francelia Billington loves Rupert Julian, her brother disapproves of any talk of marriage. This historical drama is set in the pre-Civil War South. Her brother chooses an English nobleman for Billington. However, she has other plans and runs away with Julian on the night her brother announces her engagement to the Englishman. The couple is caught and the prospective bride finally agrees to her brother's plans. The Civil War erupts and disrupts all wedding plans. All three men volunteer and are later listed as killed in action. Heartbroken over the triple loss, Billington decides to become a nun. Suddenly Julian returns – his death had been mistakenly reported – and proposes marriage to the woman he loves.

Neon Bible, The (1996), Iberoamericana. Dir. Terence Davies; Sc. Terence Davies; Cast includes: Jacob Tierney, Gena Rowlands, Diana Scarwid, Denis Leary, Leo Burmester.

Terence Davies's slow-paced and sad coming-of-age drama is based on a novel by John Kennedy Toole. It focuses on David, a lonely youth, played by Jacob Tierney, and is set in the South in the 1940s. David's working-class father continually beats the boy's unstable mother. He also treats his son with contempt. When the father goes off to World War II and is killed in battle, the family is left penniless. Aunt Mae, a floozy played by Gena Rowlands, comes to live with them and brings joy and entertainment into the boy's solitary life. She is a flashy saloon singer who has experienced her own hard times and has come to stay with the impoverished family. Mae turns out to be David's best friend and confidante, suggesting a world outside the boy's own experiences.

Nigger, The (1915). Dir. Edgar Lewis; Cast includes: William Farnum.

A political boss persuades William Farnum, an aristocratic Southerner, to run for governor. This drama is based on the 1909 play by Edgar Brewster Sheldon. Once elected to office, Farnum plans to sign a Prohibition bill that would ruin the politician's liquor business. The boss tries to blackmail the governor by saying he has proof that Farnum has black blood in him. He threatens to expose him to the press. Farnum doesn't buckle, signs the bill, loses his girlfriend and resigns from office. He then leaves for the North, where he hopes to improve the plight of blacks in the U.S.

Pharaoh's Army (1995), CFP. Dir. Robby Benson; Sc. Robby Benson; Cast includes: Chris Cooper, Patricia Clarkson, Kris Kristofferson, Richard Tyson.

This historical drama is based on a vague 1862 incident in Kentucky. A Union captain (Chris Cooper) leads a small cavalry troop onto a farm owned by defiant Sara (Patricia Clarkson). The soldiers are stranded there for a while when one of the troops is accidentally wounded. Soon a relationship develops between the benevolent and inexperienced captain and the embittered owner. The link between the two grows more profound and personal, and they begin to reach out to each other. Suddenly the reality of the war intrudes and the relationship is severed. Everyone is forced to choose his or her primary loyalty.

Places in the Heart (1984), Tri-Star. Dir. Robert Benton; Sc. Robert Benton; Cast includes: Sally Field, Lindsay Crouse, Ed Harris, Amy Madigan, John Malkovich, Danny Glover.

In this drama, a handful of white-hooded Klansmen, suddenly and for no apparent reason, decide one night to beat up a black worker (Danny Glover), who has been helping a widow (Sally Field) bring in her cotton crop.

Ploughshare, The (1915), General Film Co.. Dir. John H. Collins; Sc. Mary Imlay Taylor; Cast includes: Robert Conness, Bigelow Cooper, Bessie Learn, Henry Leone, Frank A. Lyon.

Robert Conness inherits his father's estate and is appointed guardian of his mischievous half-brother, Jim. This historical drama is set in the antebellum South. Conness is later elected governor and falls in love with Gertrude McCoy, who likes the governor's brother, Jim. Meanwhile, the young woman's father learns that Jim has made a country girl pregnant. McCoy agrees to marry the governor, and Jim duels and kills McCoy's brother. When a stranger is charged with the killing, she pleads with Jim to confess to the murder. He confesses, is sentenced and then escapes, with McCoy's assistance. The governor becomes involved in the incident and subsequently resigns from office. His wife finally confesses everything during a trial and the couple is reunited. Jim is reported killed in South America.

Pudd'nhead Wilson (1916), Par. Dir. Cecil B. DeMIlle; Cast includes: Theodore Roberts, Alan Hale, Thomas Meighan, Florence Dagmar, Jane Wolff.

Theodore Roberts portrays the title character, a lawyer, who solves a crime by checking fingerprints and thus saves a suspect from a jail sentence. Cecil B. DeMille's drama is based on the 1894 novel by Mark Twain. The freed prisoner is a young mulatto (Thomas Meighan) who is actually white. It seems that his mother, a black slave, had switched two babies born the same day, hoping to save her baby boy from a lifetime of slavery and hardship. Her son was accepted as white, and the white child grew up in bondage. Aside from Twain's original use of fingerprint identification in the story, set in the South between 1830 and 1850, critics commended the author for his courageous treatment of the theme of race relations. Republic released a low-budget hayseed comedy titled *Puddin' Head* in 1941, starring Judy Canova, but it had nothing to do with Twain's original story.

Rosewood (1997), WB. Dir. John Singleton; Sc. Gregory Poirier; Cast includes: Jon Voight, Ving Rhames, Don Cheadle, Bruce McGill, Loren Dean, Esther Rolle.

A false charge of rape by a white woman against a black man results in the destruction of a prosperous black town in Florida in 1923. Rosewood is based on an actual, overlooked racial incident. Unfortunately, the main character is depicted as a Western hero. Played by Ving Rhames, he is a loner returning from World War I, looking to settle down on his own land. Many of the blacks in the community take a liking to him and invite him to a barbecue party. When her secret lover beats a white married woman, she accuses a black stranger of raping and beating her. The enraged whites form a lynch mob and go on a senseless rampage of murder and destruction. Thee white mob is filled with smoldering hatred and jealousy of some of the more successful blacks of Rosewood and it turns on the black community and virtually destroys the town and kills many of its innocent inhabitants. They hunt down the falsely accused suspect and torture him before they murder him.

Shenandoah (1965), U. Dir. Andrew V. McLaglen; Sc. James Lee Barrett; Cast includes: James Stewart, Doug McClure, Glenn Corbett, Patrick Wayne, Rosemary Forsyth.

A strong-willed Virginia patriarch tries to keep his family untouched by the Civil War that rages around his farm in this historical drama set in 1863. James Stewart portrays a widower who struggles unsuccessfully to keep his six sons and one daughter safe from the ravages of war. When his 16-year-old son is mistakenly taken prisoner as a Confederate soldier and his prize horses are almost confiscated, Stewart and his family become involved in the conflict. He sets out with some of his sons to rescue the boy. During the search, one of his sons is killed by a Confederate sentry while another son, who has remained to care for the farm, is murdered by a looter.

Following several action sequences, Stewart and his sons fail to find the boy and return home. Stewart goes to his wife's gravesite on his farm and tries to make sense of the turbulence around him. "It's like all wars, I suppose," he concludes as if addressing his wife. "The undertakers are winning it, the politicians will talk a lot about the glory of it and the old men will talk about the need of it.

But the soldiers – they just want to go home." Meanwhile, the boy has escaped from a prisoner-of-war camp and returns to the town church where his family hails him. The film, which depicts some of the tragedies of the war, became the basis for a successful Broadway musical of the same name.

Tortured Heart, A (1916), Fox. Dir. Will S. Davis; Sc. Will S. Davis; Cast includes: Virginia Pearson, Stuart Holmes.

This domestic drama is set in the pre-Civil War South. Virginia Pearson, a young woman leaves her baby on the doorstep of the local reverend and plans to take her own life. Pearson goes down to the river and tries to drown herself. However, she finds a body and substitutes that body for her own. Given a new lease on life, Pearson takes a job as the reverend's housekeeper, but she reveals nothing about her relationship to Liza, her daughter, who grows into a beautiful young woman. Pearson tries to discourage Liza from eloping with Stuart Holmes, a roguish young man unworthy of the innocent young woman. Not heeding the advice, Liza runs off with Holmes, who is soon killed in a brawl. Liza returns home and learns the truth from her mother. She then marries a faithful young man who has always loved her.

8

The Courtroom and Early Justice

The Emancipation Proclamation of 1863 and the constitutional amendments that followed the American Civil War changed the legal status of black people, but a series of U.S. Supreme Court decisions struck down federal statutes designed to enforce the amendments. The most important of these decisions declared unconstitutional a law that outlawed racial discrimination by private individuals but upheld state-enforced segregation. For decades after Reconstruction, the absence of adequate federal laws permitted local governments to discriminate against black people in employment, housing, public accommodations, the courts and voting. For years, Southern courts and communities took advantage of these lax laws to impose severe restrictions upon their black citizens. These became known as "Jim Crow" laws, and they severely restricted the voting and legal rights of African-Americans.

*

Early Hollywood courtroom films rarely touched upon civil rights at all. Later productions, such as *They Won't Forget* (1937), *Intruder in the Dust* (1949) and *To Kill a Mockingbird* (1962) did investigate a racist legal system. In more recent years Hollywood began to release dramas that showed a Southern legal system relatively free of the earlier racism. Most notably among these "politically correct" courtroom dramas were *Mississippi Burning* (1988), *Ghosts of Mississippi* (1996) and *A Time to Kill* (1996).

Not all courtroom films during this period were racially charged dramas. *My Cousin Vinny* (1992), for example, proved to be the most popular courtroom comedy of the decade, while others, such as *The Rainmaker* (1997), were either suspenseful crime dramas or exposés of some form of corruption.

*

Client, The (1994), WB. Dir. Joel Schumacher; Sc. Akiva Goldsman; Cast includes: Susan Sarandon, Tommy Lee Jones, Brad Renfro, Mary-Louise Parker, Anthony LaPaglia, J. T. Walsh.

Joel Schumacher's drama is based on John Grisham's novel. The action takes place somewhere near Memphis and centers on young 11-year-old Brad Renfro, whose life is in danger because he witnessed a murder. Renfro realizes he needs a lawyer. He searches for a trustworthy lawyer and settles on Susan Sarandon, who has faced some hard times of her own. She is tough but sharp enough to understand the boy's emotional needs. Because of her drinking problem, Sarandon has lost custody of her own children. Sarandon and Renfro soon find themselves threatened by crooked gangsters, corrupt politicians and an overly ambitious prosecutor (Tommy Lee Jones).

The victim's body is missing and gangsters, mob lawyers, the police as well as Sarandon and Renfro search for it. Following several suspenseful complications, Sarandon and Renfro find the body and solve the mystery. The lawyer and her client have grown very close to each other. In the final scene, they embrace before the boy leaves with his mother and little brother for the safety of a government protection program in another state.

Some of the best dialogue involves the boy and his lawyer. When they first meet, Sarandon asks, "Where are your parents?" "Where are yours?" Refro fires back. "Are you even injured?" "Do I look injured?" the boy replies. "Well," the lawyer says, trying to discourage him, "we only do injuries." Well," the young potential client cracks, "I'll just go get hit by a truck and come back." Later, when they discuss her drinking problem, she assures him, "I have been sober for three years." But the streetwise boy is suspicious, and replies, "Yeah right, that's what all the drunks say, how they're gonna get sober and all. They even say they love you but they don't. And then they come home wasted and beat on you and your mother so bad that you gotta hit 'em in the face with a baseball bat!" "You're talking about your daddy, aren't you?" Sarandon asks. "Yeah," the boy replies, "well, I got rid of him. . . . And then my father became my ex-father, and now I got you, and you're a drunk and a bad lawyer too! So now I'm getting rid of you, you're fired, okay?"

Court Martial (1928), Col. Dir. George B. Seitz; Sc. Anthony Coldeway; Cast includes: Jack Holt, Betty Compson, Doris Hill, Pat Harmon, Frank Lackteen.

Court Martial is a Civil War drama about a group of Southern guerrillas. The film stars Jack Holt as a Union officer appointed by President Lincoln to bring in the leader (Betty Compson) of the marauders. Holt, working under cover, gains the confidence of the guerrillas, falls for the leader and saves her life during a cavalry battle. In turn, she rescues Holt when the other members discover he is a Northern agent. When he returns to his post, he is court-martialed for helping the leader instead of capturing her. As he is about to face the firing squad, Compson appears. Although mortally wounded by a member of her own gang, she is determined to save Holt's life.

The plot of the film may be pure fiction, but the depiction of organized guerrilla bands terrorizing Union communities behind the lines is based on fact. Several groups, including Mosby's Raiders, Morgan's Raiders and Coleman's Scouts, proved very effective in disrupting Union communications, carrying out acts of sabotage and diverting Northern troops from the front lines. Some of these guerrillas continued to operate throughout the conflict.

Devil's Advocate, The (1998), WB. Dir. Taylor Hackford; Sc. Jonathan Lemkin, Tony Gilroy; Cast includes: Keanu Reeves, Al Pacino, Charlize Theron, Jeffrey Jones, Judith Ivey.

In Taylor Hackford's drama, Keanu Reeves is a hotshot Florida defense attorney who is recruited by John Milton (Al Pacino, portraying the Devil), the head honcho of a prestigious New York law firm. Milton is impressed with the young lawyer's performance in the courtroom in his home state and invites Reeves to join his firm in New York. Milton presents Reeves with a luxurious apartment and turns over high-profile cases for him to handle. Reeve's large fees alert his astute Southern wife who soon grows suspicious of the entire setup. At one point Milton tempts the young lawyer not only with worldly riches but a beautiful woman, and seduces him with "Your vanity is justified." Following a string of complications and some special effects that tend to go overboard, the film concludes suggesting the usual battle between good and evil is an internal struggle and concerns free will. At least one critic commented "New York is a helluva town," although little of the city is shown on screen.

Ghosts of Mississippi (1996), Castle Rock. Dir. Rob Reiner; Sc. Lewis Colick; Cast includes: Alec Baldwin, Whoopi Goldberg, James Woods, William H. Macy, Bill Cobbs.

Rob Reiner's drama depicts the long, frustrating efforts to convict the murderer of Medgar Evers in the State of Mississippi. Whoopie Golberg, as Mrs. Evers, tries to open the case, and her efforts seem to bear fruit when Alec Baldwin, an assistant district attorney, volunteers to help her. After being ignored by so many other white officials before, Mrs. Evers soon grows suspicious of Baldwin. "When you hate," she explains at one point, "the only one that suffers is you because most of the people you hate don't know it and the rest don't care."

The boastful and proud murderer Byron De La Beckworth, played by James Woods, poses a formidable obstacle for the widow and the D.A. At one point, he brags, "You ain't never going to get 12 people to convict someone for killing a nigger in the State of Mississippi." But in the spirit of *To Kill a Mockingbird* (representing the Old South) and *A Time to Kill*, the good guys finally win and the guilty killer is dragged off to prison.

Inherit the Wind (1960), UA. Dir. Stanley Kramer; Sc. Nathan E. Douglas; Harold Jacob Smith; Cast includes: Spencer Tracy, Fredric March, Gene Kelly, Dick York, Harry Morgan, Claude Akins.

In 1960, Hollywood returned to an old theme – the famous and controversial "monkey trial" of the 1920s. Noted Chicago lawyer Clarence Darrow clashes with silver-tongued orator William Jennings Bryan. This drama is based on Jerome Lawrence and Robert E. Lee's thinly disguised play about the famous Scopes trial of the mid-1920s that was held in Tennessee. Spencer Tracy portrays Henry Drummond (Clarence Darrow, in real life), an admitted agnostic who defends a Southern teacher on trial for teaching Darwin's theory of evolution – a violation of the law in Tennessee. "I came here," the brilliant attorney says, "to defend the right to be different." Fredric March, as the bombastic prosecuting attorney Harrison Brady (William Jennings Bryan, in real life), considers the teaching of evolution pushed by big-city intellectuals and "agnostic scientists" as a threat to the fundamentalist belief in the Bible.

Gene Kelly portrays the cynical and caustic reporter E. K. Hornbeck, loosely based on the real life Baltimore journalist H. L. Mencken. He rarely misses an opportunity to sneer at and mock the Southern townspeople and Brady for their religious beliefs. When an elderly lady asks him if he would like a nice clean place to stay, the cynic retorts sardonically, "I had a nice clean place to stay, and I left it to come here."

During the trial Drummond and Brady engage in a battle of wits over personal and religious issues. Drummond defends a person's right to think and concludes with an attack on fanaticism, bigotry and ignorance. "Fanaticism and ignorance is forever busy," he charges, facing a prejudiced judge, "and soon, with banners flying, and with drums beating, we'll be marching backward, backward through the dark ages of that 16th century when bigots burned a man who dared bring enlightenment and challenge to the human mind!" Brady insists that the people need their idea of faith, a sort of "golden chalice of hope." Both sides suggest a metaphorical struggle between the present and progress. Although Brady wins the support of the local crowds, Drummond wins a moral victory in the courtroom when his teacher-client is fined the small sum of one hundred dollars. A disappointed Brady collapses. When the courtroom empties, the reporter insults Brady. "A giant once lived in that body!" Drummond reminds the reporter. He then packs a copy of the *Bible* and Darwin's *On the Origin of the Species* into his brief case. The astonished journalist calls Drummond a hypocrite who still believes in religion. Drummond, in turn, berates the reporter and taunts him with leading a barren and lonely existence.

*

The film was based on the actual Scopes Monkey Trial, in 1925, in Dayton, Tennessee. John T. Scopes (1900-1970), a high school teacher, was accused of having violated a Tennessee law that forbade the teaching of the theory of evolution in public schools. According to the law, evolution contradicted the account of creation in the Bible. The trial received worldwide publicity and was conducted in a circus-like atmosphere. The press labeled it the Monkey Trial because, according to popular belief, evolution meant that humans were descended from monkeys. William Jennings Bryan served as the state's prosecutor while Clarence Darrow was the defense attorney.

Intruder in the Dust (1949), MGM. Dir. Clarence Brown; Sc. Ben Maddow; Cast include: David Brian, Claude Jarman Jr., Juano Hernandez, Porter Hall, Elizabeth Patterson, Will Geer.

Clarence Brown's racially charged drama is based on the novel by William Faulkner. It is set in the Deep South and concerns an elderly black (Juano Hernandez) who is accused of murdering a white man. Hernandez quietly awaits his fate in a local jail and refuses to defend himself to David Brian, the white lawyer assigned to him, who thinks the case hopeless. A young white (Claude Jarman Jr.), a friend of the prisoner, decides to investigate the crime on his own and eventually proves his innocence. However, at the end the prisoner reveals that he is just as bigoted as his white accusers.

Judge Horton and the Scottsboro Boys (1976), NBC. Dir. Fielder Cook; Sc. John McGreevey; Cast includes: Ellen Barber, Paul Benjamin, Larry Butts, Rony Clanton.

Fielder Cook's incisive television drama was the only film or television production to deal with the tragic "Scottsboro case." The racial case initially took place early in the 1930s in Alabama and eventually grew into an international cause célèbre in 1931.

*

At that time, the U.S. was a vastly differently country from what it is today. America was in the midst of the Great Depression with millions unemployed. The poor could not afford many necessities – including the cost of transportation. For many, hopping a freight car was the only escape from town and unemployment. On the evening of March 25, 1931, nine young black men, two white women and a group of young white men boarded a freight car outside of Scottsboro, Alabama. The mixture was combustible and predictable – an altercation erupted. The whites were forced off the train and, their egos deflated in the supercharged racial atmosphere, they immediately reported the incident to the local sheriff.

A posse formed, the train was halted and the blacks forcibly removed and jailed. What happened next is unclear. Some reports indicated that the two young white women fabricated the charges against the blacks while other reports charged that the young white men manufactured the entire story. Whatever the case, local armed white mobs were aroused, circled the jail and threatened to lynch the prisoners. Within two weeks of their arrest, the "Scottsboro Boys" – one of whom was only 12 years old, another disabled and a third, blind – were tried and found guilty. Despite the fact that a medical examination of the women contradicted their testimony, eight of the nine blacks were sentenced to death.

The American Communist Party saw an opportunity to demonstrate the evils of the capitalist system and immediately sprang to the defense of the blacks. The Communists set up the International Labor Defense Committee, which collected monies and raised the profile of the case to national and international consciousness. In 1932 the Committee brought the case to the U.S. Supreme Court and, in Powell vs. Alabama, the conviction was thrown out on the grounds that the men were poorly represented.

Nevertheless, the State of Alabama was relentless and refused to drop the charges; the young men were retried the following year. Under cross-examination by defense attorney Samuel Lefkowitz, one of the women admitted that she had contrived the accusations. Despite this admission, the all-white jury returned the same guilty verdict.

The case made its way back up to the U.S. Supreme Court in 1935 where, in Norris vs. Alabama, it was once again thrown out, this time on the grounds that blacks were systematically excluded from the jury, rendering the entire trial unconstitutional.

The case returned to the Alabama courts where it was argued over and shifted between the various jurisdictions. Finally, in 1937, the State of Alabama and the attorneys for the black prisoners agreed to release the five youngest defendants immediately and to parole the four others within a year. Despite the agreement, it was only in 1943 that three of the four remaining prisoners were released. In 1948, the last black defendant escaped to Michigan, which refused extradition requests from the State of Alabama.

Finally, in 1976, the governor and the parole board of Alabama closed this sad chapter by pardoning the last surviving Scottsboro defendant.

Long, Hot Summer, The (1958), TCF. Dir. Martin Ritt; Sc. Irving Ravetch, Harriet Frank Jr.; Cast includes: Paul Newman, Joanne Woodward, Anthony Franciosa, Orson Welles, Lee Remick.

Martin Ritt's sexy and violent drama is based in part on William Faulkner's novel *The Hamlet.* It centers on Mississippi redneck Paul Newman, who has a penchant for burning down the property of his enemies. He wanders into the town controlled by Orson Welles, a domineering father who has bullied most of the townspeople and has transformed his daughter (Joanne Woodward) into a young old maid.

Faulkner won his first Pulitzer Prize in 1954 for *The Fable* in which he hoped for a spiritual rebirth of mankind. His second Pulitzer Prize was awarded for *The Reivers* in 1962 and it appears to be a blissful reconstruction of his early life in Mississippi. Mark Rydell's picaresque screen adaptation of the novel is set in 1905 Mississippi. Steve McQueen, as a lively and ribald resident rogue, leads a youth astray as they head for Memphis and the end of innocence. The visitors go through a series of familiar incidents in this bawdy nostalgic drama. The boy becomes involved in a scrape in a bordello as he tries to defend the reputation of one of the lovely young professional women. The woman then sleeps with the corrupt sheriff in order to spring the youth from jail. "Sometimes," McQueen figures, "you have to say goodbye to the things you know and hello to the things you don't."

*

Mississippi Burning (1988), Orion. Dir. Alan Parker; Sc. Chris Gerolmo, Willam Bradford Huie; Cast includes: Gene Hackman, Willem Dafoe, Frances McDormand, Brad Dourif, R. Lee Ermey.

This explosive drama is based on the true story of the murder of three young Northern civil rights workers – Chaney, Goodman and Schwerner. The three young men volunteer to help the voter registration drive in Mississippi and are murdered. FBI agents Gene Hackman and Willem Dafoe are assigned to investigate their disappearance and they soon find the volunteers' bodies. Hackman, the older and more streetwise agent who was raised in the South, tries to educate the younger, less experienced Dafoe, who believes in following procedure. They don't much like each other and they struggle for control of the investigation. Hackman befriends the unhappy and neglected wife of the local racist sheriff, who has an alibi concerning the time of the triple murder. When one of the terrorized local blacks suggests he could help in the investigation, the Ku Klux Klan burns down his father's house. The murderers are finally identified and brought to trial. The story gives us some insight into the segregated lives of blacks who lived under the "Jim Crow" laws in the South. The film, based on the book *Three Lives for Mississippi* by W. B. Huie, suggests that the South and the nation matured as a result of the civil rights movement.

My Cousin Vinny (1992), TCF. Dir. Jonathan Lynn; Sc. Dale Launer, Paul Schiff; Cast includes: Joe Pesci, Ralph Macchio, Marisa Tomei, Fred Gwynne.

Inexperienced Brooklyn lawyer Joe Pesci journeys to a small Southern town with his girlfriend Marisa Tomei to defend his nephew in court. In this rollicking comedy, the nephew, Ralph Macchio, and a fellow student have been wrongly arrested for theft. Pesci has several very funny clashes with the local judge, Fred Gwynne – reflecting the lack of communication between their two quite different worlds. The clash between the two cultures is particularly apparent when Brooklynite Pesci tries to defend his clients and mispronounces "two youths" as "two yoots." The reserved judge, nettled early on by the Northern lawyer's attire and lack of preparation, is finally flabbergasted by Pesci's use of language and is forced to inquire, "What's a 'yoot'?" Eventually, Pesci wins the case, thanks to the mechanical and technological expertise of his girlfriend, who amazes both the judge and the prosecuting attorney. In the end, it is Tomei who wins the contest for laughs. The comedy serves as a good-natured, broad burlesque of a slow-talking Southern judge and prosecutor versus a fast-talking New York lawyer.

Rainmaker, The (1997), Par. Dir. Francis Ford Coppola; Sc. Francis Ford Coppola; Cast includes: Matt Dillon, Danny DeVito, Mickey Rourke, Jon Voight, Claire Danes.

In this drama, Matt Dillon portrays a young Tennessee lawyer who has worked hard to get through law school. Flashy charlatan Mickey Rourke, a hotshot lawyer who is facing problems with the law, hires Dillon. Danny DeVito, another employee who has never passed the bar exam but knows his way around the law and the courthouse, persuades young Dillon to leave Rourke and join him in a separate practice. "A lawyer," DeVito begins to explain his own basic code of ethics, "should fight for his client, refrain from stealing money and try to tell the truth." Each takes a liking to the other and they open shop in an abandoned office. One of Dillon's first clients is an elderly woman who plans to leave her money to a television evangelist. Dillon notices that the client's son is dying but the insurance company refuses to pay for his health benefits.

Dillon fights the powerful insurance company. The insurance company hires a prestigious law firm, headed by Jon Voight, a high-priced and amoral lawyer with a battery of assistant attorneys. The inexperienced Dillon eventually beats Voight in a suspenseful and rewarding courtroom sequence. He wins a large, multimillion-dollar suit against the company, but the insurance company soon files for bankruptcy. Dillon narrates the film and contributes several lawyer jokes ("How do you know when a lawyer is lying? His lips are moving," and "What's the difference between a hooker and a lawyer? A hooker will stop screwing you after you're dead"). After an incompetent judge and a corrupt insurance company lawyer help him, Dillon sarcastically comments: "Sworn in by a fool and vouched for by a scoundrel, I'm a lawyer at last."

Sound and the Fury, The (1959), Dir. Martin Ritt; Sc. Irving Ravetch, Harriet Frank Jr.; Cast includes: Yul Brynner, Joanne Woodward, Margaret Leighton, Stuart Whitman.

Martin Ritt's film is based on William Faulkner's novel. Joanne Woodward plays the lead, a young Southern woman of independent spirit. Faulkner writes penetratingly about Southern social disintegration and transition. The film focuses on the decadent remnants of the Compsons, a former eminent family of a small Southern town.

The novel was written in a stream-of-consciousness style, which was quite radical for the time. Faulkner describes how the wealthy Compson family destroys itself while the local blacks in the novel endure with their simple, religious faith. He continually revised the novel until it was finally published in 1929.

Story of Temple Drake, The (1933), Par. Dir. Stephen Roberts; Sc. Oliver H. P. Garrett; Cast includes: Miriam Hopkins, Jack LaRue, William Gargan, William Collier Jr., Irving Pichel.

Miriam Hopkins portrays the title character, a hedonistic, pleasure-seeking young woman, whose father is a wealthy judge. This drama is based on William Faulkner's novel *Sanctuary* which was published in 1931. Hopkins embodies Southern decadence in this dramatic attack on Southern aristocracy. In Tony Richardson's later remake, *Sanctuary* (1961), Lee Remick portrays Temple Drake, a Southern young woman and product of the Jazz Age. Bradford Dillman, a spoiled college student, takes her to a bootlegger's site. Once there, Candy Man (Yves Montand) rapes her and she ends up as his mistress in a New Orleans bordello.

Faulkner's popularity rocketed after the publication of *Sanctuary.* He followed up *Sanctuary* with *Absalom, Absalom!* (1936), *Sutpen* (1936), *Requiem for a Nun* (1952), *The Unvanquished* (1938) and *Go Down Moses and Other Stories* (1942). *Requiem,* the novel, was integrated into Richardson's 1961 film remake of *Sanctuary.*

Faulkner, who won the Nobel Prize for literature in 1949, usually jumps right into his story without an introduction of any sort. He writes in long sentences with elaborate sentence structure and is sometimes dull. Faulkner's novels are interrelated. The characters reoccur and there are allusions to incidents in other novels. In most novels the narrative is sequential; however, some of them mix past and present – mirroring the way we ourselves sometimes think. Faulkner presents the dark side of the Southern tradition. He describes good struggling against the evil, subconscious side of human nature. In one of his later works, *Intruder in the Dust* (1948), Faulkner reverses himself and takes an optimistic view of the South's future.

*

They Won't Forget (1937), WB. Dir. Mervyn LeRoy; Sc. Abem Kandel, Robert Rossen; Cast includes: Claude Rains, Edward Norris, Allyn Joslyn, Linda Perry, Cy Kendall, E. Alyn Warren.

A hard-hitting attack on prejudice and intolerance, Mervyn LeRoy's social drama concerns murder and mob psychology in a small Southern town. The coed victim (Lana Turner) was assaulted and killed on Confederate Memorial Day. Politically ambitious prosecutor Claude Rains exploits the murder by targeting as chief suspect a Northern teacher, Robert Hale (Edward Norris), employed at the local college. He dismisses another possible suspect, an African-American janitor, saying, "Anyone can convict a Negro in the South." News-hungry reporter Allyn Joslyn arouses provincial bigotry as the story bursts into national headlines. Cries of "Prejudice" emerge from both the North and the South. To protect the convicted Norris from an angry lynch mob, authorities move him onto a train and rush him to prison. The angry mob storms aboard, drags him from the train and hangs him. In the last scene a reporter muses to Rains, "Now that it's over, I wonder if Hale really did it?" The prosecutor quietly replies, "I wonder."

The film was adapted from the novel *Death in the Deep South* by Ward Greene. Both novel and film were based on the famous 1913 Leo Frank Case.

An earlier, silent film titled *Thou Shalt Not Kill* (1915), loosely based on the tragic events of the Frank case, was directed by Hal Reid. A television production concerning the Leo Frank case and using actual names and places, entitled *The Murder of Mary Phagan*, appeared in 1988 and featured Jack Lemmon as the governor.

*

The mix of murder, religion and race fueled the passions that surrounded the trial of Leo Frank in Atlanta in 1913. Leo Frank was born in Texas in 1884 and then, together with his parents, moved to Brooklyn, New York, where he grew up. He graduated with a Bachelor's degree in mechanical engineering from Cornell University in 1906 and then moved to Atlanta where he soon became superintendent of the National Pencil Factory. Four years later, in 1910, he married Lucille Selig, a local young woman, and he seemed destined for a happy, ordered middle-class life.

The Hearst publications ignited the spark, and others supplied the fuel for the fatal result. Taking his clue from Hearst, another, smaller populist publisher, Tom Watson, raised the ante in his newspaper, *The Jeffersonian*. He began calling for the conviction of the Northern Jew, Leo Frank, who "had a ravenous appetite for the forbidden fruit – a lustful eagerness enhanced by the racial novelty of the girl of the uncircumcised." With these sensational writings, *The Jeffersonian*'s circulation increased from about 21,000 to 85,000. Frank was perceived both as a Northern "carpetbagger" and a Jew – a double whammy – and soon the public was whipped into a frenzy against Frank.

At this point, Jim Conley, a black janitor at the pencil factory, stepped into the maelstrom and provided additional testimony against Frank. Although Conley had been caught washing new bloodstains from his shirt, the police accepted Conley's deposition implicating Frank, who was indicted on the strength of Conley's testimony. Luther Rosser and Reuben Arnold, two of Atlanta's top criminal attorneys, represented Frank, while Solicitor General Hugh Dorsey presented the state's case. Rosser and Arnold immediately noted that the medical examiner waited nine days to perform an autopsy and that the examination was so substandard that it was never really determined whether the girl had been raped prior to her murder.

Experts examined Frank's handwriting and concluded that he did not write the two notes found at the murder scene. Conley came to the witness stand and swore that the defendant confessed to murdering Phagan and that Frank then forced him to move the victim's body. A number of female employees who uniformly disliked Frank as an employer were then called to the witness stand and they all provided damaging testimony.

Prior to sentencing, Judge Roan asked Frank and his lawyers to absent themselves from the courtroom when the jury announced their verdict. In case of an acquittal, the judge was afraid that an incensed mob might lynch the defendant or his attorneys. Frank, Rosser and Arnold agreed to absent themselves during the reading of the jury verdict.

The jury found Frank guilty of murder and Atlanta celebrated when Judge Roan sentenced him to death. Frank then hired the eminent private detective William Burns and simultaneously began a legal appeal. Burns was able to obtain several affidavits from some of the prosecution's female witnesses indicating that the police had coerced their testimony. Burns proved his worth by locating some love letters that Conley had written while in prison on a previous offense. Handwriting experts noted a number of similarities between the two notes found next to Phagan's body and Conley's letters.

The appeal was procedural and based on the fact that Frank was not in the courtroom when the jury's decision was read. The case went to the U.S. Supreme Court, which voted 7 to 2 to reject the appeal on April 19, 1915.

The only avenue open for Frank now was a direct appeal to the Governor of Alabama, John Slaton. The governor was at the end of his term and he didn't expect to run again, so he was fairly well insulated from public pressures. Meanwhile, nine U.S. governors and seven Senators requested that Slaton pardon Frank. According to the *New York Times*, the political support for Frank was without precedent in the history of the United States. Governor Slaton responded favorably and commuted Frank's death sentence to life imprisonment. In his announcement on June 20, 1915, the governor stated:

> Two thousand years ago, another governor washed his hands of a case and turned over a Jew to a mob. . . . If today another Jew were lying in his grave because I had failed to do my duty, I would all through life find his blood on my hands.

The commutation didn't sit well with Tom Watson, the publisher of *The Jeffersonian*. He continued his attacks on Frank and, on the morning of August 17, 1915, a mob broke into the County Sheriff's office in Marietta, Georgia, dragged Leo Frank out and hanged him. No one was ever convicted for Frank's murder.

As a postscript to the entire episode, in 1985, Alonzo Mann, who had worked in Frank's office and was now close to death, decided to break seven decades of silence and offered eye-witness testimony that Jim Conley had murdered Mary Phagan. The State of Georgia in 1986 responded by granting Leo Frank a posthumous pardon.

*

Time to Kill, A (1996), WB. Dir. Joel Schumacher; Sc. Akiva Goldman; Cast includes: Samuel L. Jackson, Matthew McConaughey, Sandra Bullock, Kevin Spacey.

When a young black girl is brutally raped by two white no-account bullies, the child's father (Samuel L. Jackson), a hardworking laborer, seeks help from Matthew McConaughey. This hard-hitting racially charged drama is set in a small Southern town. McConaughey is a sympathetic local white lawyer. Although his client can't pay the expenses, the attorney feels conscience-bound to take the case – despite the local pressures against him. Pert Sandra Bullock is a paralegal who journeys down from the North and volunteers her service to the lawyer. During the trial, an all-white jury fails to convict the two rapists. The enraged father shoots both the defendants on the courtroom staircase. The lawyer is now forced to defend Jackson, while an aroused group of bigots, dressed in Ku Klux Klan robes, go into action. For starters, they kidnap the paralegal and leave her hanging tied to a tree at night. Later on they start a riot on the main street outside the courthouse. Although the lawyer succeeds in exonerating the jailed father, audiences may sense that the entire film, although well made and exhilarating in the final triumph of good over evil, belongs to a world of fantasy.

To Kill a Mockingbird (1962), U. Dir. Robert Mulligan; Sc. Horton Foote; Cast includes: Gregory Peck, Mary Badham, Philip Alford, John Megna, Frank Overton.

Robert Mulligan's social drama is based on the novel by Harper Lee. It focuses on six-year-old Scout, her ten-year-old brother Jem and their lawyer-father Atticus Finch (Gregory Peck), a widower. They all live together in a small Southern town during the Depression. The two children enjoy frolicking through the streets and woods but give a wide berth to the mysterious house of the eccentric Boo Radley. One day Tom Robinson, an African American, is falsely accused of raping a white girl and the children attend the trial. The two children see prejudice at first-hand. Atticus loses the case, but before he can file an appeal, his client is shot to death, alleging trying to escape.

One night the alleged rape victim's father has an altercation with Atticus and tries to attack the two Finch children, but Boo Radley knifes him to death. Later, when Atticus learns that Radley killed the drunken father in order to protect his children, Scout proposes that the matter should be closed and listed as an accident. To protect Radley, she reminds her father that "it would be sort of like shooting a mockingbird, wouldn't it?"

9

Reconstruction and the Carpetbaggers

What is the "New South"? Obviously, there are certain characteristics that delineate the "New South" from the "Old South," but exactly what are they? For starters, the Northern victors in the Civil War destroyed the old plantation system that had been the backbone of the antebellum South. Although the lord and manor and feudalism had disappeared hundreds of years ago in Europe, it still was alive and well in the "Old South" in the form of the plantation system. The entire region had been dependent upon its the two most important crops – tobacco and cotton –and the destruction of the old society tangentially stimulated a diversification in agricultural crops. In turn, this diversification tended to weaken the concentration of power in the hands of a few large planters and eventually produced a more democratic society.

In the long run, the Northern victory not only undermined the large planters, but it stimulated the development of industry in the South. From the Reconstruction period onward, Southern cities with their attendant industries grew in population and significance. Labor-management disputes began to resemble those in the North and unions began to make their appearance.

In some ways, the Northern triumph in the Civil War resembled the victory of the Allies over Germany and the U.S. over Japan following World War II. In all these instances, victory was unconditional and the United States imposed a new and democratic society over the defeated powers.

Spike Lee's documentary *Four Little Girls* (1997) describes Birmingham, Alabama in the throes of the civil rights movement. Four black children die as a result of a church bombing and one of the white civic leaders remarks:

> Birmingham was built in the late 1800s by the barons in the North who realized we had every combination – we had peo-

> ple, natural resources, we had river transportation. It was known as the 'Magic City' because it grew so fast. It was a violent town . . . a town of union violence condoned by the unions, by the police and by the steel industry. You had a tradition of violence growing out of an industrial setting, with an overlay of rural violence coming in from the rural countryside and the traditional Old South racism.

A number of common Southern themes of the Reconstruction period found their way into literature and film. Many Southerners were bitterly hostile to the "damn Yankees" and Reconstruction and never forgot the "lost cause." Novels and films depicted the rise of the KKK, Southern chain gangs and the general decadence of the post-Civil War period.

Southerners threw the derogatory term "carpetbaggers" at Northern opportunists – government agents, politicians, businessmen, and adventurers who moved to the South in order to make their fortunes during the 12-year Reconstruction period following the Civil War (1865-1877). They often came with nothing more than a valise (a carpetbag). They were supposed to help reconstruct the economy of the South and assist the newly enfranchised freedmen, but, unfortunately, many only enriched themselves.

Former Confederate leaders and soldiers were temporarily banned from voting or holding political office, so carpetbaggers became politicians with the support of newly-emancipated slaves. Although a few established corrupt governments, many helped broaden black voting, improved education, and restored Southern cities and roads. Nevertheless, most carpetbaggers were bitterly resented by white Southerners.

Birth of a Nation, The (1915), Mutual. Dir. D. W. Griffith; Sc. D. W. Griffith, Frank Woods; Cast includes: Lillian Gish, Mae Marsh, Henry Walthall, Miriam Cooper, Mary Alden, Ralph Lewis, George Siegmann, Walter Long.

The second half of D. W. Griffith's classic Civil War drama, entitled "Reconstruction," depicts the racial tensions in the South. Stoneman assigns his protege, Silas Lynch, a mulatto, to oversee the town of Piedmont. Lynch abuses the white citizens and, to rub salt into the wounds, he wants a white girl for his wife. Griffith indicates that the whites have no alternative but to look to the Ku Klux Klan for help. The director makes these hooded monsters into heroes. He shows them as avengers who ride into town in their white robes and right all the imagined wrongs done to the white citizens. In the dramatic climax, Ben Cameron, the leader of the Klan and the hero, assembles his fellow Klan members and saves Elsie who is Lynch's prisoner. At the same time, the KKK "cleanses" Piedmont of Lynch's followers.

Griffith's innovative camera and visual techniques – his use of masks, close-ups, panoramic shots of battle scenes, tracking shots, and his first sustained use of crosscutting in a feature – help to enhance the spectacle. His tableaus, "historical facsimiles," include Lincoln signing the first call for 75,000 volunteers, General Sherman's march to the sea and Booth's assassination of Linncoln at Ford's Theater. These historical re-enactments add dramatic power and authenticity to the work.

Griffith's attempts at showing the human suffering caused by war and the tragedy of a nation torn by prejudice and geographical differences were undermined by his depiction of blacks as subhuman and his glorification of the Klan. Both he and the film have been attacked on these grounds. Film critic Richard Schickel calls the film a "flawed masterpiece." Black leaders and other critics have labeled it blatantly racist. After President Wilson viewed the film he described it as "history written in lightning." He was later forced to retract his statement under severe criticism. When the feature was originally released, blacks rioted in several cities. The film so incensed African-Americans that they formed the National Association for the Advancement of Colored People for self-protection.

Buck and the Preacher (1972), Col. Dir. Sidney Poitier; Sc. Ernest Kinoy; Cast includes: Sidney Poitier, Harry Belafonte, Ruby Dee, Cameron Mitchell, Julie Robinson, Denny Miller.

Sidney Poitier's Western is set in the years following the Civil War and focuses upon a wagon train of freed slaves who seek new homes and new lives in the West. Southern plantation owners are short of field hands and send a group of hired guns to kidnap the former slaves back to Louisiana to work in the cotton fields. They burn the blacks' wagons, supplies and tools to "encourage" them to return to Louisiana. Poitier, as the wagon master, teams up with con-man preacher (Harry Belafonte) to protect the black farmers. Too many stereotypes work against the plot, which wastes the skills of some very talented actors.

Copper Canyon (1950), Par. Dir. John Farrow; Sc. Jonathan Latimer; Cast includes: Ray Milland, Hedy Lamarr, Macdonald Carey, Mona Freeman, Harry Carey Jr.

John Farrow's action drama is a cleverly disguised Reconstruction period film in the guise of a typical Western. Former Confederate soldiers and their families migrate to the West, where they settle down to work in the copper mines. Unfortunately, they have trouble getting their product to market because of scheming Northern businessmen whose local representative (Hedy Lamarr), a saloon owner, controls business and politics in the region.

Ray Milland, a former Confederate officer, arrives, posing as a traveling trick-shot performer. But like the mythical Robin Hood or Zorro characters, he secretly foils the syndicate's plans and protects his fellow Southerners. Milland's forays against the forces of injustice follow the pattern of the KKK riders in defense of Southern whites depicted by Griffith in *Birth of a Nation*.

Symbolizing North-South reconciliation, Lamarr falls in love with Milland while a Union officer shows a similar interest in a young Southern woman. There is no racial strife in the plot, which is devoid of black characters.

Drango (1957), UA. Dir. Hall Bartlett; Sc. Hall Bartlett, Jules Bricken; Cast includes: Jeff Chandler, John Lupton, Joanne Dru, Morris Ankrum, Ronald Howard.

Union officer Jeff Chandler is assigned to a Georgia community during the Reconstruction period following the Civil War. The townspeople distrust Chandler because he was a Union officer under General Sherman during his infamous march to the sea when he sacked Atlanta. Ronald Howard tries to incite the townspeople against Chandler and almost succeeds re-igniting the war. But the people slowly start to accept the Chandler's sincerity. In order to avoid bloodshed, Donald Crisp, Howard's father, is forced to kill his uncontrollable son.

Hitchin' Posts (1920), U. Dir. John Ford; Sc. George C. Hull; Cast includes: Frank Mayo, Beatrice Burnham, Joseph Harris, J. Farrell MacDonald, Mark Fenton.

Hitchin' Posts is a sprawling tale that begins in the South and ends on the frontier in the West. Ford's silent drama centers on Jefferson Todd, a Southern gentleman, played by Frank Mayo. Todd loses his land in the Civil War and then becomes a gambler on a Mississippi riverboat where he wins four prize racehorses from Colonel Bereton. Bereton soon commits suicide and the captain asks Todd to inform the colonel's daughter, Barbara. Now penniless, she journeys to the West to become a homesteader. Todd, meanwhile, battles against Castiga, a longtime foe, over an oil claim. Castiga perishes by drowning, and Todd marries Barbara.

Jesse James (1927), Par. Dir. Lloyd Ingraham; Sc. Frank M. Clifton; Cast includes: Fred Thomson, Nora Lane, Montagu Love, Mary Carr, James Pierce.

This film mixes historical fact and fiction in its account of the famous bandit's exploits in the 1860s and '70s. This silent action drama opens with Jesse James, played by Fred Thomson, joining Quantrill's raiders during the conflict. At one point, he is almost caught as a spy but manages to escape. When the war ends, James learns that his mother has been hurt by Union sympathizers and is about to be evicted from the town. He returns to seek revenge on those who have mistreated his mother but ends up as an outlaw. Although the film includes the characters of Frank, Jesse's brother, and Bob Ford, the man who betrayed the bandit, the plot has little historical accuracy.

Little Colonel, The (1935), TCF. Dir. David Butler; Sc. William Consulman; Cast includes: Shirley Temple, Lionel Barrymore, Evelyn Venable, John Lodge Sidney Blackmer.

David Butler's comedy drama is set in the South in the 1880s. Colonel Lionel Barrymore remains bitter about losing the war, so when his daughter (Evelyn Venable) elopes with a Northerner, the colonel disinherits her. Times are hard for the couple and the wife is forced to return with her daughter (Shirley Temple) to a small cottage near the colonel's estate. Soon Temple brings the family together. Kindly family servant Bill Robinson does a famous staircase dance with the daughter.

Men of Texas (1942), U. Dir. Ray Enright; Sc. Harold Shumate; Cast includes: Robert Stack, Leo Carrillo, Anne Gwynne, Broderick Crawford, Ralph Bellamy, Jane Darwell.

Chicago newsman Robert Stack and his photographer-assistant Leo Carrillo are determined to record the true story of Texas in this patriotic action tale set during the period of Reconstruction. However, Stack must first resolve his differences with the villainous Broderick Crawford. Between his several confrontations, he woos Southern belle Anne Gwynne while Carrillo supplies the comedy relief in this standard fare. Carrillo played a similar role as assistant to newsreel cameraman Clark Gable in *Too Hot to Handle* (1938). Crawford again played the heavy a decade later in *Lone Star* (1952), another historical film about Texas.

Rebel in Town (1956), UA. Dir. Alfred Werker; Sc. Danny Arnold; Cast includes: John Payne, Ruth Roman, J. Carrol Naish, Ben Cooper, John Smith, James Griffith.

An accidental killing re-ignites tensions between a former Confederate family and the victim's Union parents in this post-Civil War drama. While a Southern father (J. Carrol Naish) and his four sons are traveling West, one of the boys hears the click of a pistol behind him and spins around and fires instinctively. He discovers too late that he has killed a child with a toy gun. The father of the dead child, a former Union officer (John Payne), wants revenge for the senseless killing. After a lot of soul-searching on both sides, revenge is replaced with forgiveness. Ruth Roman plays Payne's wife. Ben Cooper, Naish's sensitive son, defies his own father and sympathizes with Payne. John Smith plays the trigger-happy son in this suspenseful and intelligent little film.

Rio Conchos (1964), TCF. Dir. Gordon Douglas; Sc. Joseph Landon, Clair Huffaker; Cast includes: Richard Boone, Stuart Whitman, Tony Franciosa, Wende Wagner, Warner Anderson, Edmund O'Brien.

In this Western action drama, four men start out to retrieve 2,000 repeating rifles that former Confederate soldiers have stolen from the U.S. army. Captain Stuart Whitman, who is responsible for the loss, and Jim Brown, Whitman's loyal sergeant, reluctantly take along Apache-hater Richard Boone who knows the arms dealer and unscrupulous killer Tony Franciosa who speaks Spanish fluently.

Following several complications and confrontations with bandits and hostile Apaches, they come face to face with Edmond O'Brien – as his prisoners. He is a demented former Confederate officer who has made himself a general and hopes to establish his own empire in the Southwest with his own troops. He shows Boone around the mansion he is building on the banks of the Rio Conchos and his land. "What do you think of this?" he boasts. "Chihuahua instead of Louisiana, the Rio Conchos instead of the Mississippi – back to life again as if sprung from the ashes. You thought I was mad? You don't even know what tomorrow's date is? April 9. It was just two years ago that Lee surrendered to Grant. We had better soldiers, better men, a superior cause, winning all the battles – still we did not win the war. Because we were insufficiently ruthless! We allowed our own code of honor to destroy us!" To help him fulfill his dream, O'Brien sells the stolen rifles to the warring Apaches in exchange for gold. O'Brien encourages the Apaches to kill all the American civilians and troops in the area. A friendly young Apache woman frees Whitman, Brown and Boone and they proceed to destroy the rifles, munitions and O'Brien's dream of conquest.

Tennessee Johnson (1942), MGM. Dir. William Dieterle; Sc. John Balderston, Wells Root; Cast includes: Van Heflin, Ruth Hussey, Lionel Barrymore, Marjorie Main.

In this biographical drama, Van Heflin portrays the title character, Andrew Johnson. The film follows Jackson from the backwoods of North Carolina to the White House.

Andrew Johnson (1808-75), who eventually became the 16th vice-president (1865) and 17th president of the U. S. (1865- 69), was born in Raleigh, North Carolina. He was the son of poor servants. Johnson moved to Tennessee and, in 1827, established a tailor shop and married schoolteacher Eliza McCardle (1810-76). She taught him to read and write. He prospered in his trade and eventually made enough money to buy a few slaves.

In 1829 he was elected councilman and later served as mayor of Greenville. In turn, he was elected alderman, mayor, state senator, U.S. representative and, eventually, U.S. Senator. Johnson remained alone among Southern senators in supporting the federal government.

When the Civil War broke out, Johnson remained loyal to the Union. Lincoln was re-elected in 1864, and Johnson became his Vice-President. Johnson succeeded to the Presidency upon Lincoln's assassination. He opposed many of the harsh policies imposed upon the South by the U.S. Congress during the Reconstruction years and it was precisely this obstruction that led to his impeachment. Thaddeus Stevens led a group of Johnson's congressional enemies and brought charges against him. The U.S. House of Representative indicted Johnson, but the Senate failed – by just one vote – to convict him.

Johnson's popular appeal rested upon his identification with the common man. However, the obverse side of this characteristic was his brashness and ill-advised straight talk, traits that got him into political difficulty throughout his career.

Texans, The (1938), Par. Dir. James Hogan; Sc. Bertram Millhauser, Paul Sloane, William Wister Haines; Cast includes: Joan Bennett, Randolph Scott, May Robson, Walter Brennan, Robert Cummings.

This action drama is a remake of the silent *North of '36* (1924) and takes place in the years following the Civil War. Texas is recovering from the conflict and faces some of the problems of the Reconstruction period. Randolph Scott portrays a cattle driver determined to develop the Chisholm Trail as a viable and commercial route to Kansas. To accomplish this task, he battles Indians, the Ku Klux Klan and corrupt carpetbaggers. Joan Bennett, an embittered Southerner who wants to ignite another armed conflict, is another one of his problems. She plots to smuggle ammunition into Mexico in her dream of starting a second Civil War – this time with Mexico allied to the South. Scott persists against all odds as he succeeds in completing his 1500-mile trek.

Three Violent People (1956), Par. Dir. Rudolph Maté; Sc. James Edward Grant; Cast includes: Charlton Heston, Anne Baxter, Gilbert Roland, Tom Tryon, Forrest Tucker.

In this postwar Reconstruction drama, Charlton Heston, a Southern Civil War captain, returns home to his Texas ranch with his bride (Anne Baxter) and is confronted by carpetbaggers and his own troublesome brother (Tom Tryon). Crooked Northern usurpers, armed with phony tax assessments, force ranchers off their property and confiscate their cattle and horses. The embittered Tryon wants Heston to sell out and demands his share of the ranch in gold. Heston, organizes his remaining fellow ranchers in resisting the carpetbaggers, but is faced with another personal problem. He learns that Baxter, his beautiful, caring and pregnant wife, had been a prostitute. Following a foiled attempt on his life, Heston and his wife remain together to run the ranch while Tryon is killed in a gun battle with government troops.

Undefeated, The (1969), TCF. Dir. Andrew V. McLaglen; Sc. James Lee Barrett; Cast includes: John Wayne, Rock Hudson, Tony Aguilar, Roman Gabriel, Marian McCargo, Lee Meriwether.

Together with his adopted Indian son, Roman Gabriel, ex-Union colonel John Wayne leads a herd of thousands of horses into Mexico. They meet up with Rock Hudson, a former Southern colonel, in this Western drama set during Reconstruction. After just fighting some Confederate soldiers, Wayne learns that the Civil War has ended just three days earlier. Hudson chooses to burn his estate rather than let the carpetbaggers grab it. He leads an exodus of Southerners to Mexico, where Emperor Maximilian has invited them to settle and where the carpetbaggers cannot grab their land. Wayne and his hired hands come to the aid of Hudson and his ex-Confederates when they are attacked by a horde of Mexican bandits. Following several other complications, both colonels succeed in their separate goals

Vanquished, The (1953), Par. Dir. Edward Ludwig; Sc. Winston Miller, Frank L. Moss, Lewis R. Foster; Cast includes: John Payne, Coleen Gray, Jan Sterling, Lyle Bettger.

Confederate veteran John Payne returns home after spending time as a prisoner of war in a Union camp, in this post-Civil War drama. Payne finds corrupt carpetbaggers running his hometown. He soon learns that the paranoid and corrupt civil administrator (Lyle Bettger), who has moved into Payne's former mansion, is the chief crook. To gain proof against Bettger, Payne signs up as his tax collector – to the horror of Payne's girlfriend (Coleen Gray) and the other townspeople. Bettger is no fool and he suspects Payne, so he frames the veteran for a murder. After the usual setbacks and typical fights and shoot-outs, Payne straightens out the local problems by running the villain out of town.

Virginia City (1940), WB. Dir. Michael Curtiz; Sc. Robert Buckner; Cast includes: Errol Flynn, Miriam Hopkins, Randolph Scott, Humphrey Bogart, Frank McHugh, Alan Hale.

Michael Curtiz's Civil War drama opens in 1864, with the South facing economic bankruptcy and military defeat. The only hope for the Confederacy is a daring and desperate scheme proposed by an army officer (Randolph Scott). He plans to secretly transport $50 million in gold from Nevada's sympathetic Virginia City mine owners. Errol Flynn portrays a Union intelligence officer who escapes from a Confederate prison and then volunteers to stop the suspected wagon train of gold from reaching Confederate lines. He soon learns that Scott, his former captor and warden, plans to move the gold by wagon train from Virginia City, Nevada to Richmond, Virginia. Flynn falls in love with Miriam Hopkins, a Confederate spy who poses as a saloon singer in Virginia City and is working closely with Southerner Scott. During the chase, a band of bandits attempts to hijack the gold. Scott is killed in the encounter, but Flynn grabs the gold and buries it. Although a Union officer, Flynn wants to use the gold to help rebuild the South after the war.

When Flynn refuses to reveal the whereabouts of the gold, his superiors court-martial him and sentence him to death. In reply, Flynn explains his actions: "Their leader hoped that someday their gold would return to the South, where it belongs, to help them rebuild their homes and restore some of their pride." Hopkins travels to Washington to plead with President Lincoln to spare Flynn's life. The President promises to pardon Flynn and asks Hopkins to give her Southern friends the following message: "Tell them we're now one people, united by blood and fire. From this day forward our destiny is indivisible."

Virginia City is based on an actual Civil War incident and was photographed in Flagstaff, Arizona. It was released right before America's entry into World War II and carried an appeal for a unified nation.

10

The Ku Klux Klan

Six former Confederate officers organized the original Klan in Pulaski, Tennessee on Dec. 24, 1865. They derived the name "klan" from the Greek word "kuklos" (circle). Although the Ku Klux Klan began as a mischievous social organization, it soon turned violent and focused that violence against Northern carpetbaggers and local "uppity" blacks who rose to power in the South in 1867. The Klan's extremism received wide support in the white community which felt itself under siege and powerless against the carpetbaggers and blacks who were supported by federal troops during the Reconstruction period.

The Klansmen believed in the innate inferiority of blacks and resented federal Reconstruction policies as hostile and oppressive. They opposed the rise of former slaves to equal political and legal status with whites. Under tight supervision of the federal government, many Southerners from the Carolinas to Arkansas viewed the Klan as a sort of nineteenth century civil rights organization for whites and they supported the Klan's illegal activities. The Klan carefully escalated its harassment of blacks, liberals and carpetbaggers from burning crosses to flogging and, eventually, murder. The Klan justified these activities as essential in order to defend white supremacy and the inviolability of white womanhood.

In 1871 Congress passed the Force Bill to implement the 14th Amendment to the Constitution guaranteeing the rights of all citizens. That same year President Ulysses S. Grant issued a proclamation calling on members of illegal organizations to disarm and disband, and hundreds of Klansmen were arrested.

The principles of the original Klan were adopted by a new fraternal organization incorporated in Georgia in 1915. Officially, the new society was called The Invisible Empire. Blacks, Roman Catholics and Jews were excluded and soon became targets of defamation and persecution by The Invisible Empire. Until 1920 the society exercised little influence. Then, in the period of economic dislocation and political and social unrest that followed World War I, the Invisible Empire shed its protective cover and re-emerged as the Klan and expanded rapidly in urban areas and became active in many states. All non-Protestants, aliens, liberals, trade unionists and striking workers were denounced as subversives. Although the Klan continued to terrorize their victims, few prosecutions of Klansmen resulted, and in some communities local officials abetted them.

Exposures of the Klan led to a congressional investigation in 1921, and for a time the Klan changed its tactics. After 1921 it experienced a rapid growth of membership and became politically influential throughout the nation. One estimate of its membership, made in 1924 when the Klan was at its peak, was as high as 3 million. In that year a resolution denouncing the Klan, introduced at the national convention of the Democratic Party, precipitated a bitter controversy and was defeated.

In the 1970s, a weakened Klan made its appearance in several Southern states in response to the burgeoning civil rights movement. The membership was at about 5,000 at the end of the 1980s. A former grand wizard of the Klan, David Duke (1950-) was elected to the Louisiana House of Representatives in 1989 and ran unsuccessfully in the state's gubernatorial election in 1991.

Another Part of the Forest (1948), Dir. Michael Gordon; Sc. Vladimir Pozner; Cast includes: Fredric March, Ann Blyth, Edmond O'Brien, Florence Eldridge, Dan Duryea, John Dall.

Gordon Douglas's period drama is based on Lillian Hellman's play and peripherally touches upon the Klan. Fredric March portrays the head of the Southern Hubbard family. He is a war profiteer who betrayed 27 local soldiers during the Civil War. He flaunts his wealth in front of his Southern neighbors and shows only contempt for their "lost cause." March humiliates his ambitious son Ben (Edmond O'Brien), who eventually robs and blackmails his own father. March's whining and cowardly son Oscar (Dan Duryea) organizes Ku Klux Klan raids. Naturally, the father's monomaniacal drive for power and money corrupts his sons, Ben and Oscar. Ben finally threatens to expose his father's war crimes unless he signs over the family fortune to him. March resigns himself to his fate and turns over his property.

Birth of a Nation, The (1915), Mutual. Dir. D. W. Griffith; Sc. D. W. Griffith, Frank Woods; Cast includes: Lillian Gish, Mae Marsh, Henry Walthall, Miriam Cooper, Mary Alden, Ralph Lewis, George Siegmann, Walter Long.

D. W. Griffith's silent historical Civil War drama traces the fortunes of two families (one Northern and one Southern) who knew each other on a warm and friendly basis before the war. The work covers the saga of America's most tragic period. Almost every important historical event – from the early battles to the rise of the "Invisible Empire" of the KKK – is recreated with a realism that is reminiscent of Matthew Brady's contemporary photographs. At the close of the war, Northern carpetbaggers invade the South and appoint incompetent blacks to positions of power. Southern communities, the film suggests, were compelled to organize and combat many of the abuses of their white citizens – particularly abuses to white women. Individual scenes are powerful and brutal – the beating and flogging of captured blacks – but so are the abuses of white Southerners.

Griffith gave the cinema credibility as a medium capable of creating a work of art, his prejudiced view of the Klan sparked riots in the streets, gave rise to the NAACP and provoked litigation in the courts. Despite the political and social ramifications, the film's reputation as an almost flawless work of art and Griffith's skillful use of cinematic techniques emotionally moved millions of people and manipulated them as they had never been before. *The Birth of a Nation* may be a flawed masterpiece, as film critic Richard Griffith called it, but it is the picture that created the film industry.

Black Legion, The (1936), WB. Dir. Archie Mayo; Sc. Abem Finkel, William Wister Haines; Cast includes: Humphrey Bogart, Dick Foran, Erin O'Brien-Moore, Ann Sheridan, Robert Barrat, Helen Flint.

Con artists in Archie Mayo's part-crime and part-social drama make a fortune posing as leaders of a Ku Klux Klan-type of organization. Their con is to collect dues and sell members uniforms. Humphrey Bogart portrays an embittered worker who is disappointed when his prospective job goes instead to a Polish immigrant. He joins the Black Legion, a secret organization that promotes hatred of minorities and foreigners. The leaders help Bogart get his job by running his rival out of town. Bogart's life begins to come apart when he spends more time with the Legion than with his wife (Erin O'Brien-Moore). Bogart gets more deeply involved with the Black Legion, kills his best friend and is jailed for murder. The Legion threatens to kill his family if he exposes their organization, but he finally tells all at his trial. The leaders are arrested and Bogart gets a life sentence.

Chamber, The (1996), U. Dir. James Foley; Sc. William Goldman, Chris Reese; Cast includes: Chris O'Donnell, Gene Hackman, Faye Dunaway, Robert Prosky.

In this slow-paced drama, Chris O'Donnell portrays a young lawyer who journeys to Mississippi on a mission to save his grandfather (Gene Hackman) from the gas chamber. The senior citizen, an angry member of the Klan, has been found guilty of blowing up a Mississippi lawyer's office and killing the attorney's two children. O'Donnell, whose own father had committed suicide when was only ten years old, is driven to discover the entire truth about his grandfather's case. Faye Dunaway, the condemned man's daughter and O'Donnell's aunt, is a wealthy and gracious Southern hostess who, unfortunately, is burdened with a serious drinking problem that sometimes spins out of control. She objects to O'Donnell stirring up the old case when her father is about to face the gas chamber within a few weeks. She also believes her unrepentant father is guilty of the horrendous crime and deserves the death sentence. One of the better scenes in the film shows the explosion of the upper floor of the building with a statue of a Confederate soldier in the foreground. The grandson eventually proves that other Kan members, including Hackman's own brother, set off the bomb, but the Klan's code of honor kept Hackman silent over the years. Although his grandson fails to have the sentence commuted, Hackman eventually repents.

FBI Story, The (1959), WB. Dir. Mervyn LeRoy; Sc. Richard L. Breen, John Twist; Cast includes: James Stewart, Vera Miles, Murray Hamilton, Larry Pennell, Nick Adams.

FBI agent James Stewart battles the Ku Klux Klan, gangsters and Nazi spies during World War II. J. Edgar Hoover officially sanctioned *The FBI Story* and it did a very good job at promoting the agency. Vera Miles portrays Stewart's long-suffering wife while he goes off to round up such criminals as Baby Face Nelson, John Dillinger and Pretty Boy Floyd. The film is based on the book by Don Whitehead and shows a very positive picture of the FBI and its agents and gives audiences a brief glimpse into the inner workings of the bureau.

Fried Green Tomatoes (1991), U. Dir. Jon Avnet; Sc. Jon Avnet, Fannie Flagg; Cast includes: Kathy Bates, Jessica Tandy, Mary Stuart Masterson, Mary-Louise Parker.

Jon Avnet's sensitive drama is set in the South during the Depression. Idgie (Mary Stuart Masterson), an early feminist, owns and operates the local cafe in Whistle Stop, Alabama. Shocked as a young girl by the gory death of a beloved older brother, she remains a loner and a tomboy and has her own lifestyle. She does none of the things expected of respectable Southern women of the Depression Era. At one point, Sheriff Kilgore (Gary Basarba) warns that her equal treatment of blacks will only invite an unpleasant visit from the Klan – a very real threat for that time and place. But she ignores the advice.

Klansman, The (1974), Par. Dir. Terence Young; Sc. Millard Kaufman, Samuel Fuller; Cast includes: Lee Marvin, Richard Burton, Cameron Mitchell, Lola Falana, Luciana Paluzzi, David Huddleston.

Lee Marvin portrays a Southern sheriff in a racist town that is headquarters of an active Ku Klux Klan. The sheriff's deputy himself is a KKK member. When a young white woman is raped, the KKK and Cameron Mitchell, Marvin's deputy, vent their anger on an innocent black O. J. Simpson. Meanwhile, Lola Falana returns to the troubled town to visit her dying grandmother. The townspeople stir up trouble when they suspect she is an outside agitator sent to increase black voter registration.

Legion of Terror (1936), Col. Dir. C. C. Coleman Jr.'s; Sc. Bert Granet; Cast includes: Bruce Cabot, Marguerite Churchill, Crawford Weaver, Ward Bond.

Loosely based on the activities of Detroit's infamous Black Legion, the drama reveals how a secret terrorist organization threatens a local community and the national fabric of democracy. Once the gang members use the U.S. mail for their criminal acts (sending bombs to Congressmen), the U.S. Postal Service becomes interested in their activities. Government agents Bruce Cabot and Crawford Weaver are assigned to investigate the Legion. Charles Wilson portrays the sinister leader of the organization. The Legion captures Marguerite Churchill, the sister of a gang victim, along with Weaver, and both are threatened with execution. Cabot and the state police rescue them at the last minute.

Malcolm X (1992), WB. Dir. Spike Lee; Sc. Spike Lee, Arnold Perl, James Baldwin; Cast includes: Denzel Washington, Angela Bassett, Albert Hall, Al Freeman Jr., Delroy Lindo.

This broad and extensive biography traces the black leader's conversion from street thug to prison convict to religious believer. The story begins with Malcolm Little's troubled early years. The Ku Klux Klan burns down his home, murders his preacher-father and drives his mother insane. As a teenager, he dabbles in the world of whites, pursues white women and joins up with a Harlem racketeer. The next segment covers his prison years and the final part depicts his rise as a prominent disciple of Elijah Muhammad and its consequences.

Mississippi Burning (1988), Orion. Dir. Alan Parker; Sc. Chris Gerolmo, William Bradford Huie; Cast includes: Gene Hackman, Willem Dafoe, Frances McDormand, Brad Dourif, R. Lee Ermey.

Alan Parker's social drama centers on the murder of the three civil-rights workers—James Chaney, Andrew Goodman, and Michael Schwerner. Two FBI men (Gene Hackman and Willem Dafoe) arrive to investigate the disappearance of three young civil rights workers. Although they personally disagree about procedure, they do agree to organize a huge manhunt that eventually leads to the discovery of the civil rights workers' bodies. Thus far, the film follows the historical record. However, at this point the truth and Hollywood's imaginative reconstruction of the event parts ways. In an effort to "hype" the audience, the director, Alan Parker, has the FBI use non-legal terror tactics against the KKK. In two scenes the Klan burns down a home and a church while, in another scene, members flog an innocent black man. The film seems to manipulate its audience into applauding the FBI's non-legal forms of intimidation.

Places in the Heart (1984), Tri-Star. Dir. Robert Benton; Sc. Robert Benton; Cast includes: Sally Field, Lindsay Crouse, Ed Harris, Amy Madigan, John Malkovich, Danny Glover.

Field is the widow of a lawman who was accidentally killed by an intoxicated black man. The bank is threatening to take over her property for nonpayment of $240 on her mortgage. In Robert Benton's drama, Danny Glover gives a humorous eccentric performance in the endearing role of Moze. He is an itinerant black laborer who helps widow Sally Field's bring in her cotton crop, but his work gets him into trouble with the local branch of the Ku Klux Klan. Although Glover helps save the widow's farm from foreclosure, local bigots drive him off his newfound home.

The film won two Academy Awards for Best Actress (Sally Field) and Best Original Screenplay. The production also earned Academy Award Nominations for Best Picture, Best Supporting Actor (John Malkovich), Best Supporting Actress (Lindsey Crouse), Best Director (Robert Benton) and Best Costume Design (Ann Roth).

Stars in My Crown (1950), MGM. Dir. Jacques Tourneur; Sc. Margaret Fitts; Cast includes: Joel McCrea, Ellen Drew, Dean Stockwell, Alan Hale, Lewis Stone.

Jacques Tourneur's drama is based on the novel by Joe David Brown and focuses on prejudice in a Southern town. Joel McCrea portrays a preacher who moves into town with a Bible in one hand and a pistol in the other. He helps the community deal with a typhoid epidemic and KKK terrorist acts. In between these crises, McCrea supports the new doctor in town, Amanda Blake, who is the target of unfounded allegations. Naturally, Blake and McCrea get involved. All of the events occur during one year in the life of the community.

Storm Warning (1950), WB. Dir. Stuart Heisler; Sc. Daniel Fuchs, Richard Brooks; Cast includes: Ginger Rogers, Ronald Reagan, Doris Day, Steve Cochran, Hugh Sanders.

New York fashion model Ginger Rogers visits her sister (Doris Day) in a small Southern town, where she witnesses some Klansmen raid the local jail, remove a prisoner and then kill him. When she arrives at Day's home, she is shocked to recognize her sister's husband, Steve Cochran as one of the Klansmen. Her pregnant sister pleads with Rogers to keep everything quiet and Rogers agrees. Ronald Reagan, the local district attorney, fails to persuade Rogers to appear as a witness. However, when Cochran slaps both sisters around after Rogers refuses his sexual advances, she decides to testify against him. The Klan then kidnaps Rogers but she is saved when her sister arrives just in time with D.A. Reagan to the rescue.

The film was shot in a Southern-looking town near Los Angeles – Corona, California. Although the production focuses on the Klan, there were no blacks in the entire cast.

11

Discrimination

Although the Emancipation Proclamation of 1863 and the constitutional amendments that followed the American Civil War changed the legal status of blacks, a series of U.S. Supreme Court decisions struck down federal statutes designed to enforce the amendments. The most significant of these Supreme Court decisions declared unconstitutional a federal law that outlawed racial discrimination by private individuals and upheld state-enforced segregation.

In 1941, President Franklin D. Roosevelt issued an executive order forbidding discrimination in employment by a company involved in government defense contracts. Some states followed and began to legislate against discrimination on their own. On the national level, the unanimous Supreme Court decision in May 1954, in Brown v. Board of Education, declared the intentional segregation of black children in public schools to be *ipso facto* a violation of the 14th Amendment to the Constitution.

Congress passed the Civil Rights Act of 1957, but only the right to vote was expressly addressed. The federal Civil Rights Act of 1964 superseded state legislation and outlawed racial discrimination in most hotels, restaurants and other public facilities. The law prohibited private employers and unions from discriminating because of race and it banned registrars from applying different standards to white and black voting applicants, a provision that was strengthened by the Voting Rights Act of 1965. The 1964 law also authorized the U.S. attorney general to file an action when a "pattern or practice" of widespread discrimination was found.

In the same year, 1964, Congress established the Equal Employment Opportunity Commission and, in 1968, the Fair Housing Act barred racial discrimination in the sale, rental, or financing of housing, which used federal money. In 1972, state governments were prohibited to racially discriminate against job applicants.

Hollywood was afraid to tackle serious race relations' problems during the first half of the twentieth century. In the movies, blacks and other minorities were usually relegated to menial or supporting roles. In fact, the studios picked up and then reflected the stereotypes of blacks that were prevalent on stage and in popular literature of the times. Blacks and other minorities were often depicted as lazy, slow-witted, untrustworthy and often cowardly. When African-American performers were hired, they often were relegated to playing maids, servants, chauffeurs or other domestics – and chiefly as comic relief. Occasionally, the more talented performers like Bill "Bojangles" Robinson, Paul Robeson and Lena Horne, were permitted to display their specialty numbers. There were rare moments, in such films as *Imitation of Life* (1934) when Hollywood investigated racial issues. But it was not until after World War II that Hollywood thought the country was ready to accept serious films on race and subsequently turned out productions such as *Pinky* (1949) and *Nothing But a Man* (1964). The industry discovered that it could make money by confronting racism head-on rather than ignoring it altogether.

Although, until the last two or three decades, women were subject to all sorts of legal restrictions in the real world, in the fantasy world of the movies women were major players. However, unlike contemporary releases, women were always given "feminine" or supportive positions and very rarely assumed roles as doctors, lawyers, engineers or soldiers. Reflecting the advance of women within general society, Hollywood has looked for scripts that have assigned women more assertive roles as "shakers and movers."

American Indians were pictured hostile to whites, but their power was usually limited. Occasionally, a friendly or "good" Indian was assigned a supporting role.

Hollywood occasionally tackled other types of prejudice, including such dramas as *Between Heaven and Hell* (1956), about social differences; *Shock Corridor* (1963), about the treatment of mental patients and institutions; *Easy Rider* (1969), about those with different lifestyles; and comedies such as *Biloxi Blues* (1988), which address regional differences.

*

Between Heaven and Hell (1956), TCF. Dir. Richard Fleischer; Sc. Harry Brown; Cast includes: Robert Wagner, Terry Moore, Broderick Crawford, Buddy Ebsen, Robert Keith.

Wealthy Southern landowner Robert Wagner enters the military service following the Japanese attack on Pearl Harbor in this World War II drama. The film is based on the novel by Francis Gwaltney. Wagner dislikes blacks as well as poor whites and even exploits his sharecroppers. He enters the service with his local National Guard unit and they are all sent to the Pacific. When Wagner threatens a fellow bigot, an officer, he is transferred to a dangerous hill, where tough, illiterate and psychopathic Broderick Crawford is in charge of a group of men who hate his guts. Miracle of miracles, Wagner sees in Crawford a lower class version of himself and is appalled by it. He turns over a new leaf and becomes a good guy.

In the meantime, Crawford befriends sharecropper Buddy Ebsen. Eventually Crawford also sees the error of his ways and, during a furious battle, he saves his pal's life. Both are wounded and sent home.

Biloxi Blues (1988), Raster. Dir. Mike Nichols; Sc. Neil Simon; Cast includes: Matthew Broderick, Christopher Walken, Matt Mulhern, Corey Parker.

Mike Nichols's comedy drama is based on Neil Simon's play. Matthew Broderick plays Simon's young alter ego, Eugene Jerome, and the film follows Jerome into World War II. Near the end of the conflict, the youthful Brooklynite is drafted into the army and shipped to Biloxi, Mississippi, where he and his fellow recruits undergo ten tough weeks of basic training. He clashes several times with his demanding sergeant, Christopher Walken, who resents this Northerner, particularly since Jerome is from New York. "There's something about you New York boys that riles my ass," Walken complains. You don't appreciate the Army, do you?" "There are some things I like," Jerome innocently confesses. "Such as?" the suspicious sergeant asks. "Mail," the youth replies. "I like getting my mail."

Birthright (1939), Micheaux. Dir. Oscar Micheaux; Sc. Oscar Micheaux; Cast includes: Carman Newsome, Alec Lovejoy, Ethel Moses.

Advertised as "A story of the Negro and the South," Oscar Micheaux's drama is based on the novel by T. S. Stribling. The plot concerns a black Harvard graduate faced with racism. He tries to found a school for black children in a rural town in Tennessee. His goal is to "uplift the race." Director Spike Lee, half a century later, used the phrase as a subtitle for his film *School Daze* (1988). Micheaux was an early black producer-director-writer of black films, that virtually included all-black casts. These films, often known as "race" films, catered chiefly to black audiences in the South and North.

Black Like Me (1964), Continental. Dir. Carl Lerner; Sc. Carl Lerner, Gerda Lerner; Cast includes: James Whitmore, Sorel Brooks, Robert Gerringer, Al Freeman Jr., Roscoe Lee Browne, Clifton James.

James Whitmore, a white writer, masquerades as an African-American in this flawed drama, based on the book by John Howard Griffin. His purpose is to write a series of magazine articles on race relations in America. Whitmore stains his skin black and hitchhikes across several states. He confronts various Americans who often question him about the sexual activities of his (black) race. This obvious exploitation angle is just one of the weaknesses of the film. Another obvious error is Whitmore's Northern accent – although he is supposed to be from the South. Perhaps the most glaring weakness is when Whitmore keeps using his real name interviewing people while his articles – with his name and photographs as a black and a white man – appear nationally. Yet none of his interviewees ever recognizes him. The film was one of many released in the 1960s that specifically dealt with racism. Some of these other films were: the Western *Sergeant Rutledge* (1960), the psychological drama *Pressure Point* (1962), the Southern rural drama *To Kill a Mockingbird* (1962) and the racially charged *In the Heat of the Night* (1967).

Easy Rider (1969), Col. Dir. Dennis Hopper; Sc. Terry Southern, Dennis Hopper, Peter Fonda; Cast include: Peter Fonda, Dennis Hopper, Jack Nicholson, Robert Walker Jr., Luana Anders.

Two social dropouts, seeking freedom from society's restraints, motorbike from California to Louisiana in this landmark youth drama. Peter Fonda portrays Captain America, sporting the Stars and Stripes on the back of his jacket and his helmet. Longhaired and mustachioed Dennis Hopper, dressed in buckskins, plays Billy. Both pals, disgusted with the Vietnam war and with the general violence in the country, head for New Orleans's Mardi Gras. After concluding a drug deal in Mexico, they hide the money in their bikes and head out across the West toward their goal.

They meet various people on their journey and, along the way, meet Jack Nicholson. "Be a helluva good country," he muses during a moment of contemplation. "I can't understand what's going on with it." During one evening at their campfire, they are beaten up by some resentful "townies" and Nicholson is killed. Near the end of their journey, two men in a pickup truck try to run them off the road. After Hopper shows his contempt for them, the two men turn around and blast him with their shotguns. His bike explodes in flame as the camera shifts to the sky. Their unfulfilled journey has ended in assassination and reckless violence, a metaphor for the whole country.

Finian's Rainbow (1968), WB. Dir. Francis Ford Coppola; Sc. E. Y. Harburg, Fred Saidy; Cast includes: Fred Astaire, Petula Clark, Tommy Steele, Don Francks, Keenan Wynn.

Fred Astaire portrays Finian, a simple Irish immigrant, who travels to the South with his daughter, Petula Clark. The musical fantasy is based on the play by E. Y. Harburg and Fred Saidy. Astaire filches a crock of gold from a leprechaun in the mythical Rainbow Valley and plans to bury it. The work blends social comment and whimsical musical entertainment. The story describes how a bigoted Southern judge (Keenan Wynn) misuses one of the three wishes bestowed by the leprechaun and is turned into an African-American. During the story, leprechaun Tommy Steele falls in love with Finian's daughter and is transformed into a human being. Al Freeman Jr. plays an educated black botanist who imitates the stereotyped shuffling black for Wynn's annoyed benefit.

Imitation of Life (1934), U. Dir. John M. Stahl; Sc. William Hurlburt; Cast includes: Claudette Colbert, Warren William, Ned Sparks, Louise Beavers, Rochelle Hudson, Fredi Washington.

Claudette Colbert goes into partnership with her black maid Louise Beavers and both make a lot of money – and have a lot of problems. In the drama, based on a story by Fannie Hurst, each has a daughter. Beavers' girl is so light-skinned that she can pass for white. The young woman (Fredi Washington), unable to adjust to either world, is miserable. Meanwhile, Colbert falls in love with Warren William, but finds that she cannot marry him because her daughter, Rochelle Hudson, has also fallen in love with him.

Intruder, The (1962), Pathé. Dir. Roger Corman; Sc. Charles Beaumont; Cast include: William Shatner, Frank Maxwell, Beverly Lunsford, Robert Emhart, Jeanne Cooper.

A brazen, unstable merchant of hate in a Southern town instigates the white residents to oppose integration. This provocative drama is based on the novel by Charles Beaumont. A series of horrifying incidents follow. A black preacher is murdered; a white editor is beaten; and a black student is nearly lynched. At the end, the incensed mob turns against the hate merchant (William Shatner) when it learns that Shatner hopes to gain personally and to ride the wave of hatred to political office.

Liberation of L. B. Jones, The (1970), Co. Dir. William Wyler; Sc. Stirling Silliphant, Jesse Hill Ford; Cast includes: Lee J. Cobb, Anthony Zerbe, Roscoe Lee Browne, Lola Falana, Lee Majors, Barbara Hershey, Yaphet Kotto.

Veteran film director William Wyler turned to the themes of Southern bigotry and racism. Wyler's last film is based on Jesse Hill Ford's novel *The Liberation of Lord Byron Jones*. Jones, the title character (Roscoe Lee Browne), a wealthy black Tennessee funeral director, is cursed with an unfaithful wife (Lola Falana) who is having an affair with a white police officer (Anthony Zerbe). When Jones seeks a divorce, Zerbe's lawyer friend (Lee J. Cobb) prefers to avoid an open court case involving a liaison between a black woman and a white cop. Zerbe and fellow sadistic cop Arche Johnson press false charges against Jones and brutally murder and then castrate him. Lawyer Cobb discovers the truth but, along with the mayor, covers it up. Yaphet Kotto, an angry young black, returns home to avenge Jones's death. He pushes Johnson, the corrupt cop, into a harvesting machine, which mutilates him. Kotto then leaves town, together with Cobb's nephew and wife. In its violence and negative views of Southern racism, the film is reminiscent of the works such authors as Tennessee Williams and William Faulkner.

Nothing But a Man (1964), Dir. Michael Roemer; Sc. Michael Roemer, Robert Young; Cast includes: Ivan Dixon, Abby Lincoln, Gloria Foster, Julius Harris.

In this simple, honest and poignant drama, a Southern black man and his wife struggle and go through hell. Ivan Dixon portrays a young railway worker who marries schoolteacher Abby Lincoln, the daughter of a preacher. Dixon tries to live in peace and in dignity, but faces a problem when he refuses to play the role of the conventional black. His fellow workers warn him, as does his father-in-law, but he refuses to yield and his marriage subsequently suffers. When he is blacklisted for organizing other oppressed black workers, he seeks help from his reverend, but is ignored. Instead, he is charged with being a troublemaker. "You've been stoopin' so long, Reverend," Dixon retorts, "that you don't even know how to stand straight no more. You're just half a man."

Pinky (1949), TCF. Dir. Elia Kazan; Sc. Philip Dunne, Dudley Nichols; Cast includes: Jeanne Crain, Ethel Barrymore, Ethel Waters, William Lundigan, Basil Ruysdael.

Jeanne Crain portrays the title character, an African-American, light-skinned young woman who returns home after passing for white. This film is based on the novel by Cid Ricketts Summer and, for its time, was a bold examination of racism. The title "Pinky," according to blacks, is the term given to light-skinned African-Americans who can pass for white. Jeanne Crain has passed herself off as white while studying nursing in Boston. When she returns to the South and her grandmother (Ethel Waters), she reverts to her black heritage. She is in love with a white New England doctor (William Lundigan) who wants to marry her, but she is reminded of the indignities that she would have to face in the South. She realizes the impracticality of a mixed-race marriage and rejects Lundigan's offer and remains at home. A crusty old belle of a decaying Southern family (Ethel Barrymore) leaves Pinky her estate and, using the proceeds, she organizes a school and nursing home for blacks.

The film bristles with confrontational scenes. Two drunken white police officers try to rape Pinky and there is a legal challenge to a black person's right to inherit a white person's property. The film followed two similar dramas: *Home of the Brave* and *Lost Boundaries*.

Soldier's Story, A (1984), Col. Dir. Norman Jewison; Sc. Charles Fuller; Cast includes: Howard E. Rollins Jr., Adolph Caesar, Dennis Lipscomb, Art Evan, Denzel Washington.

African-American army officer Howard E. Rollins Jr. is assigned by his Washington, D.C. superiors to investigate a black sergeant's murder at a 1940s Southern military base. The suspenseful mystery is based on Charles Fuller's Pulitzer Prize-winning play. Rollins faces the usual stiff resistance and prejudice from some of the white officers at this segregated backwater Louisiana post as he tries to carry out his assignment. At times, Rollins displays his own prejudices. In probing the killing and the victim, the investigator exposes an ugly picture of both white-black and black-black racial tensions. Adolph Caesar, the murdered sergeant, was nominated for an Oscar for his searing portrayal of a man tormented by his brutal authority and self-hatred.

Stay Hungry (1976), UA. Dir. Bob Rafelson; Sc. Bob Rafelson, Charles Gaines; Cast includes: Jeff Bridges, Sally Field, Arnold Schwarzenegger, R. G. Armstrong.

Jeff Bridges plays a wealthy Southerner from an aristocratic family who develops real estate. Bridges meets R. G. Armstrong, the owner of a bodybuilding gym, and offers to buy his property. Armstrong refuses and Bridges slowly immerses himself in the gym and enters a new and entirely different world. He meets Sally Field, a working girl, and they fall in love. His more earthy side emerges from all of these experiences, but his family considers Field too common and they frown upon his new friends.

Tick . . . Tick . . . Tick . . . (1970), MGM. Dir. Ralph Nelson; Sc. James Lee Barrett; Cast includes: Jim Brown, George Kennedy, Fredric March, Lynn Carlin, Don Stroud.

George Kennedy portrays a tough but fair-minded small-town Southern sheriff who retires. His retirement clears the way for the election of Jim Brown, an African-American, as sheriff. The drama seems like an obvious attempt to exploit the successes of at least two similar racial films – Stanley Kramer's *Guess Who's Coming to Dinner?* (1967) and Norman Jewison's *In the Heat of the Night* (1967). Kennedy pledges to help his replacement with any new problems from the wary local malcontents. Brown shows his even-handedness by arresting lawbreakers, both white and black. But when he arrests a white man from another town for killing a child in a hit-and-run accident, he faces a major problem. The young man's powerful father organizes a white mob to help free his son by force. Brown receives help from Fredric March, the elderly town mayor, and Kennedy, the former sheriff. Ultimately, Brown mobilizes the townspeople to stop the hostile whites from the other side of the county.

Wild River (1960), TCF. Dir. Elia Kazan; Sc. Paul Osborn; Cast includes: Montgomery Clift, Lee Remick, Jo Van Fleet, Abert Salmi.

In this drama about the creation of the Tennessee Valley Authority, Director Elia Kazan closely examines the problems caused by the dam's construction. Resident farmers clash with Washington bureaucrats when the Tennessee Valley Authority has to flood certain lands to make room for new dams. The drama takes place during the Depression and the general historical background is fairly accurate. The federal government sends engineer Montgomery Clift to the South to persuade certain landowners to relocate. But 80-year-old widow Jo Van Fleet stubbornly refuses to leave her property and opts instead to resist the TVA. Her husband cleared the land decades ago and she intends to remain here.

From the start, Clift meets resistance from the community. Clearing some of the land is moving slowly. "Why don't you get more men?" Clift asks. "I can't," the local supervisor explains, "unless we use coloreds." "Well?" Clift returns. "If I use coloreds," the supervisor says, "the whites would quit." "Oh," Clift replies, "for a minute there I forgot where I was." Some local residents try to force Clift out, but Clift refuses to leave until his job is completed. He eventually wins the confidence of the widow's granddaughter, Lee Remick, and then the widow herself.

*

The Tennessee Valley Authority, the TVA, was created by Congress in 1933 in order to operate Wilson Dam and to develop the Tennessee River and its tributaries for navigation, flood control and the production and distribution of electricity. A board of three officials appointed by the U.S. President administers the TVA. The main offices of the TVA are in Knoxville, Tennessee. Power generated in TVA plants is distributed to more than seven million people in Tennessee and parts of Alabama, Virginia, Georgia, Kentucky, North Carolina, and Mississippi.

The TVA conducts research and development programs in forestry, fish and wildlife preservation, watershed protection, and air and water quality control. The power program is self-supporting through the sale of electricity. Although the TVA achieved remarkable successes almost from its inception, the program was the target of bitter attacks by local residents who were forced off their land and by business people who considered the project a threat to competing private electrical companies.

12

Feuds and Feuding

The most famous of all feuds – that of the Capulets and the Montagues – was but a tempest in a teapot compared with some Southern feuds. However, whereas the Capulets and the Montagues were members of the aristocracy, the aggrieved parties in Southern feuds were usually members of the lower classes.

The feud was characterized by a prolonged state of hostility between two social groups, such as clans or families, and was usually accompanied by acts of violence. Feuds were generally motivated by an initial episode involving an insult or injury that called for revenge. The hostilities frequently continued even after the initial triggering event passed from the memory of the participants. In most cases, feuds occurred in isolated areas, where legal means of redress of grievances either were not available or were considered inadequate by the affected groups. Family feuds were common in such areas as the mountain regions of the southeastern U.S.

Of course, the most famous Southern feud was between the extended members of the Hatfield and McCoy families in Appalachia during the nineteenth century. The feud began during the Civil War and lasted for decades afterwards and often erupted into violence. The Hatfields hailed from Logan County, West Virginia while the McCoys came from Pike County, Kentucky. In 1882, the feud escalated quite a bit when Johnse Hatfield and Rosanna McCoy tried to elope. During the brouhaha that followed, Ellison Hatfield was shot. Since he was shot in Kentucky, the police there arrested the shooters, three McCoy brothers. The leader of the McCoy clan, "Devil Anse" Hatfield, together with other members of the family, ambushed the police, freed the prisoners and brought them back to West Virginia. Ellison Hatfield eventually died and the three McCoy brothers were killed in a subsequent shootout.

Both families had ties with the local police and were usually released soon after their arrests. In 1888 Kentucky police crossed the border into West Virginia, arrested several Hatfield family members and initiated an interstate battle. When the local communities eventually turned against the violence of both families and began to support the authorities, the feud began to diminish. This particular feud became the subject of several films, including one released during the sound era.

*

Hollywood began producing family feuds back in the early silent film days and included such classics as Buster Keaton's classic comedy *Our Hospitality* (1923). Numerous sound comedies set among Southern mountain people, exploited local family feuds. The popular 1930s comedy team of Wheeler and Woolsey were effective in poking fun at the feud in George Stevens's *Kentucky Kernels* (1935). Twenty years later the feud retained much of its popularity as a laugh-getter in William Beaudine's comedy *Feudin' Fools* (1952). The film was a weak entry in the otherwise popular "Bowery Boys" comedy series. At least one screen version of Mark Twain's classic novel of *Adventures of Huckleberry Finn* contains a feud. After Huck finds a temporary home with the friendly Grangerford family, he discovers that they are engaged in a deadly feud with their neighbors, the Shepherdsons.

*

Kentucky is the natural venue for feuds in numerous silent as well as sound films. A feud between two families erupts when Dorothy Gish, the daughter of one clan, refuses to marry someone chosen for her, in Joseph Henabery's routine rural drama, *Children of the Feud* (1916). Instead, she loves Sam De Grasse, a local doctor and the son of a judge. The rejected suitor tries to shoot the doctor, but kills the sheriff by mistake. Humorist Will Rogers starred in George Marshall's rural comedy *In Old Kentucky* (1935), about feuding families.

*

Kentucky served as background for a number of serious dramas as well. In D. W. Griffith's silent Civil War drama *In Old Kentucky* (1909), two brothers fight on opposite sides. The younger brother has joined the Confederate cause and is sent with dispatches through the Union lines. His own brother, a Union soldier, captures him, but he escapes and hides in his mother's home. A malicious Indian kidnaps a white settler's sweetheart, but a young Indian woman, friendly to the whites, rescues her in *A Kentucky Pioneer* (1910). A band of Indians rise up in pursuit and a battle rages before the white woman is returned to her lover. A father is killed in a California mining accident and his partner sends the dead man's daughter to her uncle in Kentucky. Rupert Julien's drama *A Kentucky Cinderella* (1917) is set in the antebellum South. The mountain people of a famine-stricken part of Kentucky, are forced to get rid of their dogs in Howard Bretherton's mountain drama *Hills of Kentucky* (1927). The film is based on the story "The Untamed Heart" by Dorothy Yost. *Daniel Boone* (1936), a biographical drama loosely based on the legendary frontiersman, stresses action rather than character development. Daniel Boone, played by George O'Brien, leads his people to Kentucky where they build their settlement. John Wayne stars as the hero of George Waggner's drama *The Fighting Kentuckian* (1949). The film tells how some Americans cheat French settlers in Louisiana out of their land in the days following the War of 1812. Wayne returns with a troop of Kentucky riflemen from fighting with Andrew Jackson against the British. He resigns from his command in order to help the French settlers. In a more recent production, Patrick Swayze portrays a cop in John Irvin's crime drama *Next of Kin* (1989). Swayze returns to his roots in rural Kentucky to avenge the brutal death of his brother. The film tries to cover the trilogy of family honor, family ties and backwoods culture.

*

Children of the Feud (1916), Triangle. Dir. Joseph Henabery; Sc. Bernard McConville; Cast includes: Dorothy Gish, Sam De Grasse, Alan Sears, Alberta Lee, Elmo Lincoln.

A feud between two families erupts when Dorothy Gish, the daughter of one clan, refuses to enter into an arranged marriage. In Joseph Henabery's routine rural drama, Gish loves Sam De Grasse, a local doctor and the son of a judge. The rejected suitor tries to shoot the doctor, but kills the sheriff by mistake.

Cumberland Romance, A (1920), Realart. Dir. Charles Maigne; Cast includes: Mary Miles Minter, Monte Blue, John Bowers, Guy Oliver, Martha Mattox, Robert Brower.

This rural drama is based on John Fox's *A Mountain Europa.* John Bowers plays an eastern engineer who journeys to the Cumberland Mountains where he meets Easter Hicks (Mary Miles Minter) and soon falls in love with her. To complicate matters, a local young theological student (Monte Blue) also loves the young woman. The engineer and Hicks are engaged and his wealthy eastern parents arrive for the wedding. The bride's father attempts to shoot Blue, but Hicks steps in to take the bullet. She is wounded but, at that moment, she realizes that she really loves Blue.

Feud, The (1919), Fox. Dir. Edward Le Saint; Sc. Charles Kenyon; Cast includes: Tom Mix, Eva Novak, Claire McDowell, J. Arthur Mackley, John Cossar, Lloyd Bacon.

Tom Mix plays a dual role in this tragic romance about star-crossed lovers set both in pre-Civil War Kentucky and the West. Jere Lynch loves Betty Summers (Eva Novak), but since they are from rival feuding families, Jere is warned to stay away from Betty. He kills Betty's brother who had killed Jere's father. Jere then leaves for the West and promises to send for Betty. Betty's sister tells her Jere has been killed, so Betty marries a cousin. In the meanwhile, Jere learns that Betty has marries someone else, so he gets another wife. Indians kill Jere and his wife, but their son is spared. Betty's daughter travels West, meets and marries Jere's son and effectively ends the feud

Feudin' Fools (1952), Mon. Dir. William Beaudine; Sc. Bert Lawrence, Tim Ryan; Cast includes: Leo Gorcey, Huntz Hall, Bennie Bartlett, David Gorcey, Bernard Gorcey.

A routine and weak comedy in the otherwise popular "Bowery Boys" series, this entry revolves about one of the boys who is bequeathed a Kentucky plantation. He and his pals journey to his estate and soon become entangled in a hillbilly feud. It seems that the Smiths and the Joneses are two warring clans out for blood. When the "Bowery Boys" mistakenly address their neighbors, the Smiths, as "Joneses," all hell break loose. All ends well when both clans join forces when bank robbers invade the home of the Joneses.

Fighting Cressy (1920), Pathé. Dir. Robert T. Thornby; Sc. Fred Myton; Cast includes: Blanche Sweet, Russell Simpson, Edward Piel, Frank Lanning.

A long-standing feud between two Kentucky clans spills over into the California gold fields. This drama is based on *Cressy*, Bret Harte's 1889 novel. Cressy McKinstry, played by Blanche Sweet, treats Joe Masters with contempt. Masters is a cousin of the Harrisons, her family's sworn enemies. However, in spite of outward appearances, McKinstry secretly loves him. Following several personal complications and a dispute over land rights, McKinstry and Masters resolve their differences and the two feuding families make peace.

Heart o' the Hills (1919), FN. Dir. Joseph De Grasse, Sidney Franklin; Sc. Bernard McConville; Cast includes: Mary Pickford, Harold Goodwin, Allan Sears, Claire McDowell, Fred Huntley, Sam De Grasse.

John Fox wrote the original novel about life in the Kentucky hills, where people live by their own code. Mary Pickford portrays the daughter of a mountaineer in the film version of the novel. A man ambushes her father and later marries her mother. Although they are too young right now, Pickford and her stepbrother are so angry over the marriage that they plan to marry each other out of spite. During a furious dance, Pickford starts a jealous fight. She leaves the mountains for the city and she gets an education. She then returns home as a smart, educated young woman and is now able to protect her mother from her abusive husband who beats his unfortunate wife. The son joins in and kills his stepfather. The young couple, who have been in love for years, are now reunited.

Hill Billy, The (1924), Allied. Dir. George Hill; Sc. Marion Jackson; Cast includes: Jack Pickford, Lucille Ricksen, Frank Leigh, Ralph Yearsley, Jane Keckley.

George Hill's silent drama, based on John Fox's story *Valley of the Wolf*, superbly portrays mountain life. To gain possession of land rich in coal, Frank Leigh kills Jack Pickford's father and marries the widow. Lucille Ricksen, Leigh's niece, teaches Pickford to read and he falls in love with her, but Ricksen's uncle forces her to marry his son. Pickford is falsely accused of killing the prospective bridegroom, Leigh's son. Pickford then pursues Leigh, who is drowned during the course of the pursuit. At the end he rescues the woman he loves.

Kentuckians, The (1921), Par. Dir. Charles Maigne; Sc. Frank Tuttle; Cast includes: Monte Blue, Wilfred Lytell, Diana Allen, Frank Joyner, J. H. Gilmour.

Frank Tuttle's effective drama, based on John Fox's tale, captures the characters of the novel. Monte Blue portrays the mountaineer who testifies before the State Legislature on behalf of the hillbillies against the big money people from the city. The city people are trying to gerrymander the rural communities in order to dilute their political power. Blue falls in love with the governor's daughter. However, the young woman does not reciprocate his feelings and decides to marry a city slicker rather than Blue. He then returns to the mountains and tries to educate his own people.

Kentucky (1938), TCF. Dir. David Butler; Sc. Lamar Trotti, John T. Foote; Cast includes: Loretta Young, Richard Greene, Walter Brennan, Douglas Dumbrille, Karen Morley.

Richard Greene, the son of a banker, returns to his home in Kentucky to enter his father's business. He meets Loretta Young, a local belle, in this romantic drama about horseracing and breeding. Her grandfather (Walter Brennan) still harbors a grudge in a continuing family feud against the Greene family dating back to 1861 and the Civil War. Greene decides to hide his true identity and plans to approach Young by training her racehorse. When Young discovers her trainer's true identity, she initially rejects him but loves conquer all and they finally reconcile.

Kentucky Kernels (1935), RKO. Dir. George Stevens; Sc. Bert Kalmar, Harry Ruby, Fred Guiol; Cast includes: Bert Wheeler, Robert Woolsey, Mary Carlisle, Spanky McFarland, Noah Beery.

Bert Wheeler and Robert Woolsey, two unemployed magicians, live in a shack near the waterfront in George Stevens's comedy about Kentucky feuds. They persuade neighbor Paul Page not to commit suicide but, instead, to adopt

Spanky, an orphan, to help him forget an unrequited love affair. But when Page soon returns to his girlfriend, the two pals are left with Spanky who, they soon learn is a lost heir. The trio journeys to Spanky's estate, but discover that the town is a hotbed of family feuds and get trapped in the middle of a raging battle. The film abounds in the comedy team's one-liners. "I always say it with flowers," Robert Woolsey announces as he hands a rose to secretary Margaret Dumont. "What," she asks, "only one rose?" "You know me, I don't talk much," Woolsey quips. In another scene, the pair are tied to a tree by a rival clan in preparation for a firing squad and are asked if they have any final request. "I'd like to say goodbye to my mother," Woolsey says. "Where is your mother?" "In Australia," he replies. When Wheeler suspects a crooked lawyer of trying to cheat Spanky out of his inheritance, he calls the man a weasel. "Why," the lawyer protests, "I was never so insulted in my life!" "That's your fault," adds Wheeler. "You don't get around much!"

Little Shepherd of Kingdom Come, The (1920), Goldwyn. Cast includes: Jack Pickford, Clara Horton, Pauline Starke, J. Park Jones.

Jack Pickford portrays the title character in this a rural drama about feuds in the Old South. The story is based on the famous 1903 novel by John Fox. Pickford, a mountain lad, walks down the Blue Grass Mountains of Kentucky into the town. The film was remade in two sound versions, one in 1933 and the other in 1938. A contemporary critic found both the book and the early film dated and possibly of little interest to film audiences. *The Little Shepherd* returned to the screen in 1928 as *Kentucky Courage*. Andrew V. McLaglen's 1961 color and sound version was released with Fox's original title.

*

John Fox (1862?-1919), the novelist who developed the genre of the mountain feud, was always too vain to admit his exact date of birth. He first attended Transylvania University and then transferred to Harvard where he graduated in 1883. He began his literary career as a reporter for the *Sun* and then the *Times* in New York City. In 1888, Fox moved south to Virginia where he worked in mining but soon changed careers and became a freelance journalist for *Harper's Weekly*. In 1898, he was assigned to cover the Spanish-American War as a correspondent for *Harper's Weekly*. His reporting was so insightful that *Scribner's Magazine* hired him as a correspondent in 1905 to cover the Russo-Japanese War.

Unfortunately, Fox's assignments as a reporter were becoming fewer and far between, so he decided to try to write about the people he knew best, the mountain people and the miners of Kentucky, West Virginia and Tennessee. His stories are full of local color and, in general, are sentimental and light reconstructions of his life in Virginia.

Mountain Music (1937), Par. Dir. Robert Florey; Sc. J. C. Moffitt, Duke Atteberry, Russel Crouse, Charles Lederer; Cast includes: Bob Burns, Martha Raye, John Howard, Terry Walker.

In this routine hillbilly comedy, two feuding Arkansas families try to marry Bob Burns to young woman from an opposing clan in an effort to end their feuding. Burns disappears so that his brother, who loves the intended bride, can marry her instead. Burns then meets Martha Raye, an entertainer. The film includes two charming songs, "Mamma Don't Allow No Music Played in Here" and "Good Morning."

Our Hospitality (1923), Dir. Buster Keaton, Jack Blystone; Sc. Jean Havez, Joseph Mitchell, Clyde Bruckman; Cast includes: Buster Keaton, Natalie Talmadge Keaton, Joe Keaton, Joe Roberts.

In this silent comedy, Buster Keaton portrays a nineteenth-century New Yorker who inherits a Shenandoah Valley. He arrives in a contradictory world of blood feuds and Southern hospitality. This crazy place especially intimidates Keaton when he discovers he is a member of one of the feuding families. When Keaton is indoors in an opposing clan's homestead, he is treated as an honored guest. But once outside, he is fair game for anything that comes along. Meanwhile, he falls in love with the daughter of a longtime rival clan. A wild, frenetic chase through the mountains and a thrilling waterfall rescue closes this comical film.

Roseanna McCoy (1949), RKO. Dir. Irving Reis; Sc. John Collier; Cast includes: Joan Evans, Farley Granger, Richard Basehart, Raymond Massey, Charles Bickford.

Irving Reis's 1949 fictional drama depicts the famous hillbilly feud between the Hatfields and the McCoys. Joan Evans and Farley Granger are the two star-crossed lovers who precipitate the killings. Raymond Massey and Charles Bickford portray the patriarchs of the two warring clans in a disappointingly weak script.

*

Trail of the Lonesome Pine, The (1936), Par. Dir. Henry Hathaway; Sc. Grover Jones, Harvey Thew, Horace McCoy; Cast includes: Fred MacMurray, Henry Fonda, Sylvia Sidney, Beulah Bondi, Fred Stone.

John Fox's successful 1908 book, *The Trail of the Lonesome Pine,* sold well over a million copies. His books were made into a number of films. *The Trail of the Lonesome Pine* spawned three films, two silents in 1915 and 1923, and Henry Hathaway's definitive color version in 1936, which offered splendid scenery. Fred MacMurray, a city stranger, becomes involved in the lives of a backwoods Kentucky Mountain family which is feuding with a neighboring clan. MacMurray tries to educate Sylvia Sidney, the daughter, and soon grows to love her. Henry Fonda, her brother, objects to the affair and is killed before the feud ends. This was the third remake of Fox's novel and the first color and sound version.

13

Southern Decadence and Dark Shadows

Antebellum Southern literature was dominated by romanticism, sentimentality and nostalgia. English writers such as Sir Walter Scott and the romantic poets were extremely popular. However, in the post-war years, Mark Twain, with his stories of life along the Mississippi, and Edgar Alan Poe of Richmond, Virginia presented two views of the South that were as different from each other as they were from the earlier saccharine Southern romantic novels. In the 1920s and '30s, a Southern literary renaissance which was in stark contrast to all of these earlier schools and which was characterized by stark realism burst upon the intellectual world. Many of these Southern authors began to critically dissect their characters and environments. They analyzed their characters' motivations and lives. They wrote about crooked politicians, corrupt old patriarchs, hedonistic narcissists and dangerously seductive women. Sexual aberrations dominated these novels and plays. In general, the literature was dubbed "Southern gothic."

In contrast, the Hollywood studios, in the first three decades of the twentieth century, were still producing romantic, sentimental and nostalgic images of the South. The studios were developing scripts using such nineteenth century literature as Harriet Beecher Stowe's *Uncle Tom's Cabin*. Beginning with the late 1940s, however, the studios began to shift to the Southern gothic – or more realistic, albeit more distorted – perceptions of the region. Hollywood now started using the "gothic" scripts developed by leaders of the Southern literary renaissance in the two preceding decades. Southern novels that were adapted for the screen included William Faulkner's *The Sound and the Fury* (1959) and *Sanctuary* (1961), Tennessee Williams's *A Streetcar Named Desire* (1951) and *Baby Doll* (1956), Lillian Hellman's *Toys in the Attic* (1963) and Carson McCullers' *Reflections in a Golden Eye* (1967). All of these films painted a world of doom and gloom, peopled by dysfunctional characters who lived in decrepit old mansions.

All Fall Down (1962), MGM. Dir. John Frankenheimer; Sc. William Inge; Cast includes: Eva Marie Saint, Warren Beatty, Brandon de Wilde.

John Frankenheimer's drama is based on the novel by James Leo Herlihy. The parents of adolescent Brandon de Wilde send him to Florida to get his older brother Warren Beatty, whom he idolizes, out of jail. The two young men return home and de Wilde becomes infatuated – from a distance – with visiting Eva Marie Saint. She, however, is attracted to the narcissistic Beatty. The uncaring Beatty seduces her and she becomes pregnant. When Beatty refuses to marry Saint, she takes her own life. The shock of the suicide makes de Wilde realize how bad his brother really is and he plans to kill him. But when de Wilde confronts him, Beatty breaks down in tears. De Wilde now understands how pathetic his brother really is and decides not to kill him. Freed of domination by his older brother, de Wilde now becomes mature in his own right. Ironically, playwright William Inge, who wrote the screenplay, committed suicide, just as his character Saint does in the film.

Baby Doll (1956), WB. Dir. Elia Kazan; Sc. Tennessee Williams; Cast includes: Karl Malden, Carroll Baker, Eli Wallach, Mildred Dunnock, Lonny Chapman.

Karl Malden portrays a Mississippi bumpkin who lives in a rural area and runs a cotton gin. Elia Kazan's sexually provocative drama is based on the play *27 Wagons Full of Cotton* by Tennessee Williams. The opening scene shows Malden peering lecherously through a small hole in a wall at Baker, his luscious blonde wife. Malden promised not to sleep with her until she reached age 20, so he tries to keep his vow but is still frustrated and thus becomes a voyeur. She is lying on a crib-like bed and wearing baby doll pajamas, with her thumb in her mouth. She suddenly catches her voyeur-husband spying on her. "Archie Lee!" she exclaims. "You're a mess. Do you know what they call such people? Peepin' Toms!" "Hey," he replies, "there's no need for a woman that sleeps in a baby's crib to stay away from her husband."

Malden, who plays Archie, fears his treacherous neighbor, Sicilian Vacarro (Eli Wallach), and sneaks onto his property to set fire to his equipment. Wallach is equally suspicious of Malden and decides to check on his adversary by spending a day with Malden's virginal and overdeveloped wife (Carroll Baker). The film never establishes whether Wallach rapes her or not. *Time* magazine called the feature "just possibly the dirtiest American picture ever legally exhibited." Williams wrote the screenplay for the film version of his play.

Bastard Out of Carolina (1997), Showtime. Dir. Angelica Huston; Sc. Ann Meredith; Cast includes: Jena Malone, Jennifer Jason Leigh, Dermot Mulroney, Ron Eldard.

Angelica Huston's impressive drama centers on an eleven-year-old girl called Bone (Jena Malone), who was born out of wedlock to an irresponsible mother (Jennifer Jason Leigh). While the screen focuses on her birth certificate stamped "illegitimate," the protagonist narrates her own story. "There I was, certified a bastard by the state of South Carolina." To offer her a semblance of a stable life, her mother marries Dermot Mulroney). Bone develops a love for her stepfather but he is soon killed in a car accident. Leigh's new husband (Ron Eldard) is a violent and sexually abusive man and the film shows a series of heart-rending scenes. Leigh's brothers beat Eldard, but she returns to him and Bone suffers further abuses at his hands. Finally, Bone leaves her mother and moves in with her kind and loving aunt. "Who would I be when I was 15, or maybe 30?" she ponders tearfully. "Would I be as strong as she had been? As hungry for love as she had been, as desperate, as determined, ashamed? I wouldn't know. And I was already who I was going to be – someone like her, like my mama – a bastard – a bastard out of Carolina."

Beguiled, The (1971), U. Dir. Don Siegel; Sc. John B. Sherry, Grimes Grice; Cast includes: Clint Eastwood, Geraldine Page, Elizabeth Hartman, Jo Ann Harris, Darleen Carr, Mae Mercer.

This strange film is set during the Civil war and is based on the novel by Thomas Cullinan. Wounded Union soldier Clint Eastwood convalesces at a Southern girls' school. The young women grow more than curious about their male guest. Their sexual interest in the visitor leads envious headmistress Geraldine Page to amputate the soldier's leg out of spite. He berates her for cutting off his leg and confronts her with her sexual frustrations. After he angrily kills one of the girls' turtles, they retaliate by daily feeding him poisoned mushrooms until he dies.

Cat on a Hot Tin Roof (1968), MGM. Dir. Richard Brooks; Sc. Richard Brooks, James Poe; Cast includes: Elizabeth Taylor, Paul Newman, Burl Ives, Jack Carson, Judith Anderson.

Richard Brooks's screen version of the Tennessee Williams's steamy play depicts a planter family headed by Big Daddy (Burl Ives), who is dying of cancer but is unaware of it. He is about to celebrate his latest birthday with his wife, his two sons and their wives. The younger son, Brick (Paul Newman), is present with his young wife (Elizabeth Taylor) as is Big Daddy's older son, Gooper (Jack Carson), and his wife. Daddy's wife (Judith Anderson) is also in attendance.

Brick, suspects his wife is unfaithful and keeps her at a distance. Since they have no children, Big Daddy wants to leave his of $10 million fortune to the obnoxious Gooper and his equally obnoxious wife. Taylor decides to lie and tells her in-laws that she is pregnant, thereby hoping to inherit part of the estate. "What's that smell in this room?" Big Daddy asks sarcastically. "Didn't you notice it, Brick? Didn't you notice the powerful and obnoxious odor of mendacity in this room?" Brick, realizing that his wife really loves him, decides to try to give up some obsession with a dead friend and to have a child. The film avoids the play's controversial premise of Brick's homosexuality.

In general, Williams felt that life was meaningless. His characters move through a void and, although they want to establish relationships with others, they are unable to do so: Big Daddy in *Cat on a Hot Tin Roof* is in love once again but is dying of cancer and unable to make any meaningful human contact. The work, in which Williams returned to his Southern roots, earned the playwright a Pulitzer Prize.

Chase, The (1966), Col. Dir. Arthur Penn; Sc. Lillian Hellman; Cast includes: Marlon Brando, Jane Fonda, Robert Redford, E. G. Marshall, Angie Dickinson, Janice Rule, Miriam Hopkins.

Arthur Penn's steamy and violent drama based on Horton Foote's novel and play. Marlon Brando portrays the sheriff of a small corrupt Texas community inhabited chiefly by bigots, hoodlums and nymphomaniacs. The sheriff, the only decent citizen in the town, is encouraged by his long-suffering wife (Angie Dickinson) to defy banker Marshall. Instead, Brando is determined to capture fugitive (Robert Redford) who is returning to visit his wife (Jane Fonda) and settle old scores. "I hate this job," Brando complains to his spouse, who constantly reminds him that they have no children. "I ain't raisin' no children over a jail," he insists.

Dear Dead Delilah (1972), AE. Dir. John Farris; Sc. John Farris; Cast includes: Agnes Moorehead, Will Geer, Michael Ansara, Patricia Carmichael, Dennis Patrick.

Veteran screen actor Agnes Moorehead portrays a dying, nasty matriarch. She is confined to a wheelchair in her mansion where a fortune is supposedly hidden. The film is a generally weak Southern gothic horror tale. The depraved relatives swoop down upon her in a race to find the money. Somehow, the film, considered rather repulsive by many critics and lacking in any redeemable qualities, has acquired a devoted cult following of fans who delight in the morbid proceedings on the screen. This was Moorehead's last film before she died of lung cancer in 1974.

Deliverance (1972), WB. Dir. John Boorman; Sc. James Dickey; Cast includes: Jon Voight, Burt Reynolds, Ned Beatty, Ronny Cox.

John Boorman's stark and brutal drama, based on the novel by James Dickey. A canoe journey in the backwaters of Georgia brings unexpected results to four urban executives. Four pals, Jon Voight, Burt Reynolds, Ned Beatty and Ronny Cox, decide to take a weekend trip down a river about to be dammed for a new reservoir. Beatty, an insurance salesman, addresses an elderly mountain man who is pumping gas into the visitors' vehicle. "I like your hat," he says sarcastically. But the old hillbilly replies, "You don't know nothin'!" The four men embark on their river journey. When they camp for the night, Reynolds, as their acknowledged leader, remarks, "Machines are gonna fail, and the system's gonna fail, and survival – who has the ability to survive – that's the game." But Cox criticizes Reynolds and says to the others, "He wants to be one with nature, but he can't hack it."

An unanticipated confrontation with local vicious hillbillies tests the foursome's survival skills and suggests the unexpected and potentially hidden violence of nature. In one unpleasant and gruesome scene, Voight and Beatty wander into the woods, where two rifle-wielding hillbillies assault them. One man rapes Beatty at gunpoint while Voight is tied to a tree. Reynolds, using his bow and arrows, kills one of the men and rescues Voight. The second hillbilly escapes. The four men, shaken by the experience, contemplate whether to report the incident or simply bury the dead man and forget their ordeal. Against the decision of Cox, who prefers to report the crime and death, the others vote to bury the hillbilly. The river soon kills Cox and Reynolds is badly hurt, so Voight asserts leadership. The pacific Voight, who was unable to kill a deer at the beginning of the film, tracks down the second hillbilly and kills him. On their way back, the local sheriff (played by author Dickey) has problems figuring out what happened during the trip. "We'll wait and see what comes out of the river," he says.

One of the most memorable sequences involves Ronny Cox and the toothless son of a local hillbilly family. The mute inbred boy, who sports a moronic stare, begins to play his banjo. Cox then plays his own guitar, and the two engage in a contest as one keeps replying to the other. The frenzied playing ends with the boy the obvious winner. He then loses his moronic expression and replaces it with a dead and ominous stare – instilling a sense of dread that seems to forecast unsettling events for the remainder of the drama.

The film, with its primary theme of human cruelty, implies that these traits are inbred in some hillbilly communities of the South. The secondary theme seems to be appropriated from *Darwin's Origin of the Species* - survival of the fittest in the struggle for existence.

Delta, The (1997), Strand. Dir. Ira Sachs; Sc. Ira Sachs; Cast includes: Shayne Gray, Thang Chan, Rachel Zan Huss.

White middle-class teenager Lincoln Bloom (Shayne Gray) from Memphis leads two lives in this somber drama. He spends most of his time with his fretful girlfriend and other buddies, who drive around aimlessly, drink beer and smoke pot. Occasionally, he drifts off to a remote rural section where gay men cruise around and sometimes he visits a porno video shop. One evening he meets John, the immigrant son of a Vietnamese woman and a black soldier. John confesses his love for Bloom, and both take off down the Mississippi River, a journey that lands them in hot water with the law.

Fugitive Kind, The (1959), UA. Dir. Sidney Lumet; Sc. Tennessee Williams, Meade Roberts; Cast includes: Marlon Brando, Anna Magnani, Joanne Woodward, Maureen Stapleton, Victor Jory.

Sidney Lumet's morbid drama is based on the play *Orpheus Descending* by Tennessee Williams and it stars Marlon Brando, Anna Magnani and Joanne Woodward. Val Xavier (Marlon Brando) attempts to forget his wild life as a guitar player in New Orleans' hot spots and resigns himself to working in a small Mississippi town as the hired hand and lover of Lady Torrance (Anna Magnani). His employer is married to an older, dying man who she doesn't love and she is sexually frustrated. Her father had sold liquor to blacks and, in retaliation, some of the townies burned down his wine garden, so she also hates the townspeople. Brando meets the seductive Joanne Woodward, who tries to have sex with him in a nearby cemetery.

Home From the Hill (1960), MGM. Dir. Vincente Minnelli; Sc. Harriet Frank Jr., Irving Ravetch; Cast include: Robert Mitchum, Eleanor Parker, George Peppard, George Hamilton.

Vincente Minnelli's drama is based on the novel by William Humphrey. Robert Mitchum, a Southern landowner, comes into conflict with his wife (Eleanor Parker) and his two sons, one of whom is illegitimate. Mitchum's extramarital affairs strain his relationship with his wife. Besides their son (George Hamilton), Mitchum has another son (George Peppard), born out of wedlock and approximately the same age as Hamilton. In one particularly poignant scene, the two half-brothers acknowledge their family ties. Hamilton loves Luana Patten and impregnates her but, seeing his parents' bitter relationship, he's afraid to marry her. Peppard steps in, marries Patten and adopts the child. Patten's own vengeful father (Everett Sloane) shoots and kills Mitchum, and, in turn, Hamilton kills Sloane.

Hush . . . Hush, Sweet Charlotte (1964), TCF. Dir. Robert Aldrich; Sc. Henry Farrell, Lukas Keller; Cast includes: Bette Davis, Olivia de Havilland, Joseph Cotten, Agnes Moorehead, Cecil Kellaway.

Robert Aldrich's horror drama opens in 1927 in a Louisiana plantation mansion. Bette Davis is a Southern belle involved with a married man. Her father warns the married neighbor to end the affair with his daughter. At a grand ball that evening in the mansion, the lover appears to tell Davis their affair is over. Soon, a mysterious meat cleaver severs one of his hands and then his head. The drama then shifts to the present. Davis lives alone in her mansion, now condemned by the authorities, surrounded only by her memories, which threaten her already-shaky sanity. Her cousin (Olivia de Havilland), who secretly covets Davis's fortune, arrives to support her own claims to the estate. She is helped by the family physician, Joseph Cotten. Strange and horrifying incidents then unfold.

Midnight in the Garden of Good and Evil (1997), WB. Dir. Clint Eastwood; Sc. John Lee Hancock; Cast includes: Kevin Spacey, John Cusack, Jack Thompson, Irma P. Hall, Jude Law.

Director Clint Eastwood's dark drama captures much of the charm of Savannah. John Cusack, as a writer, journeys to the city and is mesmerized by its scenery, its quaint architecture, its history and its eccentric, talkative characters. He meets a gay antique dealer (Kevin Spacey) whose friendly, cavalier ways and lifestyle fascinate the writer. "This place is fantastic!" Cusack tells his New York agent on the telephone. "It's like *Gone With the Wind* on mescaline!"

When a young male hustler is found dead, Spacey falls under suspicion of murder. "Savin' face in the light of unpleasant circumstances," his lawyer announces, "is the Savannah way." One of the more outrageous characters is the transvestite who calls himself "The Lady Chablis" and who playfully taunts the writer and other characters – particularly during a courtroom scene. The film highlights the city of Savannah – its lush squares, its Spanish moss and its eerie graveyards. For good measure, Berendt even throws in some Southern aristocrats, fading Southern belles and voodoo rituals.

The drama is based on the successful novel by John Berendt, but appears slower-paced than the novel.

Murder of Crows, A (1999), Trademark. Dir. Rowdy Harrington; Sc. Rowdy Harrington; Cast includes: Cuba Gooding Jr., Tom Berenger, Marianne Jean-Baptiste, Ashley Lawrence, Eric Stolz.

Cuba Gooding Jr. portrays a disbarred Southern lawyer who decides to write a book about his experiences in this mystery drama. He inadvertently meets an elderly gentleman who allows Gooding to read his own manuscript about a complex series of murders. The stranger dies and Gooding, in possession of the man's fascinating book, decides to plagiarize it. The novel concerns the murder of several lawyers and becomes a sensational success, bringing Gooding fame and fortune. However, he is soon arrested as the murderer in a series of killings he describes in detail in his novel. The original author is dead and his manuscript destroyed, so Gooding cannot prove his innocence. He finds himself entrapped in a web of intrigue spun by an extremely clever – and perhaps deranged – murderer. An experienced police officer (Tom Berenger) assigned to the case is certain that Gooding is the killer.

Opposite of Sex, The (1998), Sony. Dir. Don Roos; Sc. Don Roos; Cast includes: Christina Ricci, Martin Donovan, Lisa Kudrow, Lyle Lovett, Johnny Galecki.

Christina Ricci portrays Dedee, a tough 16-year-old obnoxious blonde from Louisiana. After desecrating her stepfather's grave, she leaves home, visits her gay schoolteacher half brother and seduces his young lover. She then announces she is pregnant. "I don't have a heart of gold," she narrates to the audience, "and I don't grow one later, O.K.?" She hops from one outrageous experience to another – while hurting those around her who care for her. After she finally abandons her baby, she realizes, too late, the meaning of relationships and the repercussions of casual sex.

Reflections in a Golden Eye (1967), WB. Dir. John Huston; Sc. Chapman Mortimer, Gladys Hill; Cast includes: Marlon Brando, Elizabeth Taylor, Brian Keith, Julie Harris, Robert Forster, Zorro David.

John Huston's quirky pre-World War II Southern gothic drama is based on the novel by Carson McCullers. Marlon Brando portrays a U.S. Army major and a latent homosexual. The story is set in Georgia at an army base and abounds in sexual aberrations and is populated with neurotics, psychotics and self-absorbed bores. McCullers treats her characters in this novel harshly and in contrast to the sympathetic treatment she netted out to figures in *The Heart Is a Lonely Hunter* and *A Member of the Wedding*.

In *Reflections in a Golden Eye*, Elizabeth Taylor is Brando's simple-minded, sensual wife and she taunts her repressed husband about his inability to satisfy her. She turns to Brian Keith, a fellow army officer and insensitive hypocrite, with whom she has an affair. Keith's wife (Julie Harris) had cut off her breasts after an unfortunate childbirth. Her houseboy (Zorro David), an effeminate Filipino, offers her some sympathy while her husband attends the major's wife.

To make matters more complicated, Robert Forster enters the picture. He has a fetish for women's underwear and steals into Taylor's bedroom at night to caress her undergarments. In the meantime, Brando is waiting Forster for a rendezvous, but discovers that he has gone to Taylor's room instead. Enraged, Brando kills Forster. Overall, the film does not fully develop the major's complex and disastrous marriage. Instead, it just presents a series of shocking incidents in which the characters confront and address each other, but the confrontations do not give cohesiveness to the story. Huston's stalwart attempt to capture the author's atmosphere and prose fell short of his target.

The Rose Tattoo (1955), Par. Dir. Daniel Mann; Sc. John Michael Hayes; Cast includes: Anna Magnani, Burt Lancaster, Marisa Pavan, Ben Cooper, Virginia Grey.

The Rose Tattoo was written by Tennessee Williams in 1951 and was set in a small town in Louisiana inhabited chiefly by Italian-Americans. It came to the screen in director Daniel Mann's flavorsome 1955 production. Anna Magnani portrays an Italian widow and Burt Lancaster plays a wild truck driver who attempts to seduce her but is put off. This was a departure from Williams's usual material in that, this time, his chief protagonist was a strong Italian woman living in isolation, trying to raise her teenage daughter. When she learns that her dead husband had an affair with another local woman, she decides to end her isolation and accepts Lancaster's proposition.

Sanctuary (1961), Dir. Tony Richardson; Sc. James Poe; Cast included: Lee Remick, Yves Montand, Bradford Dillman, Harry Townes, Odetta.

This moody and realistic drama is based on William Faulkner's novels *Sanctuary* and *Requiem for a Nun.* The film is set in Mississippi in the late 1920s. Lee Remick portrays Temple Drake, a young Southerner and product of the Jazz Age. Odetta (Nancy Mannigoc), a black woman, is sentenced to death for the murder of Remick's baby. In an effort to save Odetta, Remick reveals the truth to her father, the governor.

She tells her father of her happy college years when she was in love with Bradford Dillman. Years later she reveals that she was raped by a well-known bootlegger, Yves Montand. She is subsequently fascinated by Montand and follows him to New Orleans where she is installed in a brothel. Odetta serves as her maid.

Remick enjoys her life with Montand – until he is supposedly killed in a car accident. She then returns home, marries Dillman, her old beau, and settles into a quiet, conventional life. They have two children, when suddenly Montand, who escaped death in the accident, reappears and Remick is tempted to run off with him. Odetta wants to stop Remick from making the worst decision of her life, so, for some crazy reason, she smothers the baby. The governor is stupefied by his daughter's sordid story, but lets the execution stand. Remick visits Odetta for the last time and realizes that she has sacrificed her life to save her own. Faulkner's work was previously filmed as *The Story of Temple Drake* (1933).

The book resurrects the image of the good and loyal black servant reminiscent of earlier Hollywood films.

Sling Blade (1997), Miramax. Dir. Billy Bob Thornton; Sc. Billy Bob Thornton; Cast includes: Billy Bob Thornton, Dwight Yoakam, Natalie Canerday, J. T. Walsh, John Ritter, Lucas Black.

Billy Bob Thornton wrote, directed and starred in this soulful and startling drama set in a small Arkansas town. The story centers on Karl Childers (Thornton), a psychologically disturbed patient who has just been released from a mental hospital. He was confined since age 12 for murdering his mother and her lover after finding them in bed together. He used a "sling Blade" – a machete-type long-handled tool as his weapon. Once outside, he finds work as a repairman and meets Frank (Lucas Black), a 12-year-old fatherless boy, with whom he soon identifies. Linda (Natalie Canerday), the boy's mother, allows Karl to sleep in her garage and invites him to share meals with her and her boy. Problems arise for Karl when he witnesses Doyle, Linda's heavy-drinking boyfriend, mistreat Frank and his mother. Doyle insults and mocks Karl as well. Karl, recalling his own abuse at the hands of his father, cannot bear to see his surrogate family, especially young Frank, being abused.

The bond between Karl and the boy is so overwhelming, that Karl finally strikes out against Doyle in an effort to protect the two victims in the only way he knows how – with tragic consequences for Doyle and Karl. The sensitive poignant drama is reminiscent of *To Kill a Mockingbird,* in which the retarded Boo Radley character protects lawyer Finch's two children who had befriended the lonely recluse.

Sound and the Fury, The (1959), Dir. Martin Ritt; Sc. Irving Ravetch, Harriet Frank Jr.; Cast includes: Yul Brynner, Joanne Woodward, Margaret Leighton, Stuart Whitman.

Martin Ritt's drama is a weak version of author William Faulkner's penetrating novel about Southern life. The film focuses on the social disintegration of the Compson family, a formerly eminent family of a small Mississippi town. Yul Brynner, as Jason, a stepson, takes control of the decrepit estate and the decadent remnants of the family whose only heritage is their family name. Brynner is bent on keeping the family name and honor intact. However, he is completely self-centered and is entirely focused on making money. One Compson brother is a weak alcoholic and the other is a mute idiot. Years ago their promiscuous sister (Margaret Leighton) abandoned her illegitimate daughter Quentin (Joanne Woodward), who has developed into a fiercely spirited young woman. She now tries to abandon her wild life and returns to her family. However, she fails to find any affection from her family, so she seeks it in a lecherous traveling carnival mechanic (Stuart Whitman). After a while, Brynner recognizes Quentin's integrity and, despite her defiance, decides to help her. Ethel Waters is an African-American servant, a foil character. Her patience and compassion provide a sharp contrast to the selfish and self-destructive Compsons.

Southern Comfort (1981), TCF. Dir. Walter Hill; Sc. Michael Kane, Walter Hill, David Giler; Cast includes: Keith Carradine, Powers Boothe, Fred Ward, Franklyn Seales, T. K. Carter.

Walter Hill's frightening drama focuses on a group of National Guardsmen in Louisiana. They want to share their camaraderie and plan a weekend outing in the swamps, but their friendship ends in tragedy. "It's all set," one guardsman (Keith Carradine) promises his comrades as they start out. "Noleen and her bayou queens. Just a little something for morale. And let me add, Sergeant, that these women are expecting some smart unit military penetration." Carradine also invites an African-American guardsman who is anxious to join them. "In the spirit of the new South," Carradine jokingly adds, "I have made full arrangements." He befriends Powers Boothe, a newcomer to the squad, fresh from the Texas Guard. "The Louisiana Guard," Carradine boasts satirically, "has done really important things – like beating up on college kids and tear-gassing niggers. We have a long and noble tradition." Later, he remarks to Boothe: "RC Colas and Moonpies. We ain't too smart, but we have a good time."

The sergeant leads the squad into the swamp in an exercise in survival in a hostile environment. Their weapons only shoot blanks. The men soon get lost in the swamp and, without permission, innocently borrow some canoes from some local backwoods Cajuns. However, the Cajuns don't take to this so well and they soon chase the visitors. One guardsman playfully fires blanks at the Cajuns on shore. The Cajuns are unaware of the blanks and return live fire and kill one of the guardsmen. The others try to escape from the area, but they are unfamiliar with the swamp. The pursuers pick off the guardsmen one by one. Keith Carbine and Powers Boothe make it back to a Cajun festival and try to blend in as best they can. But they, too, are in danger of being shot – until a U.S. army truck and helicopter finally rescue them.

Story of Temple Drake, The (1933), Par. Dir. Stephen Roberts; Sc. Oliver H. P. Garrett; Cast includes: Miriam Hopkins, Jack LaRue, William Gargan, William Collier Jr., Irving Pichel.

The Story of Temple Drake is loosely based on William Faulkner's novel *Sanctuary.* Miriam Hopkins portrays the title character, a hedonistic, pleasure-seeking young woman (whose father is a wealthy judge). In this dramatic attack on Southern aristocracy, she embodies Southern decadence in the age of Prohibition. The flirtatious Hopkins discovers the seamier side of life when her car breaks down one night and she and young William Collier Jr., two rich youngsters, seek help. They run to a shack occupied by a tough gang of hoodlums, led by Jack LaRue. The gangster ejects Collier and rapes the terrified young woman. He then murders several innocents and frames Irving Pichel, a fellow mobster. Laurie kidnaps Hopkins and brings her to the big city where he sets her up in his bordello. She begins to enjoy her new life but soon has a fight with Laurie and kills him with his own gun. The death remains unnoticed and Hopkins returns home with a reputation somewhat tarnished but she somehow manages to resume her former life as a Southern belle. When she learns that Pichel is falsely accused of the earlier murder, she disregards her own reputation and decides testify on his behalf. She tells her story in the presence of attorney William Gargan, her former boyfriend.

Because of its controversial content, the Hays Office attacked the film. The following year, in 1934, the Catholic Church opened its Legion of Decency in an effort to condemn similar films. However, Paramount and its writers remained fairly faithful to the original material. It was remade in 1961 under Faulkner's original title, *Sanctuary*, with Lee Remick and Yves Montand.

Storyville (1992), Spelling/Davis. Dir. Mark Frost; Sc. Mark Frost, Lee Reynolds; Cast includes: James Spader, Joanne Whalley-Kilmer, Jason Robards, Charlotte Lewis.

This Byzantine Southern gothic drama includes murder, mistresses and mayhem. James Spader, as the scion of a wealthy and political Louisiana family, is running for political office. Separated from his wife, he is lured into an affair with an attractive Vietnamese woman (Charlotte Lewis). When he awakens, there is a body next to him and Lewis has vanished. Spader is accused of the murder. He discovers that a secret video was made of him and he desperately wants to get the film that will clear him of the murder. Spider must face the prosecuting attorney who turns out to be his former lover. Jason Robbers is a sinister member of Spader's family who had murdered Spider's father. So much for family relationships. Meanwhile, a corrupt police officer on the vice squad is out to find Spider guilty. Lots of scenes are shot in New Orleans.

Streetcar Named Desire, A (1951), WB. Dir. Elia Kazan; Sc. Oscar Saul; Cast includes: Vivien Leigh, Marlon Brando, Kim Hunter, Karl Malden, Rudy Bond.

Elia Kazan's 1951 screen version of Williams's play stars Vivien Leigh and Marlon Brando, with Kim Hunter and Karl Malden. Vivien Leigh, as Blanche Du Bois, a fading Southern belle, tries to salvage the last vestiges of her world of gentility from constant attacks by her brutal brother-in-law, Stanley (Marlon Brando). Dismissed from her teaching position for having an affair with one of her 17-year-old pupils, she moves in with her sister Stella (Kim Hunter) and her husband Stanley in New Orleans. Here she meets Mitch (Karl Malden), a simple bachelor friend of Stanley's, who considers marrying her. Blanche is desperate and sees in Mitch a chance for a new life. But Stanley destroys her romantic illusions when he learns of her promiscuous past and tells Mitch about it. Many critics consider this drama the best play ever written by an American.

Suddenly, Last Summer (1959), Dir. Joseph Mankiewicz; Sc. Gore Vidal, Tennessee Williams; Cast includes: Elizabeth Taylor, Katharine Hepburn, Montgomery Clift, Albert Dekker.

Montgomery Clift portrays a brain surgeon in a debt-ridden Louisiana hospital. Joseph Mankiewicz's fascinating, sometimes amoral drama is based on a play by Tennessee Williams. Katharine Hepburn, a wealthy, elderly widow, promises to donate a large sum of money if Clift performs a lobotomy on Holly, her niece (Elizabeth Taylor). Holly has been in a mental hospital since her return from South America, where the widow's son died. Although pressured by the hospital administration and Hepburn, the surgeon resists the operation. Holly tells the doctor of the horrible death of Hepburn's son. It seems that the son, a homosexual, was brutally killed by a group of young men in retaliation for his sexual advances on them. Hepburn wants the lobotomy to shut Holly up and permanently prevent her from telling the truth about her son's death. The play was remade into a British television production in 1992.

Summer and Smoke (1961), Par.. Dir. Peter Glenville; Sc. James Poe, Meade Roberts; Cast includes: Geraldine Page, Laurence Harvey, Una Merkel, John McIntire, Pamela Tiffin, Rita Moreno.

A handsome doctor (Laurence Harvey) establishes himself in a small town in Mississippi. He gets involved with Geraldine Page, a single fragile woman, in this drama based on the play by Tennessee Williams. Harvey lures Page into a passionate affair that exposes all of her repressed sexual feelings. Cad that he is, the doctor then meets the daughter of a local gambling-casino owner and drops Page. The film won several Oscar nominations.

Sweet Bird of Youth (1962), MGM. Dir. Richard Brooks; Sc. Richard Brooks; Cast includes: Paul Newman, Geraldine Page, Shirley Knight, Ed Begley, Rip Torn.

Richard Brooks's film is based on a Tennessee Williams' play. A former movie star (Geraldine Page) seeks escape in alcohol, drugs and sex. Paul Newman portrays a stud for Page, who believes her last film is a flop and that her career is coming to an end. She wants to keep young and handsome Newman around, so she promises to get him an acting job in Hollywood. Meanwhile, Newman is gathering information of Page's sleazy past, intending to eventually blackmail her.

Newman accepts Page's offer but first decides to return to his Southern roots to visit his old girlfriend (Shirley Knight). He earns the enmity of corrupt political boss Ed Begley, Knight's father. Begley ran Newman out of town after he made Knight pregnant and forced her to have an abortion. To protect his daughter from the unsavory and undesirable Newman, Begley, in the original play, has the Newman character castrated. In this production, however, Begley's son (Rip Torn) and his hoodlum friends beat Newman and badly scar his face, virtually ruining his chances to work in films as a romantic lead. Knight realizes that Newman really loves her and both leave town together. Begley remains frustrated in his failed attempt to wreak full vengeance on the drifter.

Toys in the Attic (1963), UA. Dir. George Roy Hill; Sc. James Poe; Cast includes: Dean Martin, Geraldine Page, Yvette Mimieux, Wendy Hiller, Gene Tierney.

George Roy Hill's drama, based on Lillian Hellman's Southern gothic play, involves the usual Southern gothic ingredients – incest, infidelity and lust. Dean Martin returns to his two unmarried sisters in their decaying New Orleans mansion. He brings along his childlike bride (Yvette Mimieux). Both sisters, living in genteel poverty, hope that their brother will help them financially. Eventually they learn that Martin has made his money in a real estate swindle.

One of the sisters, Geraldine Page, is sexually attracted to her ne'er do-well brother and resents Martin's young wife. The intrusion of the bride into the family transforms Page from a charming Southern belle into a cruel, venomous sister. She plots to use the young bride to betray her husband, but Martin soon discovers the truth and walks out on Page in disgust. "You never really loved me!" Martin finally exclaims to Page. "It was Jed, your own father, you really wanted! Go on, say it." Both sisters soon realize that their love for their brother is unnatural and regretfully release him. Wendy Hiller, who portrays the older and more perceptive sister, learns of Page's evil inclinations and also abandons her. Page is left alone in the big, decaying mansion to ponder her Freudian behavior.

To complete the picture of Southern lust, Hellman has Mimieux's well-to-do mother (Gene Tierney) have an affair with her black chauffeur.

Two Moon Junction (1988), Samuel Goldwyn. Dir. Zalman King; Sc. Zalman King; Cast includes: Sherilyn Fenn, Martin Hewitt, Richard Tyson, Louise Fletcher.

Young April (Sherilyn Fenn) is the daughter of a senator and a Southern heiress. She is engaged to marry handsome Chad (Martin Hewitt) in this romantic drama. After seeing the bare chest of carnival worker Perry (Richard Tyson), her romantic life is turned upside down. Her dalliance takes place a few days prior to her scheduled wedding to Chad. With her fiancé out of town on business and her family on vacation, she is free to visit the carnival and meet Perry. April is torn between her new love for Perry and her family responsibility to marry Brad. Her grandmother is suspicious of April and the carnival worker and asks the local sheriff (Burl Ives) to closely watch Perry. The wedding ceremony is the finale of the film.

View From Pompey's Head, The (1955), TCF. Dir. Phillip Dunne; Sc. Phillip Dunne; Cast includes: Richard Egan, Dana Wynter, Cameron Mitchell, Sidney Blackmer, Marjorie Rambeau.

In Phillip Dunne's explosive drama, New York lawyer Richard Egan returns to Pompey's Head, his Southern hometown. Marjorie Rambeau requests that he investigate Sidney Blackmer, her husband. She suspects Blackmer, a blind author, of being unfaithful when he surreptitiously cashes his royalty checks. Eagan discovers that Blackmer, to avoid a family scandal, has been paying blackmail money to his father's mistress, a black woman who is also Blackmer's mother. The film, based on a novel by Hamilton Basso, captures a lot of Southern local color.

Walk on the Wild Side (1962), Col. Dir. Edward Dmytryk; Sc. J. Fante, E. Morris; Cast includes: Laurence Harvey, Capucine, Jane Fonda, Anne Baxter, Barbara Stanwyck.

Texas drifter Laurence Harvey journeys to New Orleans where he finds Capucine, his first love. This violent drama of love and frustration is set in the South during the Depression era and is based on the novel by Nelson Algren. Capucine is the featured attraction in the notorious Doll House Café, a bordello owned by lesbian Barbara Stanwyck, who is unhappy about Harvey's presence. Meanwhile, Jane Fonda, a coquette he picked up during his travels on the road, stakes her own claim on Harvey. Anne Baxter portrays another attractive woman in Harvey's complicated romantic life.

14

Family Survival

Director D. W. Griffith's earliest Southern films – c. 1908 – set the pattern for future Hollywood portrayals of the region. Griffith divided the Southern population into two distinct groups – those who resided in the hills of Kentucky and surrounding environs and those who lived in the flatlands. The former, separated from the cities and towns, lived closer to nature, worked hard, were fiercely independent, suspicious of strangers, involved in feuds and were generally violent but brave. Those in the flatlands lived a more leisurely life, were paternalistic toward their black slaves or workers and were also courageous.

Other directors co-opted these attributes and used them for their characters.. Dramas like *Hills of Kentucky* (1927) described famine-stricken mountain people. Other dramas focused on life among the aristocrats. *His Enemy, the Law* (1918) concerned a former cavalry officer; *Chain Lightning* (1922) described horseracing; and *Gone With the Wind* (1939) dealt chiefly with plantation owners, other aristocrats and life in towns and cities such as Atlanta.

Georgia served as the backdrop for several film dramas. Director Mervyn LeRoy's powerful and memorable *I Am a Fugitive From a Chain Gang* (1932), based on James Allen's experiences, reveals how Allen (Paul Muni) is buffeted by fate and life. Mel Ferrer is a light-skinned African-American in Alfred L. Werker's drama *Lost Boundaries* (1949), set partly in Georgia. He and his family pass for white, but, eventually, his children discover the truth. Susan Hayward, the city-bred bride of Protestant minister William Lundigan, relates her three-year experience in the hills of Georgia, in Henry King's uplifting drama *I'd Climb the Highest Mountain* (1951). The film is based on the novel by Corra Harris. Daniel Petrie's cliché-ridden romantic drama *Buster and Billie* (1974) concerns a 1948 romance in rural Georgia between a promiscuous high-school girl and a boy who helps her find love. An army officer in John Kortney's drama *Resting Place* (1986) confronts white opposition when, in the 1970s, he tries to bury a black Vietnam War hero in an all-white Georgia cemetery. Con artist James Woods sets his target on small Georgia town braggart Bruce Dern by luring him into betting against boxer Louis Gossett Jr. in Michael Ritchie's drama *Diggstown* (1992).

Some films set in Georgia are simply crime dramas. Richard Compton's violent drama *Macon County Line* (1974), set in Georgia in 1954, is based on an actual incident where three strangers are pursued for a killing they didn't commit. A sequel, *Return to Macon County*, followed.

*

All the Way Home (1963), Par. Dir. Alex Segal; Sc. Philip Reisman; Cast includes: Jean Simmons, Robert Preston, Pat Hingle, Alice McMahon, Thomas Chalmers.

This somber drama is based on James Agee's autobiographical novel *A Death in the Family*. Robert Preston portrays the father and husband of a Knoxville, Tennessee family, circa 1915. Preston is killed in a car accident and leaves his wife, Jean Simmons, and his seven-year-old son, Michael Kearny, to face an uncertain future.

Anna Lucasta (1949), Col. Dir. Irving Rapper; Sc. Philip Yordan, Arthur Laurents; Cast includes: Paulette Goddard, William Bishop, Oscar Homolka, John Ireland, Broderick Crawford.

A number of post-World War II Southern films reverted to the ugly side of human nature. This stark drama is based on the play by Philip Yordan. In the film, Paulette Goddard's lecherous father (Oscar Homolka) throws his daughter out of the house and she is forced to become a streetwalker. When he has an opportunity to marry her off to a wealthy farmer and grab the simple man's money, Homolka forces her to return home and marry the farmer. However, she soon falls in love with the groom and blocks her father from grabbing her husband's money. The all-white film version was based on the stage play that featured an all-black cast. Arnold Laven directed a remake of the film in 1958, starring Eartha Kitt as the title character and Sammy Davis Jr. as her boyfriend.

Beloved (1998), BV. Dir. Jonathan Demme; Sc. Akosua Busia, Richard LaGravenese, Adam Brooks; Cast includes: Oprah Winfrey, Danny Glover, Thandie Newton, Kimberly Elise, Beah Richards.

Director Jonathan Demme's Southern gothic horror tale is based on Toni Morrison's popular Pulitzer-winning novel. The film stars Oprah Winfrey as Sethe, a strong woman who raises her daughter, Denver, on her own in Cincinnati during the post-Civil war years. Their home is haunted, and when Beloved, a strange, untamed girl shows up, the film suggests that perhaps she is Sethe's dead older daughter. Flashbacks reveal Sethe's terrible past – her torture at the hands of a brutal slave master, abandonment by her husband and the death of her daughter. Denver has become part of her mother's paranoia and she has to try to straighten out the entire family.

Chain Lightning (1922), Arrow. Dir. Ben Wilson; Sc. J. Grubb Alexander; Cast includes: Ann Little, Norval MacGregor, William Carroll, Joseph Girard.

Southern-bred Ann Little attempts to win enough money to take her father West for his health. She is determined to ride her horse to victory and grab the prize, in this horseracing drama. Her father, meanwhile, has taken a second mortgage on their home to pay for his daughter's tuition in finishing school in Washington, D.C.

Claudelle Inglish (1961), WB. Dir. Gordon Douglas; Sc. Leonard Freeman; Cast includes: Diane McBain, Arthur Kennedy, Will Hutchins, Constance Ford, Claude Akins.

The daughter of a farming family in the rural South, Diane McBain is the title character. The drama is based on the novel by Erskine Caldwell. McBain rejects her mother's wishes that she marry a wealthy farmer. Instead, she prefers dirt farmer Chad Everett, who is soon drafted. McBain now becomes the town floozy and men fight for her affection. When one young man is killed in a fight over her, her father finds and shoots her.

Crimes of the Heart (1986), De Laurentis. Dir. Bruce Bereford; Sc. Beth Henley; Cast includes: Diane Keaton, Jessica Lange, Sissy Spacek, Sam Shepard.

This comedy drama is based on the play by Beth Henley and focuses on three sisters (Diane Keaton, Jessica Lange, Sissy Spacek) who are all equally eccentric. They share their various problems, resentments and jealousies during a crucial reunion. Set in Mississippi, the story of the sisters' heartbreaking and mixed-up lives is a blend of craziness and poetry. The trio's acting is inspired.

Cross Creek (1983), U. Dir. Martin Ritt; Sc. Dalene Young; Cast includes: Mary Steenburgen, Rip Torn, Peter Coyote, Dana Hill.

Set in the Florida backwoods, Martin Ritt's warm drama is based on the memoirs of author Marjorie Kinnan Rawlings and her early struggle to publish a novel. Rawlings, portrayed by Mary Steenburgen, abandons the security of a marriage to a rich New Yorker in 1928 and leaves for a remote part of Florida. She purchases and orange grove and hopes to make enough money to support herself while writing that "great novel." When her gothic romances don't sell, she changes topics and writes about the Florida swamp people in such novels as *The Yearling* and *Jacob's Ladder*.

Cross Creek was selected for the book-of-the-Month Club in 1942. For this story, Rawlings interviewed local Florida "crackers" in her efforts to record the vanishing life of these people. Rollins College in Florida awarded her an honorary doctorate in 1939 for her work in describing the local folk in these remote areas.

Down in the Delta (1998), Miramax. Dir. Maya Angelou; Sc. Myron Goble; Cast includes: Alfre Woodard, Al Freeman Jr., Mary Alice, Esther Rolle, Loretta Devine, Wesley Snipes.

Maya Angelou's drama focuses on "family values." Mary Alice, as Rosa Lynn, realizes that the drugs and guns that dominate the streets of her Chicago neighborhood threaten her daughter Loretta, her grandson Thomas and her autistic granddaughter Tracy. Loretta is rejected for a cashier's job and goes directly to a liquor store and then a crack house. Shocked into action, Lynn then telephones her brother Earl in Mississippi and arranges to send her family to him for the summer. Loretta and her two children settle in Earl's large house, and her tough exterior soon softens when she is exposed to the new environment and the bucolic landscape. Under the care and patience of Earl and his wife Annie, the entire family enjoys the feeling of returning to their roots. Earl hires Loretta as a waitress in his restaurant, and his son, a successful Atlanta lawyer, played by Wesley Snipes, shows up.

Eve's Bayou (1997), Trimark. Dir. Kasi Lemmons; Sc. Kasi Lemmons; Cast includes: Jurnee Smollett, Samuel L. Jackson, Lynne Whitfield, Meagan Good, Debbi Morgan.

Ten-year-old Eve (Jurnee Smollett) is the second daughter of Dr. Louis Batiste (Samuel L. Jackson). She narrates the story, a tragic tale of a black middle-class community in Louisiana's swampy and humid Bayou country. The good doctor provides medical attention as well as pills to his patients and is especially solicitous of his female patients. His family sees little of him, even on weekends and in the evenings. The storyteller, Eve accidentally witnesses him making love to a female guest during a family gathering. His wife (Lynn Whitfield) suspects him but remains silent. His older daughter Cisely (Meagan Good) needs him for affection in her own, twisted way. They all prefer him as their hero, but he constantly disappoints them.

Her sister convinces Eve that their father is somehow immoral and puts a voodoo curse upon him. When he is shot and killed outside a bar by an enraged husband, Eve believes she has been responsible for her father's death. The film begins with her narration. "Memory is the selection of images, some elusive, others printed indelibly on the brain," she muses. "The summer I killed my father, I was ten years old." Eve and the rest of her family must live with only the memory of the man who had disappointed them in his short life.

*

A bayou is an offshoot of a river or lake in a lowland area. It is a sluggish or stagnant creek, frequently flowing through swampy terrain. The term is used mainly in the U.S. states on the Gulf of Mexico and especially in the delta region of the Mississippi River. Films using Louisiana's bayou as background ranged from dramas to biographies to horror tales. Francis X. Bushman and others face a number of dangers in an isolated mansion on the bayou in the silent horror tale *Midnight Faces* (1926).

*

Family Honor, The (1920), FN. Dir. King Vidor; Cast includes: Florence Vidor, Charles Meredith.

In this domestic drama, Florence Vidor, the daughter of a bankrupt aristocratic Southern family, struggles to put her brother through college. She hopes that, after graduation, he will eventually be able to support the family. But her brother has other intentions. He spends much of his time gambling and drinking in a local saloon owned by the mayor of the town. During a raid led by Charles Meredith, the mayor's idealistic son, a law officer is killed and Vidor's brother is charged with the death. When his case seems virtually hopeless, a witness appears and testifies that the saloon manager, not the young defendant, did the actual shooting. The student reforms and Vidor marries Meredith, whom she has met and grown to love.

Fried Green Tomatoes (1991), U. Dir. Jon Avnet; Sc. Jon Avnet, Fannie Flagg; Cast includes: Kathy Bates, Jessica Tandy, Mary Stuart Masterson, Mary-Louise Parker.

Eighty-year old Jessica Tandy, a resident of a nursing home, regales a dutiful but bored housewife (Kathy Bates) with stories of her past. This drama is told chiefly in flashbacks and is based on the novel by Fannie Flagg. Tandy tells about the now deserted town of Whistle Stop, Alabama, and a likeable pair of women who ran the local café in the 1930s. She describes the close friendship between the sparkling Idgie (Mary Stuart Masterson) and the more modest Ruth (Mary-Louise Parker). Idgie eventually rescued her pregnant friend from an abusive husband. The two then raised the child together. Bates is impressed by Tandy's stories and begins to reorganize her own life. She gives up trying to please her sluggish, ungrateful husband and finds a career selling cosmetics. She also begins to devote herself to her elderly friend, Tandy, in an imitation of Idgie helping Ruth.

Gal Young 'Un (1979) Nunez. Dir. Victor Nunez; Sc. Victor Nunez; Cast includes: Dana Preu, J. Smith, Jennie Stringfellow.

Marjorie Kinnan Rawlings's story was filmed in 1979 by Florida-based director Victor Nunez. A young idle, irresponsible bootlegger terrorizes a lonely, middle-aged widow in this drama set in Forida's rural backwoods during the 1930s. He woos and marries her and then sets about swindling her out of her money in order to expand his moonshine operation – until she finally seeks revenge.

God's Little Acre (1958), UA. Dir. Anthony Mann; Sc. Philip Yordan; Cast includes: Robert Ryan, Aldo Ray, Tina Louise, Buddy Hackett, Jack Lord.

Georgia farmer Robert Ryan believes he can find buried treasure on his farm in Anthony Mann's film version of the book. Mann took Erskine Caldwell's serious work and sort of pokes fun at the poor, ignorant farmers. Together with his two sons, Jack Lord and Vic Morrow, Ryan spends years digging for the elusive riches. He searches everywhere except on the one acre he has set aside for God. This acre is marked with a cross. But since the cross can be moved, it is constantly shifted from one spot to another in his fruitless pursuit of the treasure. The entire farm is soon pockmarked with holes as a result of Ryan's senseless search. His son-in-law, Aldo Ray, who lives in town, also seeks simple solutions to large problems. He believes he'll rejuvenate the town just by turning on the power of the closed cotton mill. He is killed turning on the power. The film ends when Ryan and his son decide to plant some crops and put something into the land rather than trying to get something out of it.

Gone With the Wind (1939), MGM. Dir. Victor Fleming; Sc. Sidney Howard; Cast includes: Clark Gable, Leslie Howard, Olivia de Havilland, Vivien Leigh, Thomas Mitchell, Hattie McDaniel, Evelyn Keyes, Ann Rutherford, George Reeves, Butterfly McQueen.

Margaret Mitchell's extremely popular Civil War novel became the basis of one of the most acclaimed and perennial films ever produced. There are few people who have not read the book or seen the Selznick production. In some ways it is a typical Hollywood product – expensive, boasting a large cast, shot in and around the studio and highly publicized. Criticism ranged from astounding to less than enthusiastic. But American and world audiences flocked to see the epic war film and the heroic and hapless love story of two strong-willed people.

The production of the film has become almost as legendary as the film itself. Clark Gable was chosen by national referendum to play Rhett Butler while Selznick and MGM tested more than a thousand candidates for the role of Scarlett. Norma Shearer, the studio's first choice, rejected the role. Eventually, English actress Vivien Leigh won the part, disturbing some that she was not an American and calming Southerners that at least a Northerner was not chosen. Several dozen writers worked on the script. Ironically, Sidney Howard, who wrote the major part of the screenplay, never saw the film; he died in an accident before the screening. Several directors had a hand in the work. George Cukor was taken off the project. Victor Fleming, who received full credit, had a nervous breakdown while working on the film and was assisted temporarily by Sam Wood.

The Civil War and the love story are the two focal points of the film. The war not only results in widespread physical destruction but it affects the psyches of two generations. The film traces the war's impact on two families, the O'Haras and the aristocratic Wilkses. Scenes of the war and its results remain as memorable as the principal characters. The burning of Atlanta, the high angle shot of the Confederate wounded sprawled along the streets and in the hospital and Scarlett shooting a Union deserter are just three such images.

Scarlett O'Hara, by far the most interesting character in the film, demonstrates a will and a strength that suggest she will survive. Men fall in love with her not for her tenderness or romantic ideas but for her strength. She marries not for love but for specific needs. Her first love is Ashley, but he rejects her and she marries Rhett Butler out of spite. Butler represents energy and experience and, although his reputation is suspect, he proudly announces, "With enough courage, you can do without a reputation." Scarlett, however, remains true to Ashley, who symbolizes the past, a South that was quickly disappearing into memory. Not until Rhett walks out on her does she finally come to terms with reality, a reality that casts a shadow over her sense of tomorrow.

Good-bye, My Lady (1956), WB. Dir. William A. Wellman; Sc. Sid Fleischman; Cast includes: Walter Brennan, Phil Harris, Brandon de Wilde, Sidney Poitier, Louise Beavers.

Young Brandon de Wilde lives with his uncle, Walter Brennan, in a ramshackle cabin near a swamp. This poignant drama is based on the novel by James Street. The boy finds a dog and cares for it, until the owner comes to claim it. His uncle, Brennan, has been very supportive of De Wilde, so that when this crisis comes, the boy is able to weather it. Sidney Poitier and Louise Beavers, two local inhabitants, befriend the uncle and his nephew.

Grass Harp, The (1995), Fine Line. Dir. Charles Matthau; Sc. Stirling Silliphant; Cast includes: Edward Furlong, Piper Laurie, Sissy Spacek, Walter Matthau, Jack Lemmon, Nell Carter.

Charles Matthau's soulful drama is based on Truman Capote's nostalgic autobiographical novella. Matthau recalls his boyhood with two eccentric maiden cousins in a small Southern town during the 1940s. The film stars Edward Furlong as the boy Collin, Piper Laurie as Dolly, Sissy Spacek as her sister Verena, Walter Matthau (the director's father) as a retired and kindly judge and Jack Lemmon as a con man. Furlong helps Dolly recognize her maternal instincts while the stern Verena remains a very practical hotel owner and businesswoman. At one point, Walter Matthau says to Dolly, "Love is a chain,"and she repeats it to young Furlong just before she dies.

*

American writer Truman Capote (1924-1984) was born in New Orleans, Louisiana, but was educated chiefly at Trinity School and Saint John's Academy, both in New York City. At age 23 he wrote his first novel, *Other Voices, Other Rooms,* about a Southern boy's search for identity. Capote also wrote *A Tree of Night and Other Stories* (1949), *The Grass Harp* (1951) and *The Muses Are Heard* (1956). Blake Edwards turned Capote's *Breakfast at Tiffany's* (1961) into a highly popular romantic comedy, starring Audrey Hepburn and George Peppard. Richard Brooks brought Capote's chilling and realistic *In Cold Blood* (1967) to the screen. It featured Robert Blake as fantasy-driven Perry Smith and Scott Wilson as Dick Hickock. The latter is a psychological misfit burdened with a grudge against society, probably because of his sexual inadequacies. These two Kansas drifters murder a family of four during a burglary in 1959. After their vicious and senseless killings, Perry says to his partner, "I thought Mr. Clutter was a very nice man. He was a real gentleman . . . I thought so right up to the moment I cut his throat." Their case drags through the courts for six years before they are executed.

Capote collaborated on the screenplay for Jack Clayton's dark and brooding drama *The Innocents* (1961), based on Henry James's story "Turn of the Screw." Deborah Kerr portrays a governess in charge of two apparently innocent children who share a corrupting evil secret.

Heart Is a Lonely Hunter, The (1968), WB. Dir. Robert Ellis Miller; Sc. Thomas C. Ryan; Cast includes: Alan Arkin, Sondra Locke, Laurinda Barrett, Stacy Keach, Chuck McCann.

Alan Arkin, a lonely, deaf mute, impresses a number of psychological and physical misfits. This sensitive drama is set in the South and is based on the novel by Carson McCullers. Sandra Locke is an idealistic young girl who is forced by her parents to quit school to support the family. Somehow, someway, Arkin helps Locke find herself.

In a second case, despite Arkin's efforts to help him, alcoholic drifter Stacy Keach drifts from one failure to another.

In yet a third episode, Percy Rodriguez, a black doctor who hates whites, has problems with his daughter Cicely Tyson. Tyson rebels against her father who wants her to go to medical school and she marries a field hand instead. Unknown to Tyson, her father is dying of cancer. When she wants her strongly-principled father to perjure himself to save her husband, the father refuses. Arkin helps reunite the two.

In yet another case, Arkin's close pal, Chuck McCann, is simple-minded and deaf. When Arkin tries to visit him in an institution, he learns that McCann has died. Despite all his attempts at reaching out, the film ends on a depressing note as Arkin ends up suicidal and alone.

Hills of Kentucky (1927), WB. Dir. Howard Bretherton; Sc. Edward Clark; Cast includes: Jason Robards, Dorothy Dwan, Tom Santschi, Billy Kent Schaeffer, Rin-Tin-Tin.

The mountain people of a famine-stricken part of Kentucky are forced to get rid of their dogs in this drama based on the story "The Untamed Heart" by Dorothy Yost. One dog becomes the leader of a foraging pack and is known as "The Gray Ghost." The animal is wounded in an attack and a local boy who has been fishing in a nearby area cleans him up and feeds him. They soon become good friends. Later, the grateful animal saves the boy from an attack by the pack and rescues a young woman from a river.

His Enemy, the Law (1918), Triangle. Dir. Raymond Wells; Sc. George E. Jenks; Cast includes: Jack Richardson, Irene Hunt, Jack Livingston, Graham Pette, Walt Whitman.

The failed romance of two lovers affects their grandchildren's lives in this romantic drama. Jack Richardson portrays a former Southern cavalry officer who temporarily leaves the young woman he loves to earn enough money for marriage. During his absence she marries someone else, in order to save her sickly father. Richardson learns of her marriage and marries a widow. He abandons her, takes his six-year-old son with him and joins a band of stage robbers. Upon his death, a sheriff raises the bandit's son who becomes a criminal lawyer. Fate has the young lawyer meet the daughter of his father's first true love. She hires him to defend her fiancé, who has been charged with murder. The lawyer gets the man off on a technicality although he is actually guilty. The young lawyer and his client fall in love after her crooked fiancé tries to retrieve some stolen loot in Mexico and is killed. Richardson and Irene Hunt portray both pairs of lovers.

Let's Do It Again (1975), First Artists. Dir. Sidney Poitier; Sc. Richard Wesley; Cast includes: Sidney Poitier, Bill Cosby, Jimmie Walker, John Amos.

In Sidney Poitier's comedy, a sequel to *Uptown Saturday Night* (1974), Atlanta milkman Poitier and Bill Cosby portray lodge brothers. They hypnotize Jimmie Walker into becoming a pro prizefighter.

Member of the Wedding, The (1952), Col. Dir. Fred Zinnemann; Sc. Edna and Edward Anhalt; Cast includes: Julie Harris, Ethel Waters, Brandon de Wilde, Arthur Franz, Nancy Gates.

Originally published as a novel in 1946 by Carson McCullers, her work underwent a metamorphosis and was produced as a Broadway play in 1950. The film starred Ethel Waters as Berenice the cook, Julie Harris as Frankie and Brandon de Wilde as her younger brother. The drama describes the adolescent experiences of a twelve-year old girl. The young girl, Frankie Addams, attempts to join her brother, Jarvis, and his bride, Janice, on their honeymoon. Frankie desperately wants to become an adult and to reach out. The black cook, Berenice, helps the young girl through this difficult period into maturity.

Miss Firecracker (1989), Corsair. Dir. Thomas Schlamme; Sc. Beth Henley; Cast includes: Holly Hunter, Mary Steenburgen, Tim Robbins, Alfre Woodard, Scott Glenn.

Hollywood again returns to explore several popular Southern themes. The dilapidated mansion is featured prominently, as is the Southern belle – both symbols of a fading, declining South. This comedy drama is based on Beth Henley's play about a family of harmless eccentrics. But this time these once-cherished and glamorized characters become objects of gentle derision. Sad, funny and lonely Holly Hunter, a young woman living in Yazoo City, a small

Mississippi town, yearns for love and wants to improve her self-image. She desperately tries to fulfil her dreams. Remembering how her cousin (Mary Steenburgen) was named Miss Firecracker in 1972, Hunter is now determined to succeed as the Fourth of July Queen. When her cousin refuses to lend her the special red dress she had worn in the earlier contest, Hunter has Alfre Woodard, the local seamstress, Popeye, sew her a special costume.

On another track, Hunter hopes to live down her previous soiled reputation as "Hot Tamale" among the young men in town and win back her self-esteem. Tim Robbins, her stormy and philosophizing cousin Delmount, arrives in town by freight train. He plans to sell the deteriorating family mansion to developers and use the money to go to an out-of-town college. He wants to learn about life. "It'd be a great relief, I believe," he explains. While all this is going on, Scott Glen, a carnival roustabout and ladies' man, shows up in town. Holly has a reunion with Scott and she finally realizes the need to be loved is more important than a foolish beauty contest. The tone of the film falls somewhere between the comedy of John Ford's *Tobacco Road* and the sordid sexual deviations described in the films of Tennessee Williams and William Faulkner.

Other Voices, Other Rooms (1997), Artistic License. Dir. David Rocksavage; Sc. Sara Flanigan, David Rocksavage; Cast includes: Lothaire Bluteau, Anna Thomson, David Speck.

This flowery and stylized drama is based on the Truman Capote's first novel. It is set in the 1930s and concerns a sensitive 13-year-old Southern boy (not unlike Capote) who seeks a close relationship with his father. Isolated and mature for his age, the boy journeys by bus and horse cart to the decrepit mansion where his long-absent father lives. Reminiscent of Carson McCullers and Lillian Hellman, the poetry-sprouting characters and the heavy Southern gothic atmosphere unfortunately work against the film.

Queen Bee (1955), Col. Dir. Ranald MacDougall; Sc. Ranald MacDougall; Cast includes: Joan Crawford, Barry Sullivan, Betsy Palmer, John Ireland, Lucy Marlow.

In this drama, based on a novel by Edna Lee, love takes a back seat to power. The central family comes from the North and settles in Atlanta. The missus, wealthy Joan Crawford, and husband, Barry Sullivan, live in a mansion. Crawford is a power-hungry type while Sullivan is laid-back and he drinks heavily in order to escape his domineering wife. Crawford, meanwhile, is going full blast and she prevents Sullivan's sister (Betsy Palmer) from marrying estate manager John Ireland, Crawford's former lover. Palmer, out of frustration, commits suicide and Ireland, in retribution, devises a car accident which kills Crawford.

Something to Talk About (1995), WB. Dir. Lasse Hallstrom; Sc. Callie Khouri; Cast includes: Julia Roberts, Dennis Quaid, Robert Duvall, Gena Rowlands, Kyra Sedgwick.

A sheltered Southern wife discovers that her husband has been unfaithful. Julia Roberts portrays Grace, the betrayed wife, who is a member of a close-knit, unruly Southern family. While driving down a street, she inadvertently sees her husband Eddie (Dennis Quaid) kissing a blonde. "You marry a guy whose nickname in college is Hound Dog," her wisecracking sister Emma Rae comments, "what did you think was going to happen?" The revelation motivates her to rebel against everything in her staid Southern life – from the ladies' committee that is working on a cookbook to her father (Robert Duvall), the dictatorial patriarch who keeps her under his thumb. She receives little support from him. Instead, he berates her. "You trying to humiliate your whole damn family?" Her mother (Gena Rowlands) explains to Grace that being kind to an unfaithful husband is part of a wife's job. On the other hand, an elderly woman in her ladies' group offers her a special perilous recipe for philandering husbands. "Sometimes a little near-death experience helps them put things in perspective," she suggests. Only her sister's outspokenness helps Grace straighten out her life – if not her marriage.

Southerner, The (1945), UA. Dir. Jean Renoir; Sc. Jean Renoir, Hugo Butler; Cast includes: Zachary Scott, Betty Field, Beulah Bondi, J. Carrol Naish, Norman Lloyd.

Jean Renoir's poignant drama shows the indomitable spirit of the Southern independent farmer – despite untold hardships. Former sharecropper Zachary Scott has bought his own farm and endures poverty, sickness, storms and ultimately the destruction of his cotton crop. After these setbacks, Scott considers taking a factory job in town to support his family, but decides to stay on the farm when he discovers that his family has renovated the farm and made it livable. Family survival in the South appeared in a series of post-World War II films, many idealizing or glorifying the independent farmer.

Staying Together (1989), Hemsdale. Dir. Lee Grant; Sc. Monte Merric; Cast includes: Sean Astin, Stockard Channing, Melinda Dillon, Jim Haynie.

This domestic comedy drama concerns the hardworking McDermott family, the residents of a Southern town. The head of the household runs a chicken restaurant, and his wife stays home in the kitchen. They have three sons who drink, smoke pot and are generally antisocial. Suddenly, wealthy city developers want to buy the restaurant and replace it with a franchise. The two son love the business and don't want to sell, but their father, who hates chickens, prefers selling and retiring to a quiet life. The crisis pulls the family apart temporarily, but everything works out at the end.

Tobacco Road (1941), TCF. Dir. John Ford; Sc. Nunnally Johnson; Cast includes: Charley Grapewin, Marjorie Rambeau, Gene Tierney, William Tracy, Dana Andrews.

Director John Ford turned the long-running and somber 1933 play by Jack Kirkland and novel by Erskine Caldwell – about the "poor white trash" of Georgia's Tobacco Road during the Depression – into a film chock-full of black humor. But it still didn't present a pretty picture of the rural South. The drama opens with the statement: "All that they were, and all that they had, is gone with the wind and the dust." Ford skirted this pessimism in his depiction of a family battered by the elements. Instead, he somehow found black comedy in characters such as Jeeter Lester and energetic Charley Grapewin and his wife, Elizabeth Patterson, as they struggle to keep their family together while trying to raise the $100 they need to pay the month's bills.

Their rowdy son, William Tracy, is of no use at all. Instead of helping his father, he only drives his car, beeps its horn and wrecks the vehicle – all in one day. On another level, the car serves as a unifying symbol for the family. They all gather around to gawk at and admire the new car – especially its color and style. However, the unity of the family is short-lived. Daughter Gene Tierney has her own agenda. She's only interested in flirting with handsome, brawny neighbor Ward Bond. Grapewin's only potential savior is his sister, Marjorie Rambeau, but she ends up spending all her money frivolously. Generally lazy, all members of the family refuse to work or plant. Grandma has walked off into the woods, never to return. Although the family eventually disintegrates, Grapewin, thanks to his sense of humor, prevails with most of his dignity. This was an unusual film for Ford, who poked fun at family values, truth, the work ethic and love of the land – themes that he so strongly supported in earlier films such as *How Green Was My Valley* (1940).

Yearling, The (1946), MGM. Dir. Clarence Brown; Sc. Paul Osborn; Cast includes: Gregory Peck, Jane Wyman, Claude Jarman Jr., Chill Wills, Forrest Tucker.

Parents Gregory Peck and Jane Wyman struggle to raise their son Jody (Claude Jarman Jr.) in backwoods Florida following the Civil War. This family drama is based on the 1939 prize-winning novel by Marjorie Kinnan Rawlings. The family farm is hammered by storms that ruin the crops and invaded by animals that kill the livestock. Yet Peck and his son stick with the land. The hardships have made Wyman stronger than her husband and she remains devoted and proud throughout their ordeals. The boy derives a lot of pleasure from raising a pet fawn. But when it becomes a yearling and starts to eat the crops, he realizes that he must make a decision between his family and the yearling.

15

Economics in the New South

After the shock of losing the Civil War, Southern politicians began to rethink their hostility towards business and industry and even their blind support of "King Cotton." Businessmen were pragmatic enough to realize that their agrarian economy was dead and the future was in large-scale industrialization. Southern intellectuals, on the other hand, didn't have to face reality and be pragmatic. They continued to live in the past and persevered in praising Southern civilization as superior to Northern capitalism. Some of these intellectuals even harbored hopes that "the South shall rise again." Despite the aberrations of these intellectuals, the post-Civil War South moved more and more away from an insulated agrarian economy and began to resemble the rest of the country.

After boll weevils damaged the cotton plants in 1915, farmers began to concentrate on raising livestock and other crops besides cotton. The iron and steel industries experienced dynamic growth during the early 20th century. Beginning in the 1930s, low-cost power provided by the Tennessee Valley Authority (TVA), a federal agency helped the growth of industries in Southern states. While farming and crops continued to play a prominent role in the economy, manufacturing created hundreds of thousands of jobs and generated billions of dollars of income for the region. Both the New Deal and the war stimulated the post-World War II Southern economy. It was precisely during this period of time following World War II that Washington began to relocate many agency offices to the South.

The cumulative effect of all of these changes was to eliminate many economic remnants of the "Old South" and to create a new economy in the "Sun Belt."The Southern environment drew Northern tourists as well as retirees who settled in areas from North Carolina to Florida. Although the economy and per capita income continued to grow in the 1980s and 1990s, the growth was unevenly distributed.

Many enthusiastic businessmen endorsed the "New South Creed"–a philosophy aimed at remaking the area into an industrial power. This Creed saw "progress" in copying the economic successes of its former Northern adversary. In the spirit of boosterism, it advertised the riches of the South and boasted of the absence of unions. Appointed and elected officials offered lenient tax breaks and carefully avoided criticism of industry. By so doing, they were successful in attracting Northern industry to the South. Overall, the "New South Creed" was moderately successful and had remarkable longevity. A number of historians credit the "New South Creed" with remarkable success in developing and exploiting the Appalachian region.

*

The 13th Amendment to the Constitution prohibited involuntary servitude except as punishment. Several Southern states passed their own versions of the 13th Amendment. To avoid these prohibitions, sharecropping was introduced. Soon, sharecropping replaced slavery as the driving engine of the agrarian economy. Sharecroppers, both black and white, and their families provided the labor for the landlords. The owners, on the other hand, provided land, animals, equipment, seed and living accommodations. Together, they split the profits.

At first, the practice seemed beneficial since it provided jobs to former slaves, but its many abuses soon outweighed its benefits. Sharecroppers were treated poorly and overworked, They were often cheated out of their money by the landowners who controlled the account books and the scales. By the end of the sharecropping era, former slaves and their children eventually joined forces with poor whites in a struggle against the landlords. Eventually, however, widespread mechanization and a decreased demand for American cotton made the system unprofitable. Both these factors – mechanization and the decline in cotton production – reduced the need for farm workers and the sharecropping system came crashing down. Although unemployment soared, the workers were finally freed from the slavery of the farm. Unfortunately, by the time *Let Us Now Praise Famous Men*, a semi-fictional exposé of a sharecropper's life by Walker Evans and James Agee, was published in 1941, the nation was preparing for war and had little time to focus on sharecroppers' problems.

*

As early as the first decade of the twentieth century Hollywood studios began cranking out numerous dramas depicting moonshiners and revenue agents. The production of illegal liquor in "stills" was a mainstay of the economy in isolated communities in Kentucky, Tennessee, North and South Carolina. Some of the earliest silent films were *The Moonshiner* (1904), two films titled *The Moonshiners*, one released in 1911 and a second issued in 1914, *The Moon-*

shiner's Daughter (three films: 1910, 1912, 1914), *The Moonshiner's Last Stand* (1913) and *The Moonshiner's Mistake* (1913).

*

One of the staple Hollywood themes was the corrupt Southern public official. Since a number of Southern communities were geographically isolated from their state capitals and, of course, from Washington, they existed as independent fiefdoms and it was in this environment that corruption flourished. Hollywood screenwriters described villains as varied as railroad magnates (*The Interloper*, 1918), plantation owners (*White Bondage*, 1937), smalltime racketeers (*The Big Shot*, 1937), corrupt business owners (*Boy Slaves*, 1938), overly ambitious businessmen (*Ruthless*, 1948) and con artists (*The Flim-Flam Man*, 1967).

*

Big Shot, The (1937), RKO. Dir. Edward Killy; Sc. Arthur T. Horman, Bert Granet; Cast includes: Guy Kibbee, Cora Witherspoon, Dorothy Moore, Gordon Jones, Russell Hicks, Frank M. Thomas.

Guy Kibbee plays a small-town veterinarian who inherits a fortune. He faces competition from a variety of businesses that are really controlled by organized crime. In this comedy, Russell Hicks, who controls the rackets, wants the naïve Kibbee to sign all his business interests over to him. Kibbee, meanwhile, tries to become a "do-gooder" in order to please his nagging wife. She wants their daughter to enter society, so, for the prestige, Kibbee bankrolls a crusading newspaper about to expose organized crime. When Kibbee congratulates one of his bookkeepers on his good work, the man responds, "I picked it up while I was doin' a stretch in Atlanta." The corrupt Hicks immediately informs Kibbee that "the best bookkeepers come from the South." The broad comedy works well in the film, which also takes a swing at public indifference. An incisive newspaper publisher exclaims: "A city of 5,000 worms are bullied by 500 rats!"

Book of Numbers (1973), AE. Dir. Raymond St. Jacques; Sc. Larry Spiegel; Cast includes: Raymond St. Jacques, Freda Payne, Philip Thomas, Hope Clark, Willie Washington Jr.

Raymond St. Jacques and Philip Thomas portray enterprising African-Americans in this low-budget black exploitation drama. The film is based on a novel by Robert Deane Phaar. Jacques and Thomas leave their jobs as waiters in the big city and try to open a numbers racket in a small Southern town during the Depression. The pair soon runs into trouble when the local white crime czar, played by Dave Greene, steps in.

Boy Slaves (1938), RKO. Dir. P. J. Wolfson; Sc. Albert Bein, Ben Orkow; Cast includes: Anne Shirley, Roger Daniel, James McCallion, Alan Baxter, Johnny Fitzgerald, Walter Ward.

Wayward juvenile delinquents are forced to work in a labor camp located somewhere in the South in this overly didactic exposé. Roger Daniel runs away from home and joins a gang of young toughs. They are arrested and brought to a privately-owned turpentine camp, where they must work in brutal conditions. They escape and are recaptured, but a kindly judge refuses to remand them to the horrible environment of the camp.

Bright Leaf (1950), WB. Dir. Michael Curtiz; Sc. Ranald MacDougall; Cast includes: Gary Cooper, Lauren Bacall, Patricia Neal, Jack Carson, Donald Crisp.

Michael Curtiz's drama is based on the novel by Foster Fitz-Simmons. Gary Cooper returns to his hometown in the South. Tobacco tycoon Donald Crisp had forced him to leave after dating Crisp's reserved daughter, Patricia Neal. Determined to succeed in business, Cooper persuades Lauren Bacall into investing in a new cigarette machine. Cooper and his colleagues clean up financially and virtually drive their local competitors – including Crisp -nearly bankrupt. "I've learned a great deal from you," inventor Jeff Cory admits to Cooper. "If I weren't an honest man, I might be able it use it." To rescue her father, Neal marries Cooper. Crisp learns of the marriage, gets depressed and takes his own life. Neal seeks revenge and informs the government of her husband's monopoly. They split up and Cooper prepares to leave town once again. Now rejected, he changes his tune and tells Bacall that he has always loved her and plans to return to her someday.

Cabin in the Cotton (1932), WB. Dir. Michael Curtiz; Sc. Paul Green; Cast includes: Richard Barthelmess, Betty Davis, Henry B. Walthall, Berton Churchill, Walter Percival.

In this drama, based on the 1931 novel by Harry Kroll, poor sharecropper's son Richard Barthelmess works as a night man at the general store. Bette Davis' father owns the business. Barthelmess falls under her spell and is torn between his feelings for Davis and his love for his childhood sweetheart, Dorothy Jordan. At one point when he tries to kiss her, Davis offers her famous line: "I'd love to kiss you, but I just washed my hair." Berton Churchill, the owner, promotes Barthelmess to bookkeeper and he soon discovers that his boss has been cheating his tenant farmers out of a large share of their profits. In the meantime, his boss wants to use the young man to spy on the farmers to determine potential troublemakers. Barthelmess soon discovers the farmers are cheating Churchill as well. He brings both sides together and has them sign an equitable contract.

*

Author Kroll was the son of a Tennessee sharecropper and therefore sympathetic to these tenant farmers. The film version of his novel depicts the sharecroppers as poor, struggling whites while, in reality, most sharecroppers were black. The radical Southern Tenant Farmers' Union of the 1930s was interracial, but the cotton pickers' strike of 1937 in southeastern Missouri was composed chiefly of black workers.

*

Coal Miner's Daughter (1980), U. Dir. Michael Apted; Sc. Tom Rickman; Cast includes: Sissy Spacek, Tommy Lee Jones, Leon Helm, Phyllis Boyens.

In the biography of singing star Loretta Lynn, a moonshiner in the hills of Kentucky tries to tempt a reluctant Tommy Lee Jones, Lynn's future husband, into making illegal whiskey. "If you keep on in the mountains," the moonshiner warns Jones, "you got three choices – coalminin', moonshinin' or movin' on down the line." Soon after, the moonshiner is shot to death.

Cocoanuts, The (1929), Par. Dir. Robert Florey; Sc. George S. Kaufman, Morrie Ryskind; Cast includes: Groucho, Chico, Harpo and Zeppo Marx, Margaret Dumont, Oscar Shaw, Mary Eaton, Kay Francis.

Set in Florida, this early comedy was the Marx Brothers' first feature film. It was based on their stage comedy routine that features a greedy Florida hotel manager and includes spurious real estate sales. The film was made in Paramount's Queens, New York studio while the brothers were performing on Broadway. The limitations of this studio setting probably led to critic Paul D. Zimmerman's caustic remark: "The camerawork showed all the mobility of a concrete fire hydrant caught in a winter freeze."

Dixie Dynamite (1976), Dimension. Dir. Lee Frost; Sc. Wes Bishop, Lee Frost; Cast includes: Jane Anne Johnstone, Kathy McHaley, Warren Oates, Duane Eddy.

Two sisters (Jane Anne Johnstone and Kathy McHaley) ask a drunken biker (Warren Oates) to help them avenge the death of their father, in this action drama A local sheriff killed their moonshining father and evicted the sisters from their family farm. In retaliation, they virtually destroy a small Southern town. Duane Eddy, Dorsey Burnette and the Mike Curb Congregation perform the songs in this routine revenge tale.

Flim-Flam Man, The (1967), TCF. Dir. Irvin Kershner; Sc. William Rose; Cast includes: George C. Scott, Sue Lyon, Michael Sarrazin, Harry Morgan, Jack Albertson.

An aging Southern con artist, portrayed by George C. Scott, travels around the South. He bilks a variety of bad guys in this engaging comedy drama based on Guy Owen's novel *The Ballad of the Flim-Flam Man.* Michael Sarrazin, his young army deserter-sidekick and assistant, proves too honest for Scott's liking. When the young partner meets the attractive Sue Lyon, Sarrazin's life takes a drastic turn. She convinces him to abandon his carefree wandering and settle down.

Several comic incidents show Scott, the veteran flim-flam man, outwitting a local sheriff (Harry Morgan) and swindling a host of gullible victims, all of whom are criminals themselves. The film treats the South and its inhabitants sympathetically, a sharp contrast to Southern gothic dramas about dysfunctional families and psychologically disturbed characters.

Hallelujah (1929), MGM. Dir. King Vidor; Sc. Wanda Tuchock; Cast includes: Daniel L. Haynes, Nina Mae McKinney, William Fountaine, Harry Gray, Victoria Spivey.

With this production, Director King Vidor tried to blend comedy, romance and tragedy into one of the earliest all-black talking features. He realistically depicted the cotton fields of the South where hardworking and singing black sharecroppers scratched out a meager living. Nina Mae McKinney portrays a vivacious young black woman, a member of the black underworld. She uses her personality, sex and dancing to charm her men. Daniel L. Haynes, as the big, brawny and rough male lead, loves his women. He falls for McKinney, who is attracted to him, and they fall in love. But lurking in the shadows is her former beau, Hot Shot, played by William Fountaine. Hot Shot returns and takes McKinney away in a broken-down buggy, which turns over and kills the young woman. Haynes pursues Fountaine into the Tennessee swamps, where he strangles his girlfriend's murderer. The film contains scenes of revival meetings, river baptisms and black choruses.

Ruth Morris, a contemporary critic, was evidently overwhelmed by Vidor's production. She wrote in *Variety* on August 28, 1929 that the drama "shows the itinerant preacher of the South and his hysterical parishioners as no picture and few books have done. It mixes the childish superstition and simple grandeur of the colored race. It's a human document." Simultaneously, another critic commented that the film "has tended to glorify the primitive Negro life of the South and the emerging race consciousness and intellectual vigor of the colored people." Although the comments were complementary, they give us more insight into the prejudices of the reviewers than into the quality of the film.

*

Heart of the Blue Ridge, The (1915), World. Dir. James Young; Cast includes: Clara Kimball Young, Chester Barnett, Robert Cummings, Edwin L. Hollywood.

An illiterate mountain girl (Clara Kimball Young) who lives with her grandfather objects to marrying a moonshiner (Robert Cummings). The rural drama is set in the Blue Ridge Mountains and is based on the novel by Waldron Baily. Rather than marrying the moonshiner, Kimball has chosen a local farmer (Chester Barnett) for her husband. Several complications and conflicts between the two rivals ensue. Cummings abducts Young and threatens to kill her family unless she marries him. Barnett finds Cummings in a cave with his captive and, in a struggle between the two men, Cummings falls off a cliff to his death. The lovers are then reunited.

*

Several comedies and dramas either referred to or were set in these picturesque mountains. Young's *The Heart of the Blue Ridge* (1915) is just one of many. James Horne's *Way Out West* (1937) is a Western satire, featuring Stan Laurel and Oliver Hardy, as two drifters in search of gold. They perform a soft-shoe shuffle in front of a Western saloon and, in one scene, sing "In the Blue Ridge Mountains of Virginia." In Clyde Ware's drama *No Drums, No Bugles* (1971), West Virginia farmer Martin Sheen, because of his opposition to the war, retreats to a remote cave somewhere in the Blue Ridge Mountains.

*

The Blue Ridge Mountains range from northern Georgia across western North Carolina and western Virginia into West Virginia. Their northern terminus is generally described as a point near Harpers Ferry in West Virginia, although some authorities include in the Blue Ridge the ranges that extend north from Harpers Ferry into Maryland and Pennsylvania. The Blue Ridge Parkway, about 3000 feet above sea level, follows the Blue Ridge Mountains through Virginia and North Carolina for more than 450 miles.

*

Hurry Sundown (1967), Par. Dir. Otto Preminger; Sc. Horton Foote, T. C. Ryan; Cast includes: Michael Caine, Jane Fonda, John Phillip Law, Diahann Caroll, Faye Dunaway.

Ruthless Southerner Michael Caine is determined to buy out his cousin's two adjoining farms. He resorts to all sorts of schemes to achieve his goal in this drama filled with social and racial tension. Caine is married to a wealthy Southern belle and, unknown to her, he sells her property to a Northern cannery. He tries to buy his cousin's property but, when this fails, he attempts to grab the land illegally. As a last resort, he encourages a race-hating mob to dynamite a dam, thereby flooding the farms, one of which belongs to his wife's old and sickly African-American nurse.

I Walk the Line (1970), Col. Dir. John Frankenheimer; Sc. A.Sargent; Cast includes: Gregory Peck, Tuesday Weld, Estelle Parsons, Ralph Meeker.

Rural Tennessee Sheriff Gregory Peck falls in love with Tuesday Weld, the backwoods daughter of a local moonshiner. John Frankenheimer's drama is set in The Cumberland Mountains. The people are poor but independent. Peck is forced to decide between love and duty – a choice that ends in tragedy. Johnny Cash sings four country songs to help enliven the film.

Interloper, The (1918), World. Dir. Oscar Apfel; Sc. Wallace Clifton; Cast includes: Kitty Gordon, Irving Cummings, Warren Cook, Isabelle Derwin.

A Southern woman inherits an estate but finds that she has no cash. She decides to work the land herself in this standard romantic drama. Meanwhile, a railroad magnate wants her property for a right of way and sends his son to negotiate. Instead, the son falls in love with the owner and they marry. The wife soon learns that her new husband is a widower but he is still in love with the memory of his first wife. Wife number two discovers that wife number one had been unfaithful but that she had destroyed all the evidence of her adultery. Thus her husband has no definite proof of her infidelity and it is precisely this uncertainty that entices her husband to keep her memory alive.

Key Largo (1948), WB. Dir. John Huston; Sc. Richard Brooks, John Huston; Cast includes: Humphrey Bogart, Edward G. Robinson, Claire Trevor, Lionel Barrymore.

Gang leader Edward G. Robinson, as Rocco, and his hoodlums take over a Florida resort owned by Lionel Barrymore and his granddaughter, Lauren Bacall. During a hurricane, they threaten and terrorize the owners and guests, including World War II veteran Humphrey Bogart. When Bogart notices how fearful the gangster is of the storm, he works on his nerves and taunts the hoodlum: "You don't like it, do you, Rocco, the storm? Show it your gun, why don't you? If it doesn't stop, shoot it."

*

Other films took advantage of the scenery and were shot off the Florida mainland – especially in the Florida Keys. The Keys are a chain of chiefly limestone and coral islands, islets, and reefs, in southern Florida. The larger islands are Key West, Key Largo, Sugarloaf Key and Boca Chica Key. For administrative purposes, both Dade and Monroe counties supervise the Keys. They were devastated in a 1935 hurricane. Several islands are popular vacation resorts, and fishing and tourism are the leading industries. A causeway extends from the mainland to Key West, the United States' southernmost city.

*

Long, Hot Summer, The (1958), TCF. Dir. Martin Ritt; Sc. Irving Ravetch, Harriet Frank Jr.; Cast includes: Paul Newman, Joanne Woodward, Anthony Franciosa, Orson Welles, Lee Remick.

Mississippi redneck Paul Newman specializes in burning down the property of his enemies. This sex-driven, violent drama of the South is based on several stories by William Faulkner. Newman wanders into the town controlled by Orson Welles, a domineering father who has bullied the citizens of the town and has transformed his daughter (Joanne Woodward) into a young old maid. Welles senses Newman as a rival and they both maneuver for advantage. Welles' broken and pitiful son (Anthony Franciosa) finally revolts against his father and tries to kill him. Some townspeople try to lynch Newman, and Welles is duped into marrying his mistress, Angela Lansbury. "I admire his manners and I admire the speeches he makes and I admire the big house he lives in," Newman earlier warns her. "But if you're saving it all for him, honey, you've got your account in the wrong bank." At times, the plot suggests the clash between the emerging new moneyed class and the former aristocracy.

Louisiana (1947), Mon. Dir. Phil Karlson; Sc. Jack De Witt; Cast includes: Jimmie Davis, Margaret Lindsay, John Gallaudet, Freddie Stewart, Dottye Brown, Russell Hicks.

Phil Karlson's biographical drama tells the true-life story of Jimmie Davis, a sharecropper's son who grew up to become the governor of Louisiana. The familiar rags-to-riches tale describes how Davis struggles to receive a good education and succeed. During his lifetime, Davis had numerous careers. He was a singing governor, a professor at a women's college and a police commissioner who knew how to survive under all conditions. Davis sings several songs in the film, including "You Are My Sunshine."

Mardi Gras (1958), TCF. Dir. Edmund Goulding; Sc. Winston Miller, Hal Kanter; Cast includes: Pat Boone, Christine Carere, Tommy Sands, Sheree North.

In this musical, Pat Boone is a cadet in a New Orleans military school who wins a date with Christine Carere, the queen of Mardi Gras. Boone is ignorant of Carere's film star status and they fall in love. But when the studio seizes the moment and launches a public relations blitz around the new romance, Boone learns her true identity and feels betrayed and exploited. The lovers soon resolve their differences in this pleasant blend of romance, comedy and music.

*

Hollywood has often used a Mardi Gras backdrop for various films. Luther Reed's musical comedy *Dixiana* (1930) includes a festive and lively finale set during Mardi Gras in New Orleans and filmed in color – rare for that period. It features the personable Bill Robinson doing an entertaining dance specialty. Bert Wheeler and Robert Woolsey, a popular contemporary comedy team, provide the comic relief.

At times, Mardi Gras provides a vehicle for wish fulfillment. For example, Betty Field, who is hard and embittered because of her ugly features, is given a beautiful face mask on Mardi Gras night, in the first of Julien Duvivier's three-part fantasy drama *Flesh and Fantasy* (1943). After she is told that beauty is only within oneself and that she will be loved for that and not her external features, she meets Robert Cummings, who falls in love with her. Hollywood occasionally used the festive activities of Mardi Gras as a contrast for incidents in its sordid crime films.

*

In religious terms, Mardi Gras is a pre-Lenten festival celebrated in Roman Catholic countries and communities. Celebrated by the French as the last of the three days of Shrovetide, it is a time of preparation immediately before Ash Wednesday and the start of the fast of Lent. It is, therefore, the last opportunity for merrymaking and hearty eating and drinking. In practice, Mardi Gras is often celebrated for a full week before Lent – with spectacular parades featuring floats, pageants, elaborate costumes, masked balls and dancing in the streets. Many different groups sponsor their own floats and themes during the parade and they all have their own crazy antics. The most famous modern Mardi Gras festivities are those held in New Orleans, La.; Rio de Janeiro, Brazil; Nice, France; and Cologne, Germany.

*

Matewan (1987), Cinecom. Dir. John Sayles; Sc. John Sayles; Cast includes: James Earl Jones, Chris Cooper, Will Oldham, Mary McDonnell, Jace Alexander, Ken Jenkins.

John Sayles's tense labor-management drama traces a conflict between coal miners and a union-busting coal company in West Virginia. Chris Cooper portrays a union organizer and former member of the Industrial Workers of the World (I.W.W., also known as "wobblies"). He arrives in the town of Matewan, a "company town" and is immediately confronted with several serious problems. He tries to bring together a diverse group of strikers – some of whom are becoming increasingly desperate. Some strikers resent the new black and Italian immigrant workers. Cooper's landlady (Mary McDonnell) has a 15-year-old son (Will Oldham) who is studying to be a preacher. James Earl Jones plays a strong pro-union worker who is unaware that he is working as a scab. Meanwhile, the coal company has eyes and ears everywhere and forces the miners out of their homes and into a tent city in the mountains. The film is based on events that preceded the 1920 West Virginia Mine War.

*

Tensions between miners and mine operators have a long and bitter history. The Coal Creek Rebellion of the 1880s was typical of this type of labor-management conflict. In the 1880s, Southern miners in Tennessee tried to join the Knights of Labor, a popular all-inclusive union of the period, and they were fired. The mine owners leased thousands of convicts from the State of Tennessee at $60 each. The owners were thus able to operate the mines with the convicts and they were able to eliminate their workers' jobs altogether. The governor rejected all petitions by the workers and agreed with the Tennessee Coal and Iron Corporation, a Northern-owned giant company. On one occasion, a group of desperate miners in one town marched to the prison gate on July 4, 1891 and, at gunpoint, freed the arrested strikers and burned the stockade.

In retaliation, the state constructed a new stockade, which was guarded by a detachment of militia. The miners once again organized and set fire to several other stockades and overpowered the militia in a number of battles. Finally, the miners hid their arrested union brothers in their homes and provided them with clothing. The prisoners escaped to adjoining states and thus avoided being arrested and jailed by Tennessee police.

The state authorities eventually starved the remaining miners into submission and defeated them in actual gun battles. Union leaders were arrested and sent to prison. But, eventually, the miners succeeded. When the mine operators began using convict labor, the miners gained public support and the owners themselves determined that the use of convict labor wasn't cost-effective. After the next election, the state legislature eliminated the use of convict labor for private corporations and released the union leaders as well.

*

Moonrunners (1974), UA. Dir. Gy Waldron; Sc. Gy Waldron; Cast includes: James Mitchum, Kiel Martin, Arthur Hunnicutt, George Ellis, Chris Forbes.

Hillbilly moonshiners Arthur Hunnicutt and his two nephews, James Mitchum and Kiel Martin, are pursued in their beat-up cars by revenue officers and the local sheriff. In this routine action drama, Chris Forbes portrays a young runaway woman who teams up with Mitchum for a shaky romance. Just to keep things rolling along, a New York syndicate tries to take control of the local moonshiners' business. The country-and-western ballads of Waylon Jennings serve as a bridge between sequences.

*

Waylon Jennings (1937-) was born in Littlefield, Texas, and loved to listen to his childhood heroes Gene Autry and Jimmie Davis. He was so sure that he could make it in the music industry that he quit high school to pursue his dreams. He talked his way into a job as a disc jockey at station KLLL in Lubbock, Texas. It was there, during one of these shows, that Jennings met Buddy Holly. Holly liked the way Waylon played and took him on board his band as a bass player. In 1968, RCA produced two of his hit songs, "Just to Satisfy You" and "Walk the Line." Some of his later songs, including "Amanda" and "Rainy Day Woman," were bolstered by his reputation as a rebel. Jennings' songs were performed on several television shows, and he appeared in a number of films, including *Nashville Rebel* (1966), *Sesame Street Presents Follow That Bird* (1985), *Chet Atkins and Friends: Music From the Heart* (1987) and *Maverick* (1994).

Moonshine County Express (1977), New World. Dir. Gus Trikonis; Sc. Hubert Smith, Daniel Ansley; Cast includes: John Saxon, Susan Howard, William Conrad, Morgan Woodward.

Susan Howard, as the oldest of three daughters, decides to take over their murdered father's bootlegging operation in this slim action drama set in hillbilly country. William Conrad, the corrupt boss of moonshining operations in the area, is trying to control the entire business. John Saxon, a fast driver behind the wheel, works for Conrad and is romantically interested in Howard, who resists the boss' efforts to dominate everyone.

Moonshine War, The (1970), MGM. Dir. Robert Quine; Sc. Elmore Leonard; Cast includes: Richard Widmark, Patrick McGoohan, Alan Alda, Melodie Johnson.

When revenue officer Patrick McGoohan learns that Alan Alda has barrels of moonshine hidden on his farm, he hires gangster pal Richard Widmark to get the contraband. This action drama about the Prohibition era is based on the novel by Elmore Leonard. Widmark's excessive use of violence and murder compels McGoohan to join Alda. Alda reveals the hiding place to Widmark and his cohorts, then booby-traps the cache and kills them all. The film benefits from its creative sets and its use of country music.

New Moon (1940), MGM. Dir. Robert Z. Leonard; Sc. Jacques Deval, Robert Arthur; Cast includes: Jeanette MacDonald, Nelson Eddie, Mary Boland, Patric Knowles, George Zucco.

This musical comedy somehow manages to include the plight of indentured servants. Their struggle to survive takes on a light note of escapism and fantasy. Plantation owner Jeanette MacDonald hires indentured servant Nelson Eddie who was once sold into servitude. This operetta is based on the stage production by Oscar Hammerstein III and is set in late eighteenth century Louisiana. After a romance develops, MacDonald discovers that Eddie is really is a French duke. A natural revolutionary leader, Eddie leads his fellow servants in revolt. They sail off and capture a pursuing ship with MacDonald and a shipment of brides aboard. An unexpected shipwreck lands them all on an island where they set up their own community.

Norma Rae (1979), TCF. Dir. Martin Ritt; Sc. Irving Ravetch, Harriet Frank Jr.; Cast includes: Sally Field, Beau Bridges, Ron Leibman, Pat Hingle, Barbara Baxley.

Poor Southern textile factory worker Norma Rae (Sally Field) falls in love with a New York union organizer (Ron Leibman) in this drama about labor-management conflicts. According to the film, textile workers in some of these plants eventually go deaf from the din of the machines. Others suffer consumption or "brown lung" disease. Leibman, a union organizer, is motivated to journey to the South in order to help organize the non-union plant. He picks Norma Rae, a divorced worker with two children, as his shop steward. Their platonic relationship soon grows into a subdued love story. Eventually, however, Norma Rae returns to her blue-collar husband, fellow worker Beau Bridges.

Ruthless (1948), EL. Dir. Edgar G. Ulmer; Sc. S. K. Lauren, Gordon Kahn; Cast includes: Zachary Scott, Sidney Greenstreet, Diana Lynn, Louis Hayward, Martha Vickers.

This nasty drama, based on the novel *Prelude to Night* by Dayton Stoddart, concentrates on ambitious Southerner Zachary Scott. He rises from poverty to a position of wealth and prestige. The use of flashbacks shows how he betrayed the people who trusted him while he figuratively climbed over their bodies. Diane Lynn, a young woman who was in love with him – until he cruelly dropped her, was one of his early victims. Louis Hayward, his former partner, received similar treatment and was forced to end his partnership with Scott. At the present time, Scott tangles with the strong and wealthy as he manipulates stock prices in order to topple Sydney Greenstreet, a corrupt tycoon, from his seat of power. Director Ulmer gained fame for another film, his low-budget film noir drama *Detour* (1944) that became a cult classic.

Shepherd of the Hills, The (1941), Par. Dir. Henry Hathaway; Sc. Grover Jones, Stuart Anthony; Cast includes: John Wayne, Betty Field, Harry Carey, Beulah Bondi, James Barton.

Trouble starts when outsiders try to steal the land of the Ozark mountain people in Henry Hathaway's drama. The film is based on the novel by Harold Bell Wright. Hillbillies manufacture their own moonshine and even drink it. In the meanwhile, revenue officers try to locate their stills. Outsider Harry Carey arrives and wants to buy some land. Since the death of mountaineer John Wayne's mother, the particular piece of land Carey wants seems cursed. Wayne has sworn to kill his father who has deserted the family and has disappeared. Carey eventually discloses he is the missing father and has been in prison for several years. Father and son join in a reunion and Wayne announces he will marry Betty Field, an attractive neighbor who loves Wayne and has befriended Carey.

Sounder (1972), TCF. Dir. Martin Ritt; Sc. Lonnie Elder 3rd; Cast includes: Cicely Tyson, Paul Winfield, Kevin Hooks, Carmen Mathews, Taj Mahal.

Martin Ritt's heartwarming drama, based on the novel by William H. Armstrong, tells the story of a struggling black family of sharecroppers during the Depression. Paul Winfield and Cicely Tyson portray the poor but devoted parents. When Winfield is sentenced to one year of hard labor for stealing some food to feed his impoverished family, his oldest son (Kevin Hooks) assumes the challenge of providing for the family. The title is the name of the family dog.

The sequel, *Part 2, Sounder* (1976), directed by William A. Graham, uses the same venue as Martin Ritt's 1972 film. Harold Sylvester and Ebony Wright play the black sharecroppers in Depression-era Louisiana. They still face the same conditions and struggle against poverty and prejudice. But Anzanette Chase, an activist teacher, provides some glimmer of hope. White landowners shut down her school when they begin to believe the "coloreds" are getting too "uppity." The sharecroppers decide to join together to build their own school in the hope that their children will have a better future.

Southerner, The (1945), UA. Dir. Jean Renoir; Sc. Jean Renoir, Hugo Butler; Cast includes: Zachary Scott, Betty Field, Beulah Bondi, J. Carrol Naish, Norman Lloyd.

In Jean Renoir's domestic drama, Zachary Scott portrays Sam Tucker, a sharecropper. He decides to work his own land, in this drama about the struggle of a family to start a Southern farm. They arrive at a dilapidated shanty on a plot of undeveloped land and, although at first discouraged, they decide to stay. Grandma Beulah Bondi complains constantly. Tucker doesn't have any water, so he tries to get some from his embittered neighbor, J. Carrol Naish, who reluctantly lets him use his well. However, Naish makes Tucker replace the worn-out rope. The family endures poverty, sickness, storms and ultimately the destruction of its cotton crop. Tucker now tries to get a factory job in town, but is persuaded to stay on the farm when his family pitches in and help him run the farm.

White Bondage (1937), WB. Dir. Nick Grinde; Sc. Anthony Coldeway; Cast includes: Jean Muir, Gordon Oliver, Howard Phillips, Joseph King.

Newspaper reporter Gordon Oliver sets out to prove that unscrupulous merchants are using short-weight scales in order to cheat their sharecroppers in this minor social drama. For his efforts, Oliver almost gets lynched but is saved at the last minute by Jean Muir, a young local woman farmer. The film, shot chiefly outdoors, uses several authentic-looking sets that add a note of realism to the production. A lot of the dialogue is very bitter. "We are all sharecroppers, ain't we?" one irate farmer asks at a secret meeting with his colleagues. "And we been cheated, too, ain't we? Boys, we have been workin' and cheated . . . for years. My pappy died workin' the cotton land. We didn't have no shoes to bury him in." In another scene, an impoverished sharecropper quotes from the *Bible*: "What mean ye that ye crush my people and grind the faces of the poor?"

Within Our Gates (1920), Micheaux Co. Dir. Oscar Micheaux; Sc. Oscar Micheaux; Cast includes: Evelyn Preer, Flo Clements, James D. Ruffin, Jack Chenault, William Smith, Charles D. Lucas.

When sharecropper Jasper Landry and his educated daughter Sylvia prepare a bill for the plantation owner, Eph plots against them. Oscar Micheaux's drama is an early all-black silent film. Eph tells the owner that Landry's bill is bogus. Landry comes face to face with the landowner, who is shot and killed. Landry stands over the body with a smoking gun and he is almost lynched.

16

The New Politics

In the antebellum period, the Democratic Party championed states' rights and its strength lay chiefly in the South. Following the war, white voters flocked to the Democrats in order to register their opposition to the Reconstruction policies of the Republicans. The Democratic Party in the South was perceived as "the white man's party" while the Republicans were viewed as "the black man's party."

The Republicans generally supported the newer manufacturing interests, railroad builders, speculators and financiers of the country. The tariff continued to be a major point of contention between the two major parties and between the North and the South. Both parties maintained their antebellum positions, with the Republicans championing high tariffs and the Democrats opposed the tariffs altogether.

Although the issue of states' rights had been tentatively solved by the Civil War, the issue, like the tariff question, simply would not disappear.

A number of minor parties emerged during the postwar period. In the long years of agricultural depression following the war, low prices for agricultural products severely affected farmers in the West and South. They organized the first farmers' associations – the Grangers and the Populists. These movements soon turned political and resulted in the formation of several farm and labor parties such as the Farmers' Alliances, the Greenback Party the Greenback-Labor Party and the Peoples' Party.

On the industrial side, factory workers were exploited by the new capitalists and were compelled to accept low pay and terrible working conditions. These factory workers organized several other independent parties, one of which was the Socialist Labor party and it opposed both the Democratic and Republican Parties.

The Great Depression of the 1930s brought about complex changes in political alignments. The Democratic Party, led by President Franklin D. Roosevelt, became the sponsor of the most far-reaching social-reform legislation in the history of the U.S. Some Republicans supported Roosevelt, but most opposed his policies. Roosevelt appropriated so many of the positions of some of these minor parties – such as the American Labor Party and the Liberal Party in New York State – that they became mere appendages of the Democratic Party. When Roosevelt died in 1945, Vice-President Harry S. Truman succeeded him. Democratic hegemony appeared to unravel, however, when the anti-cold war Progressives under Henry A. Wallace and the anti-civil rights Dixiecrats under Strom Thurmond ran their own Presidential tickets respectively in the 1948 campaign. Truman thus faced the Republican Thomas E. Dewey as well as two Democratic dissidents, but nevertheless went on to win the election.

John F. Kennedy, in 1960, and Lyndon B. Johnson, in 1964, were once again able to reassemble the Northern and Southern wings of the Democratic Party and capture the White House. In a short time, however, white Southerners began to oppose the civil rights programs of both presidents and the coalition began to untangle. Now, white Southerners reversed their earlier perceptions of the Democratic and Republican parties. The Democrats were now perceived as "the black man's party" while the Republicans were viewed as "the white man's party." As a result, Richard Nixon was able to win the presidency in 1972. The Democrats responded with a "Southern strategy" by nominating Jimmy Carter, the former governor of Georgia, as a presidential candidate in 1976. Carter defeated Republican President Gerald R. Ford in that year, but failed to beat Ronald Reagan in 1980. Under Reagan, conservative Republicans were firmly in control of their party in the 1980s, and the Republicans held a majority in the U.S. Senate from 1981 through 1986, when the Democrats regained control. After Carter's defeat and the apparent breakup of the New Deal coalition, the Democrats did not have the strong leadership in the 1980s necessary to regain the presidency until Bill Clinton arrived in 1992. Although Democrat Bill Clinton defeated President George Bush in the 1990s, both parties seemed weakened, as voters became disillusioned with politicians and appeared to be influenced more by a candidate's message and his positions on the issues rather than by party affiliation.

*

Louisiana served as a popular Hollywood backdrop for many feature films. Young jockey Edward Quillan gets involved with some unscrupulous people in Irving Pichel's turn-of-the-century drama *Gentleman From Louisiana* (1936) and he has to prove his innocence. Several years later, Bernard Vorhaus directed *Lady From Louisiana* (1941). Ona Munson portrays a lottery owner's daughter who falls in love with a crusading lawyer (John Wayne) who is out to smash her father's racket. Elia Kazan's drama *Panic in the Streets* (1950) was one of the earliest films to use Louisiana locations effectively. Gangster Jack Palance carries the bubonic plague in New Orleans and Richard Widmark, a doctor, desperately hunts him down. During the 1980s and early 1990s, Louisiana began to be a major producer of oil, natural gas, and petrochemicals. Anthony Mann's action adventure *Thunder Bay* (1953) anticipates the importance of oil to the state. The film, with its impressive wide-screen camerawork, sketches oil driller James Stewart's battle against shrimp fishermen in Louisiana Bay. Joanne Dru provides the romantic interest. A Louisiana swamp woman in Ferd Sebastian's violent action drama *Gator Bait* (1976) is forced to deal with threats against herself and her family. She succeeds in a most original – and gruesome – way. In Peter Masterson's harsh drama *Convicts* (1991), a young boy witnesses the terrible working conditions in the Louisiana cornfields of the early 1900s. Robert Duvall portrays the greedy plantation owner who uses convict labor.

*

All the King's Men (1949), Col. Dir. Robert Rossen; Sc. Robert Rossen; Cast includes: Broderick Crawford, Joanne Dru, John Ireland, John Derek, Mercedes McCambridge, Sheppard Strudwick.

Newspaper reporter John Ireland witnesses the rise and fall of a powerful Southern politician. Robert Rossen's award-winning drama is based on the Pulitzer Prize-winning novel by Robert Penn Warren. The book was allegedly inspired by the life of Huey Long, the former governor of Louisiana. Broderick Crawford portrays Willie Stark, the stand-in for Long. After starting off as an idealistic and naïve young political candidate, Stark learns to play hardball. In the movie, Stark is a crafty, brutal and hypocritical aspiring politician who rises from the backwoods of a Southern state to the position of governor. When Ireland asks his editor what's so special about Stark, his superior replies, "They say he's an honest man." Newsman Ireland follows Stark's political career from the beginning and falls for his charm and charisma. When his editor is instructed to quash further stories about Stark, Ireland quits and is hired by Stark. Ireland introduces Stark to influential members of society but these people remain skeptical of Stark.

The politician's cynical secretary-mistress, Mercedes McCambridge, is at first spellbound by Stark, but eventually grows disillusioned with the politician, as does Ireland. "There's something on everybody," Stark maintains. "Man is conceived in sin and born in corruption." He is finally slain on the steps of the state capitol at the height of his triumph by Sheppard Strudwick, a sensitive doctor, who is then gunned down by Stark's bodyguard. Stark had seduced Strudnick's sister and the gunman believed that the governor was a corrupting and dangerous force who had to be stopped. One of the most scathing indictments of political demagogues, the film won Academy Awards for best picture, best actor (Crawford) and best supporting actress (McCambridge).

Bayou (1957), UA. Dir. Harold Daniels; Sc. Edward I. Fessler; Cast includes: Peter Graves, Lita Milan, Douglas Fowley, Tim Carey, Jonathan Haze.

Architect Peter Graves arrives in New Orleans and, although he lacks confidence in his work, he nevertheless tries to convince a New Orleans politician to approve plans for a new structure. The drama is a weak depiction of Tennessee Williams' characters. Graves meets Lita Milan, Douglas Fowley's passionate daughter and falls in love with this Cajun queen. He subsequently decides to live in New Orleans, but runs into trouble with Tim Carey, who also wants Milan. Graves beats Carey in a fight.

Big Easy, The (1987), Col. Dir. Jim McBride; Sc. Daniel Petrie, Jack Baran, Gordon Greisman, Jim McBride; Cast includes: Dennis Quaid, Ellen Barkin, Ned Beatty, John Goodman, Ebbe Roe Smith.

Dennis Quaid portrays a hip homicide detective who is suspected of corruption by an uptight female assistant district attorney, Ellen Barkin. This drama is set in New Orleans and is filled with plenty of Cajun music. The two leads soon become entangled in a steamy romance while they investigate the murder of a leading organized crime figure. As their romance develops, Quaid tries to get Barkin to adopt a more laid-back attitude. "Just relax, darlin'," he suggests. "This is the Big Easy. Folks have a certain way o' doin' things down here."

Charles Ludlam portrays a well-dressed gentleman lawyer of the Old Dixie school. His gimmick is to roll his eyes and, when he appears, he dominates the screen. As a defense attorney, he is flawless in his Panama hat and summer suit. He talks a mile a minute in a high-pitched Cajun shriek. Ned Beatty plays another smooth Southerner – a police captain who really wants to go straight but can't.

Blaze (1989), BV. Dir. Ron Shelton; Sc. Ron Shelton; Cast includes: Paul Newman, Lolita Davidovich, Jerry Hardin, Gailard Sartain, Jeffrey DeMunn, Carey Garland Bunting.

Paul Newman portrays Earl Long, the flamboyant governor of Louisiana in the 1950s, who fell in love with stripper Blaze Starr. This entertaining biographical drama is based on Starr's autobiography. The film concentrates on Long, the three-time governor of Louisiana, and his relationship with the young red-headed stripper, played by Lolita Davidovich. This is Davidovich's first lead role, and it is bawdy and satirical. Blaze film provides a ribald view of Southern politics, which differs from *All the King's Men*, a more solemn 1949 drama in which Earl's older brother Huey is portrayed as a fascist demagogue. In some scenes Long uses his smarts to battle white supremacists. Near the end of the work Long asks Starr, "Would you still love me if I wasn't the fine governor of the great state of Louisiana?" And she replies, "Would you still love 'me' if I had little tits and worked in a fish house?" In one short scene, Newman kisses the real Blaze Starr – who appears as the stripper Lily – on the shoulder.

*

Several Long family members were movers and shakers in Louisiana politics. Huey Pierce Long (1893-1935), the colorful, grandiose "Kingfish," was governor of the state and then U.S. senator until he was assassinated. His wife, Rose McConnell Long (1892-1970), completed his senate term (1936-1937). His brother, George Shannon Long (1883-1958), served as a member of the U.S. House of Representatives (1953-1958) and another brother, Earl Kemp Long (1895-1960), was three times governor of Louisiana (1939-1940, 1948-1952, and 1956-1960). His son, Russell Billiu Long (1918-), was a U.S. senator (1948-1986).

*

Brubaker (1980), TCF. Dir. Stuart Rosenberg; Sc. W. D. Richter; Cast includes: Robert Redford, Yaphet Kotto, Jane Alexander, Murray Hamilton, David Keith, Morgan Freeman.

In Stuart Rosenberg's prison drama, Robert Redford plays a prisoner in a Southern jail. He witnesses lots of brutalities all over the prison. Suddenly, everyone learns that Redford is not a convict at all. He is really the new warden who wants to experience jail conditions first-hand in order to bring about reform. The film did not do well at the box-office; perhaps it came twenty or more years too late in the cycle of prison dramas.

Bulworth (1998), TCF. Dir. Warren Beatty; Sc. Warren Beatty; Cast includes: Warren Beatty, Oliver Platt.

In Warren Beatty's comedy drama, Senator J. Billington Bulworth learns that he is soon going to die and decides to be brutally candid with his audiences. Warren Beatty plays Bullworth, the political leader who decides to come clean. He has grown sick of Senate and of his own hypocrisy. He tells his listeners that money has corrupted the political system. At one point, he contracts a top gangster to kill him, but when he changes his mind, Beatty has problems canceling the contract. Oliver Platt, Beatty's aide, believes in him and continually tries to cover for his constantly disappearing boss. However, he warns Beatty that he often goes too far. At one public appearance, Beatty's wealthiest California contributors abandon him during one of his politically incorrect rants.

Damn Citizen (1958), U. Dir. Robert Gordon; Sc. Stirling Silliphant; Cast includes: Keith Andes, Maggie Hayes, Gene Evans, Lynn Bari, Geoffrey Stone, Edward C. Platt.

In Robert Gordon's drama, the governor of a Southern state invites World War II veteran Keith Andes to take over the state police. This episodic cops-and-robbers drama is based on the true exploits of World War II hero Colonel Francis C. Grevemberg. Shot in semi-documentary style, the film describes Louisiana as plagued by crime and corruption for decades. Although confronted with a tough assignment and many obstacles, Superintendent of State Police Andes meets with considerable success. He and his small force of crime fighters smash the major rackets, controlled chiefly by vice lord Edward C. Platt, and round up Platt's lieutenants.

Desire in the Dust (1960), TCF. Dir. William F. Claxton; Sc. Charles Lang; Cast includes: Raymond Burr, Martha Hyer, Joan Bennett, Ken Scott, Brett Halsey.

This seedy drama is based on the novel by Harry Whittington.Ken Scott. A simple farmer, Ken Scott, returns to his hometown after serving six years in a chain gang for a crime he didn't commit. Scott immediately visits the home of politician Raymond Burr. Scott had an affair with Burr's daughter, Martha Hyer, and when she accidentally killed her son in an automobile crash, Scott took the blame for the accident. Burr persuaded Scott to assume the responsibility and promised to take care of him upon his release from prison.

Burr's wife (Joan Bennett) witnessed the accident and had a nervous breakdown. Although Burr had also promised that Hyer would be waiting for him, she marries a local doctor. When Scott tries to claim his debt, Burr reneges on all his promises. Scott then exposes the entire family plot and destroys Burr's political career. Burr and his daughter are left alone and the film hints at incest. All in all, *Desire in the Dust* is pretentious but is still an impressive production.

In offering this film, Hollywood studios hoped to emulate the success of such steamy Southern dramas as *The Long Hot Summer* (1958) and *The Sound and the Fury* (1959). They decided to turn out a mixture of sex, deception, murder and sleaze – all within a Southern context.

Flamingo Road (1949), WB. Dir. Michael Curtiz; Sc. Robert Wilder; Cast includes: Joan Crawford, Zachary Scott, David Brian, Sydney Greenstreet, Gladys George.

Michael Curtiz's stinging drama is based on a play by Robert and Sally Wilder. Joan Crawford portrays a carnival dancer who rises in the social circles of a Southern town controlled by a corrupt political boss. Lane Bellamy (Crawford) is stranded in the town ruled by Titus Semple (Sydney Greenstreet) and becomes romantically involved with Fielding Carlyle, the local sheriff. Carlyle is just Greenstreet's weak puppet. For some strange reason, Greenstreet feels threatened by Crawford and organizes a campaign to drive her out of town. Meanwhile, he convinces the sheriff, whom he is grooming for the governor's seat, to marry a local socialite. Crawford is unable to find work and is arrested on a bogus morals charge. After her release, she finds a job as hostess at a nearby roadhouse, where she meets David Brian, who is the state's chief political boss. They marry and move to the exclusive Flamingo Road. The sheriff, who has degenerated since his marriage, commits suicide, and the corrupt Semple is accidentally killed in a gunfight. Bellamy and her husband begin their new life together in relative peace and quiet.

Forrest Gump (1994), Par. Dir. Robert Zemeckis; Sc. Eric Roth; Cast includes: Sally Field, Tom Hanks, Gary Sinise, Mykelti Williamson, Robin Wright.

Tom Hanks portrays the title character, a slow-witted young man raised by his mother in Alabama. This very popular comedy drama is based on the novel by Winston Groom. Gump's life story, set in the 1950s through the 1970s, unfolds at a leisurely pace. Heavily dependent on the director's special effects, the film shows Gump with at least two presidents and other notable personalities as he blunders through life from one good fortune to another.

The opening scene shows Gump joining a young woman on a bench, as she waits for a bus. He offers her a chocolate, remarking, "My mother used to say life was like a box of chocolates because you never know what you're gonna get."

Because of his ability to run fast, he gets a college scholarship and is awarded "All American" for his achievement in football. During the Vietnam War he befriends a fellow soldier who is killed in battle, goes on to save the lives of several buddies and becomes an immediate war hero. "Have you found God yet?" a lieutenant asks him. "I didn't know I was supposed to be looking for him," Gump innocently replies. Later, members of the antiwar movement, whom he meets through Robin Wright, his childhood sweetheart, use him to address a large crowd of protesters at the Washington Monument.

One particularly interesting scene shows him with Governor George Wallace, who is blocking the entrance of a state university in an attempt to prevent black students from entering the school.

He finally settles down with his erratic and wandering girlfriend, who introduces him to his son, the result of his one earlier affair with her.

It's a Joke, Son! (1947), Eagle-Lion. Dir. Ben Stoloff; Sc. Robert Kent, Paul Gerard Smith; Cast include: Kenny Delmar, Una Merkel, June Lockhart, Kenneth Farrell, Douglas Dumbrille.

Ben Stoloff's mediocre political comedy features Kenny Delmar, who played Senator Clagborn, the lead character on Fred Allen's popular radio program. Once again, Delmar portrays a Southern politician. In this film, the Daughters of Dixie nominate Delmar's shrewish wife for state senator. Some Northern carpetbaggers decide to nominate Delmar himself for the same position so as to split the vote and make room for their own candidate. Delmar is kidnapped but manages to arrive back at the count where he wins the nomination and establishes himself once and for all as the head of the family.

Lion Is in the Streets, A (1953), WB. Dir. Raoul Walsh; Sc. Luther Davis; Cast include: James Cagney, Barbara Hale, Anne Francis, Warner Anderson.

James Cagney stars in Raoul Walsh's drama. The film is based on the novel by Adria Locke Langley and portrays Hank Martin, a backwoods swamp peddler who turns politician by crusading for the impoverished sharecroppers. He eventually runs for governor in the cotton-growing state. Barbara Hale plays his schoolteacher wife with conviction. "Brighten up, sweet-face, brighten up," Martin says to her, "'cause you married a winner, not a loser!" The drama is purportedly a fictionalized tale of the career of Louisiana's Huey Long. The production took so long to film that the shock value of coming so close to the actual events was lost. The film only skirts Long's real-life romance with an "entertainer" from the Flamingo Club, portrayed by Anne Francis. None of the themes touched upon in the film are developed in any depth.

Marie (1985), De Laurentis. Dir. Roger Donaldson; Sc. John Briley; Cast includes: Sissy Spacek, Jeff Daniels, Morgan Freeman, Fred Thompson.

Peer Maas wrote the original book, *Marie: A True Story*. The book and the film are biographical dramas and the latter stars Sissy Spacek as the title character. Soon on in he story, Spacek, who is a state bureaucrat, discovers that she is expected to rubber-stamp pardons granted by corrupt state officials. When she protests, the governor dismisses her. She is forced to sue him, and the film ends in a courtroom drama in which she is vindicated. Jeff Daniels portrays the governor's legal counsel and yes man. At first Daniels poses as her defender as long as she goes along with the system, but when she asserts her independence, he shows his ugly side.

*

The story is, in large part, base on the true life experiences of Marie Ragghianti who, in 1976, became the first woman to head Tennessee's Board of Pardons and Paroles.

Phenix City Story, The (1955), AA. Dir. Phil Karlson; Sc. Crane Wilbur, Dan Mainwaring; Cast includes: John McIntire, Richard Kiley, Kathryn Grant, Edward Andrews.

Director Phil Karlson's tough and dramatic exposé portrays the wild-west character of the city of Phenix. The city was once described as an "infamous and sordid chapter in American city politics" and the film certainly buttresses this assessment. A reporter conducts interviews with prominent citizens in a newsreel-style-opening scene. The drama features Richard Kiley as ex-serviceman John Patterson. He returns home with his wife and children and finds his town overwhelmed by corrupt forces, more violent than ever. Patterson's father, Albert, a highly respected lawyer, decides to campaign for clean government. "I'm going to fight you," he announces to Edward Andrews, the head of the crime syndicate. "I'm going to put you and all those others out of business. I'm running for attorney general." When his father is murdered, young Patterson, also a lawyer, is determined to carry on his work. At a meeting with a small reform-minded group of citizens, young Patterson exclaims: "Let me give you the first quotation my dad ever taught me: 'The only thing necessary for the triumph of evil is that good men do nothing.' " After several murders, the governor sends in the state troopers. Young Patterson is swept into office as attorney general and immediately goes after the vice-czars of the city.

*

Lawyer and former state legislator Albert A. Patterson (-1954) directed the Betterment Association's legal campaign in 1951 against the mob in Phenix City, widely known as Sin City. He ran for Attorney General of the State of Alabama in 1954 and was gunned down on June 14 outside his law office in Phenix City. In response to the widespread public outrage, Governor Persons ordered in the National Guard to help clean up gambling and prostitution and to solve the numerous murders in the city. A newly organized grand jury returned 749 indictments, gambling equipment was confiscated and a reform ticket was whisked into office while the National Guard stood watch.

Romance of Rosy Ridge, The (1947), MGM. Dir. Roy Rowland; Sc. Lester Cole; Cast includes: Van Johnson, Thomas Mitchell, Janet Leigh, Marshall Thompson.

Roy Rowland's Civil War drama, which takes place in the spring of 1865, skips the conflict itself and concentrates on personal drama. Van Johnson portrays a traveling schoolteacher who woos the daughter (Janet Leigh) of a Missouri farmer (Thomas Mitchell), a man who hates the North. He suspects Johnson of being a Union sympathizer. But, by the last reel of this romantic tale, Johnson manages to reassure Mitchell. This was Janet Leigh's first screen appearance. The film was based on a story by MacKinlay Kantor.

*

MacKinlay Kantor (1904-1977) was an Iowa boy who went the route from reporter to novelist. He moved to Chicago where he worked at a number of odd jobs. Eventually he received an offer as a reporter in 1926 for the Cedar Rapids *Republican*. Unfortunately, the paper went bankrupt and Kantor was out of work.

As a last resort, he decided to write a novel. He and his wife moved back to Webster City in 1927 and, in order to survive, moved in with Kantor's grandparents and lived on four dollars a week for several months. The product of those few months was *Diversity*. However, fame still eluded him as he failed to achieve any significant notice with this, his first novel.

Kantor later developed a special interest in the Civil War. However, it took the next twenty years before he achieved international recognition with his chef d'oeuvre, *Andersonville* (1955). His novel describes the horrible conditions of the infamous Confederate prisoner of war camp where 14,000 Union prisoners died.

*

WUSA (1970), Par. Dir. Stuart Rosenberg; Sc. Robert Stone; Cast includes: Paul Newman, Joanna Woodward, Anthony Perkins, Laurence Harvey, Pat Hingle.

Cynical drifter Paul Newman gets a job as disc jockey at a conservative New Orleans radio station (WUSA). Stuart Rosenberg's naïve drama is based on Robert Stone's novel, *A Hall of Mirrors*. Newman learns of station owner Pat Hingle's practice of tailoring the news towards his own political agenda. Naturally, station manager Robert Quarry follows the owner's lead and insists that Newman concentrate on exposing welfare cheats and other "social parasites." Social worker Anthony Perkins feeds Quarry the stories. The film ends up as a ponderous cautionary drama about the dangers the extreme right wing poses in its control of the mass media.

17

New Social Conditions

In the North, in the period immediately preceding the Civil War, numerous religious leaders and especially members of Protestant denominations began to closely re-examine their own morality. The Calvinist determinist view had given way to a belief in free will and this compelled the righteous to examine various moral issues – especially slavery – in religious terms. The North considered slavery in the South a mortal sin. Southerners resented this judgment and pointed to the "wage slaves" who were exploited in Northern factories.

In recent times, the terms "family values" and "Southern Christian evangelicals" have almost become synonymous. If we go back one hundred years, however, we find that the Southern evangelical Protestants were the vanguard of a revolutionary movement which threatened to subvert traditional "family values" and risked turning society upside down as well.

Various Methodist and Baptist preachers at that time sought to emancipate women from the authority of their husbands. These young evangelical preachers maintained that women should not be forced into marriage against their will and should be allowed free choice in selecting a church. By emphasizing emotion in their services, the evangelicals welcomed the unity of Christians and opened their churches to blacks and whites.

These radical views shook the entrenched Southern Anglican Church to its core and, for a while, threatened to subvert the entire establishment. Eventually, however, the evangelical movement was co-opted and its views tailored to fit the more conservative views of mainstream Christianity. In time, Baptist and Methodist preachers grew older and they became more and more inclined to support the traditional patriarchal family. In terms of race relations, they stood the initial evangelical ideas upside down and decided to support the separation of the races.

During the 1950s most Southern schools were still racially segregated. The U.S. Supreme Court had sanctioned the concept of "separate but equal" and had thus supported separate schools for blacks and whites. Northern schools were not segregated by law but, in many cases, the separation grew out of separate housing patterns. In 1954, in Brown v. the Board of Education of Topeka, Kansas, the Supreme Court unanimously ruled that deliberate racial segregation in public schools was unconstitutional. In so doing the Supreme Court reversed an earlier Court decision and now maintained that "separate" was inherently unequal. Despite vigorous legal and non-legal challenges, by 1980 separate school systems had been eliminated in most of the South

*

Urbanization, industrialization and the civil rights movement all contributed towards changing the face of the South. The New South was transformed into a major industrial region. Whereas in earlier years, there was a net emigration from the region, in the last 20 years there has been a net immigration to the region. In the 1950s and 1960s Northern capital found an hospitable climate of non-union workers and low taxes and moved textile manufacturing plants South. During the next three decades, however, with the rise of "the global economy," many Southern textile operations moved overseas. However, Japanese and German capital sometimes replaced Northern capital and these foreigners built auto manufacturing, chemical and drug plants in the area. Two of every three Southerners are presently urban or suburban residents and the majority of Southerners work in industry. While ten percent of the 1950 cotton crop was picked by machine, in 1990 the figure rose to ninety five percent.

*

Early American films rarely embraced some of the more controversial racial issues. In later years, the movie industry films finally touched upon more serious topics, as in *Conrack* (1974) and *Foreign Student* (1994). Some features, like *Adventures of Huckleberry Finn*, *The Defiant Ones* and *Driving Miss Daisy*, experimented with the theme of bonding between white and black.

*

Socially, the "hillbillies" or "crackers" were just slightly above the African-American population in the South. The former were most likely the descendents of indentured servants in colonial days and lived in the mountainous areas which were not as fertile as land in the plain. Although they made up less than ten percent of the population and they were looked down upon, the hillbillies exerted a great influence on the imagination of various writers. Hollywood turned out a number of entertaining hillbilly comedies, musicals and dramas.

*

The Acadians were settlers in French Canada in the area called Acadia but now called Nova Scotia, New Brunswick and Prince Edward Island. In 1755, the British and French were in the midst of the Seven Years' War and were fighting for control of North America. The British were concerned about the loyalties of the Acadians and forcibly removed and then resettled them in other parts of America. American poet Henry Wadsworth Longfellow forever recorded the fate of the Acadians in his epic poem, *Evangeline.*

Some of these Acadians were forcibly resettled in Louisiana, which was then ruled by Spain. The Spanish authorities immediately moved the new arrivals to the countryside outside of New Orleans. The Acadians tried to grow the grain crops they were familiar with in Nova Scotia – oats, barley and wheat. However, the topology and climate of Louisiana were unsuitable for these crops and they failed in their initial venture. They were fortunate, however, when they grew corn for feed and when they developed cattle ranches in the prairie regions of Louisiana. These ranches soon supplied New Orleans with top quality steaks and beef.

Some of these Acadian ranchers became more successful than others and they soon began expanding their spreads. The wealthy cattle farmers eventually found it more remunerative to grow cotton than to raise cattle and so they turned their ranches into cotton plantations. These same ranchers who had been victims of British tyranny then became large-scale slaveholders themselves. The smaller ranchers were forced into marginal swampland. They became subsistence farmers and lived off their own peas, beans, rice, corn, yams and okra. To this day, the wealthier Cajuns in Louisiana continue to raise cattle while their poorer cousins grow the same subsistence crops that their ancestors did. Some of the latter continue to make homespun clothing.

*

About Face (1952), WB. Dir. Roy Del Ruth; Sc. Peter Milne; Cast includes: Gordon MacRae, Eddie Bracken, Dick Wesson, Virginia Gibson.

The film is a minor musical comedy based on the play and earlier film *Brother Rat* by John Monks Jr. and Fred Finklehoffe. Roy Del Ruth's remake zeroes in on cadets struggling to pass their finals at the Southern Military Institute. Gordon MacRae warbles several nondescript songs and Eddie Bracken tries to keep his secret wife from being 'outed.' Some of the cadets try to outsmart one of their overbearing professors.

Adventures of Huckleberry Finn, The (1993), Walt Disney. Dir. Stephen Sommers; Sc. Stephen Sommers; Cast includes: Elijah Wood, Courtney B. Vance, Robbie Coltrane, Jason Robards, Ron Perlman, Dana Ivey.

In Stephen Sommers's adventure drama, the most recent of numerous film versions of Mark Twain's classic novel, Huck runs off down the Mississippi with an escaping slave named Jim. Huck internalizes the racist views about blacks prevalent during that period, but he has never really thought about blacks. During their journey on the river Jim re-educates him. Huck finally decides that if it is a sin to help a slave escape, then he must be a sinner. When Huck and Jim drift onto the subjects of race and slavery, Huck finally admits, following Jim's explanations to him, that black people have the same feelings as everyone else and deserve his respect.

Huck's conversion is significant as it is one of the earliest reflections on race in popular American literature. However, some adults still think Twain's novel should not be taught in schools because Huck uses the word "nigger." The film eliminates the word and it prefers to entertain rather than to psychoanalyze Huck's racist attitudes. Elijah Wood portrays Huck, Courtney B. Vance plays Jim, Jason Robards, the King, and Ron Perlman, Pap Finn.

Angel Baby (1961), AA. Dir. Paul Wendkos; Sc. Orin Borsten, Paul Mason, Samuel Roeca; Cast includes: George Hamilton, Mercedes McCambridge, Joan Blondell, Henry Jones.

George Hamilton is the faith healer who helps to restore the voice of a mute young woman, known as Angel Baby (Salome Jens). This drama is set in the South and is based on the novel *Jenny Angel* by Elsie Oaks Barber. Angel Baby becomes sexually involved with Hamilton but breaks off and eventually starts her own faith-healing operation. However, she falls under the power of an unscrupulous charlatan who, unknown to Angel Baby, plants phony invalids in her audience who boast of instant cure. Disillusioned, she retreats to a nearby community where she reestablishes herself and, incidentally, helps a lame child to walk. At this point, Hamilton meets Angel Baby once again and they reunite for a happy ending to this superficial exposé of the faith-healing racket.

Bright Road (1953), MGM. Dir. Gerald Mayer; Sc. Emmet Lavery; Cast includes: Dorothy Dandridge, Philip Hepburn, Harry Belafonte, Robert Horton.

In this well-paced drama, black teacher Dorothy Dandridge is a teacher in a small Southern town who tries to help her pupils. Philip Hepburn portrays a defiant and unruly student whom Dandridge finally "turns around." Harry Belafonte, who plays the school principal, made his film debut in this production.

Brother John (1970), Col. Dir. James Goldstone; Sc. Ernest Kinoy; Cast includes: Sidney Poitier, Will Geer, Bradford Dillman, Beverly Todd.

Sidney Poitier portrays the mysterious John Kane, a world traveler with a questionable passport, in this offbeat drama that explores racial attitudes. In reality, he is an angel bent on eliminating prejudice and hatred in his Southern hometown. He makes his debut in town at the bedside of his dying sister. The District Attorney (Bradford Dillman) thinks that Poitier is an outside agitator who has come to stir up the black strikers at a local plant. Former schoolmate Beverly Todd falls in love with Poitier. Will Geer, the only doctor in town, envisions the visitor as a Christ-like figure who has returned and demonstrates mystical powers. Others treat him as a messiah while still others fear him.

Brother Rat (1938), WB. Dir. William Keighley; Sc. Richard Macaulay, Jerry Wald; Cast includes: Priscilla Lane, Wayne Morris, Johnnie Davis, Jane Bryan, Eddie Albert, Ronald Reagan.

Wayne Morris and Ronald Reagan, two energetic cadets at the Virginia Military Institute, decide to buckle down and curb their antics in the weeks preceding graduation. This comedy is based on the play by John Monk Jr. and Fred Finklehoff. Complications arise for the two when fellow cadet Eddie Albert, who is secretly married, informs them that his wife is pregnant. In addition, Reagan begins wooing Jane Wyman, the commandant's daughter. To add to their problems, they try to hide Albert's wife in the barracks before graduation and the prom. Ray Enright directed a sequel in 1940, *Brother Rat and a Baby*, with many of the same leads. The film was remade in 1952 as *About Face*.

Conrack (1974), TCF. Dir. Martin Ritt; Sc. Irving Ravetch, Harriet Frank Jr.; Cast includes: Jon Voight, Paul Winfield, Hume Cronyn, Madge Sinclair, Tina Andrews.

Jon Voight portrays Pat Conrack, a teacher who goes to a small island off the South Carolina coast. This drama is based on Pat Conrack's true story, *The Water Is Wide*. Voight soon determines that the black children on the island are not receiving an adequate education. Although Voight is sympathetic with his students, he realizes that many are illiterate and some are retarded. They have difficulty pronouncing "Conrack," so they call him "Conroy." Voight introduces his students to a wider world by teaching them about music, other religions and baseball. At first, the children and their parents resist his methods, but they soon come to accept him and his approach. However, Hume Cronyn, an education supervisor, prefers the strict three r's to Conrack's more radical approach. He removes the young teacher, but Conrack's memory remains an inspiration for the children as well as for the isolated community.

Count Three and Pray (1955), Col. Dir. George Sherman; Sc. Herb Meadow; Cast includes: Van Heflin, Joanne Woodward, Phil Carey, Raymond Burr, Allison Hayes.

In this post-Civil War drama, Joanne Woodward portrays a young woman who survives the horrors of the Civil War by taking refuge in the mountains and turning into a nature child. After the war, Parson Van Heflin, a former wild young man who has reformed, returns to his hometown determined to rebuild the local church and preach love and peace to the defeated Southerners. Following several complications, Heflin and Woodland marry and heal the community.

Defiant Ones, The (1958), UA. Dir. Stanley Kramer; Sc. Nathan E. Douglas, Harold Jacob Smith; Cast includes: Tony Curtis, Sidney Poitier, Theodore Bikel, Charles McGraw, Lon Chaney.

In Stanley Kramer's racially tense drama, Southern chain-gang convicts Tony Curtis and Sidney Poitier escape from their captors still shackled together. Although each man hates the other for his race, they are forced to cooperate in order to escape. The film turns into a metaphor for race relations in America – suggesting that we are all linked by a common history and we have to live together. Bloodhounds chase them through the woods and swamps until they are finally captured by angry townspeople. The captors tie them together and hold them in a warehouse until the sheriff arrives. In the meantime, however, Lon Chaney, a former chain gang convict, is sympathetic and frees them. They take refuge in a farmhouse with widow Cara Williams, who makes a play for Curtis. When she suggests they set up Poitier for capture while the two of them make their getaway, Curtis grows disgusted with her and the two fugitives take off.

Still pursued by the dogs and a posse, they try to hop a freight train. Poitier climbs aboard the fast-moving train but Curtis fails to make it. As he desperately holds out his hand to Curtis, Poitier falls from the train and loses his own freedom. Both tumble down a hill, where the sheriff captures them. Early in the film one law officer asks, "How come they chained a white man to a black?" The sheriff replies simply, "The warden's got a sense of humor."

Driving Miss Daisy (1989), WB. Dir. Bruce Beresford; Sc. Alfred Uhry; Cast includes: Morgan Freeman, Jessica Tandy, Dan Aykroyd, Patti Lupone.

Miss Daisy (Jessica Tandy) is a proud old Southern woman who lives with her cook. Bruce Beresford's drama is based on Alfred Uhry's stage play that spans 25 years. After she loses control of her 1948 Packard and drives it onto a neighbor's lawn, Miss Daisy's son (Dan Aykroyd) forces her to hire a chauffeur. Although she stubbornly objects, her son hires Hoke (Morgan Freeman), a mature, proud and stubborn African American. Hoke displays plenty of patience in dealing with Miss Daisy. Outwardly, he continues to acquiesce to Miss Daisy's petty demands throughout the film, but he is inwardly frustrated.

Miss Daisy is a Southern Jewish liberal, but when Hoke drives her to listen to a speech by Martin Luther King, she does not invite him in with her extra ticket. He is forced to wait outside the hall, in her car. In one quiet, poignant scene, they park their car by the side of a lake for a little picnic. A police car drives by, stops and questions the pair. Satisfied that nothing is wrong, they leave and one officer, puzzled at the sight, shakes his head at the odd couple and remarks to his partner, "An old Jew and a Negro." Near the end of her life she finally admits to Hoke, who has come to visit her in a home for senior citizens, that he is her best friend.

Foreign Student (1994), Gramercy. Dir. Eva Sereny; Sc. Menno Meyjes; Cast includes: Marco Hofschneider, Charles S. Dutton, Hinton Battle, Robin Givens, Jack Coleman.

Eva Sereny's social drama is based on the novel *The Foreign Student* by Philippe Labro. It portrays the life of a French exchange student at a Virginia college where certain traditions still dominate. It is the mid-1950s, and Phillippe (played by Marco Hofschneider) absorbs some of the local culture, but refuses to live by it. He wanders into the black section of town near a blues club. When he's chased and harassed by the locals, he runs away shouting, "I'm not a redneck! I am not a Southern gentleman! I am French!" Two black musicians recall how well they were treated in Paris and invite Phillippe inside. He has a romance with a black grammar-school teacher, who is also a part-time housekeeper for Phillippe's English professor. Their interracial love affair is dangerous for the period and raises some eyebrows around the school It also explores some of the racial attitudes in the 1950s South. A middle-aged Phillippe narrates his own story and looks back in time.

Girl of the Ozarks (1936), Par. Dir. William Shea; Sc. Stuart Anthony, Michael Simmons; Cast includes: Virginia Weidler, Leif Erikson, Elizabeth Russell, Henrietta Crosman, Janet Young.

Orphan Virginia Weidler, a young orphan girl, always seems to be in trouble. She lives in an orphanage after her mother dies but is eventually adopted by a sympathetic editor of a small newspaper. This sentimental drama takes place in an Appalachian hillbilly village. Henrietta Crosman portrays the stereotypical hillbilly granny who sports a pipe in one hand and a double-barreled shotgun in the other.

Gone Are the Days (1963), Dir. Nicholas Webster; Sc. Ossie Davis; Cast includes: Ossie Davis, Ruby Dee, Godfrey Cambridge, Sorrell Booke.

Nicholas Webster's film is based on the Broadway stage hit *Purlie Victorious* and the musical *Purlie*. The comedy drama stars Ossie Davis as Purlie Victorious Judson, an artful and glib African-American preacher. Davis tries to buy a barn that he wants to convert to an integrated church in his hometown in Georgia. He needs 500 dollars so he swindles a nearby racist plantation owner out of the money. The owner, an old Southern bigot, has daily confrontations with his college-educated son who believes in integration and "Negroes' rights." The father fumes at his son's talk of "Nigras' rights" and grumbles, "Four years of college and you still can't say the word right." Ruby Dee, one of Purlie's disciples, helps him. Following several funny scenes, Davis gets his barn. As a result, the old racist plantation owner suffers a stroke and dies. Purlie's first service in his new church provides the deceased with an integrated funeral.

Heart of Dixie (1989), Dir. Martin Davidson; Sc. Tom CcCown, Ann R. Siddons; Cast includes: Ally Sheedy, Virginia Madsen, Phoebe Cates.

Martin Davidson's drama touches a number of popular stereotypes of Southern college life. Scenes of sorority functions, formal ball-dances and the coronation of a "honeysuckle queen" give the film a particular Southern flavor. In between all of these social activities, boys serenade the co-eds at night beneath their windows and "pin" them in the daytime. "Like the song says," a sorority officer announces at the coronation, "old times here are not forgotten – look away, look away, look away, Dixieland." The queen of the ball calls the coronation "a tradition – gentility and good old Southern honor – with friendship. You get a way of life you could never turn your back on."

Despite this honeyed tradition, several coeds become entangled in a racist plot in the 1950s South.

Ally Sheedy portrays a student who is reconsidering her impending betrothal to the heir to one of the richest plantations in the Delta. She is terribly disturbed when she witnesses several white thugs and local policemen beat an innocent black man and she decides to write about it in the school newspaper. The dean threatens to expel her from the school and cancels her story, so she decides to leave the school.

At the end of the film, the school's first black student walks fearfully and bravely through a hostile crowd of whites, while protected by a detachment of state troopers. The dean is reluctantly forced to accept the new student and pleads with the crowd to disband. The film's director sticks to the politically correct, hackneyed images of Southern white bigots, passive blacks and a brutal, hard-nosed Southern establishment.

Hillbilly Blitzkrieg (1942), Mon. Dir. Ray Mack; Sc. R. S. Harris; Cast includes: Bud Duncan, Cliff Nazarro, Edgar Kennedy, Doris Linden, Lucien Littlefield.

Based on the Snuffy Smith and Barney Google comic strip characters created by Billy DeBeck, Ray Mack presents a World War II comedy. The federal government want to build a rocket base in the backwoods of Tennessee. Comic character actor Edgar Kennedy portrays a sergeant and Bud Duncan plays Private Snuffy Smith. Both men are assigned to guard the secret military site. Meanwhile, spies plot to steal the plans and destroy the site. The title remains the most interesting part of this comedy.

I'd Climb the Highest Mountain (1950), TCF. Dir. Henry King; Sc. Lamar Trotti; Cast include: Susan Hayward, William Lundigan, Rory Calhoun, Barbara Bates, Gene Lockhart.

Susan Hayward plays the city-bred bride of Protestant minister William Lundigan. In this uplifting drama based on the novel by Corra Harris, Hayward describes her three years in the hills of Georgia. She encounters an entirely different and strange world and she has to fight off an aggressive young woman who has eyes for Hayward's husband. In one particularly stark scene, the hill people fall victim to an epidemic. While all this is going on, Lundigan tries to reach out to Alexander Knox, a local unbeliever, and unsuccessfully attempts to reform Rory Calhoun, a wild youth.

In the Heat of the Night (1967), UA. Dir. Norman Jewison; Sc. Stirling Silliphant; Cast include: Sidney Poitier, Rod Steiger, Warren Oates, Lee Grant, James Patterson.

Sidney Poitier portrays a Philadelphia police detective who visits his hometown in Mississippi. Norman Jewison's drama is based on the novel by John Ball and shows Poitier clashing with the Southern sheriff. The film pulsates with racial overtones. When an important industrialist who had planned to build a factory in town is found murdered, Poitier, who is black, is immediately picked up as a suspect. "Whatcha hit him with?" sheriff Rod Steiger asks. "Hit whom?" Poitier asks. "Whom?" Steiger remarks in surprise. "Are you a Northern boy? What's a Northern boy doing down here?" Steiger promptly books him for the murder – until he checks his credentials and learns that his prisoner is an outstanding homicide detective. Poitier is ordered to assist Steiger, who resents the offer. In turn, Poitier tries to refuse the order but is countermanded. The antagonism between the two lawmen eventually dissipates as they begin to respect each other.

The victim's wife (Lee Grant) sees the sheriff's and the community's hostility towards Poitier and insists that the police accept the outside help. "What kind of people are you!" she cries out in anger. Some local young bigots attack Poitier and he clashes with an aristocrat of the Old South. Eventually, Poitier helps Steiger solve the murder. In the best Hollywood tradition, both men part as friends with a deeper understanding and appreciation of each other.

Johnny Ring and the Captain's Sword (1921), Temple. Dir. Norman L. Stevens; Sc. Russell H. Conwell; Cast includes: Ben Warren, Frank Walker.

Supposedly based on a true incident, Norman L. Stevens' drama describes the religious conversion of Russell H. Conwell (Ben Warren). Conwell is a Union captain and, during the course of the war, is honored by the townspeople with a special sword. The officer, an avowed atheist, assigns young religious orderly Johnny Ring (Frank Walker) to polish and care for the sword but prohibits him from reading the Bible publicly. The boy, however, prays for the captain. During one battle the orderly is mortally wounded trying to save the precious sword. Conwell, who is now a captain, is also wounded in battle but he survives. In terrible pain, he promises that if God permits him to live, he will do His work in the name of the dead orderly. Eventually Conwell survives, redeems his pledge and becomes a Philadelphia minister.

Lords of Discipline, The (1983), Par. Dir. Franc Roddam; Sc. Thomas Pope, Lloyd Fonvielle; Cast includes: David Keith, Robert Prosky, G. D. Spradlin, Barbara Babcock.

David Keith, a senior cadet at the Carolina Military Institute, has been assigned to subtly look after Mark Breland, the academy's first black cadet. This brutal drama is based on the novel by Pat Conroy and specifically zeroes in on racism. Keith is appointed to keep Breland safe and to keep a special watch over him on "hell night," when seniors are permitted to pull stunts on lower classmen. When, as a result of one of these "pranks," one young man dies, Keith goes undercover to find the perpetrators. Eventually he discovers that a secret society called "The Ten" has been terrorizing what they deem "undesirables." As tensions grow and the number of incidents escalates, Keith just manages to rescue Breland from several serious attacks by the society. Keith and a few other students discover that the administration itself has sanctioned the violence. Robert Prosky portrays the school's second-in-command who is both congenial and nefarious.

Mummy's Curse, The (1944), U. Dir. Leslie Goodwins; Sc. Bernard Schubert; Cast includes: Lon Chaney, Peter Coe, Virginia Christine, Kay Harding, Dennis Moore.

Leslie Goodwins's horror drama is set in the Cajun country of Louisiana. An Egyptian prince (Lon Chaney) was buried alive as a punishment for trying to resurrect his dead girlfriend and somehow winds up in Louisiana. Only a handful of American films have dealt with the Cajuns or even touched upon Cajun themes.

Night of the Hunter, The (1955), UA. Dir. Charles Laughton; Sc. James Agee; Cast includes: Robert Mitchum, Shelley Winters, Lillian Gish, Evelyn Varden, Peter Graves, Billy Chapin, Sally Jane Bruce.

Robert Mitchum plays a demented ex-convict and self-appointed preacher who marries widow Shelley Winters. Charles Laughton's sometimes overly atmospheric drama is based on the novel by Davis Grubb. Prior to hanging, Winters' first husband shared a prison cell with Mitchum. Mitchum learned the police never recovered the money from the deceased's bank heist. Winters' husband had stashed away a large sum of money and Mitchum is determined to get his hands on it. Mitchum murders Winters but her two children, Billy Chapin and Sally Jane Bruce, still refuse to tell their stepfather where the money is hidden. They flee from him and find refuge with Lillian Gish and her flock of orphans. Gish is a kindly guardian of young souls. "Children," she muses, underscoring the film's allegory of innocence and evil, "are man at his strongest. They abide." Mitchum relentlessly pursues the two children until he is arrested for Winters' murder. The children return the money, which was hidden in the little girl's doll, and find a new life of peace and security with Gish. James Agee's script, set chiefly in the rural South during the Depression, is considered rather arty by some critics.

Passion Fish (1992), Miramax. Dir. John Sayles; Sc. John Sayles; Cast includes: Mary McDonnell, Alfre Woodard, David Strathairn, Vondie Curtis Hall, Angela Bassett.

Mary McDonnell is May-Alice, the soap opera star whose life is suddenly changed when she is paralyzed in an accident. She goes back home to Louisiana to recover and is filled with resentment. Prior to the accident her career had been going downhill and she was divorced. Now it seems that she has hit rock-bottom. May-Alice was always a headstrong woman who wanted to control things around her, but now she is confined to a wheelchair. She drinks wine all day long and takes out her bitterness on all those around her. She has trouble hiring a full-time companion, and a bunch of them are soon fired or quit on their own. Not easy to work for, she finally settles on Chantelle, an African-American (Alfre Woodard), who is a strong woman, also.

Determined to keep the job, Chantelle understands that May-Alice needs less coddling and a lot less wine, and tries to take charge. But a struggle of wills ensues as May-Alice fights. At one point, Chantelle ignores May-Alice's objections and pushes the actress and her wheelchair out of the house, forcing her to wheel herself back in. "But it's all uphill," she complains, as Chantelle leaves. "So's life," Chantelle fires back. The two fight but, when all things are considered, they really balance each other. As May-Alice becomes more self-sufficient, she learns that Chantelle is recovering too – from a drug-addicted past. Chantelle has also left behind a daughter who is now living with her grandfather. Living isolated in the bayou and faced with new identities and responsibilities, the two women begin to change for the better

Road to Richmond, The (1910), Selig.

This silent Civil War drama recounts how two cadets meet at West Point, become friends and eventually fight against each other. In the antebellum period, the Northerner visits his Southern friend and meets the latter's sister. Later on during the war, the Union soldier captures his former roommate during a battle, but the Confederate soldier manages to escape. However, in a later scene his war wounds prevent him from completing his assignment – blowing up a bridge. His sister destroys the bridge for him and then jumps into the river below. The Northerner, who has advanced with his troops, jumps into the river after her and rescues her. In turn, the Confederates capture him. The girl speaks to General Lee on his behalf and the prisoner is freed. D.W. Griffith uses the two circumstances – the friendship between a Union officer and a Confederate officer and a visit by a Northerner to a Southern home in the antebellum period – in *The Birth of a Nation* (1915).

Song of the South (1946), RKO. Dir. Harve Foster, Wilfred Jackson; Sc. Dalton Raymond, Morton Grant, Maurice Rapf; Cast includes: Ruth Warrick, James Baskett, Bobby Driscoll, Luana Patten, Lucile Watson, Hattie McDaniel.

Bobby Driscoll portrays a boy who journeys with his mother to live on his grandmother's Southern plantation during the Reconstruction era. This Disney feature is based on *Tales of Uncle Remus* by Joel Chandler Harris. The film blends animation with real-life action. When his parents separate, the boy is confused and decides to run away. He meets James Baskett, a former slave who, who entertains him with folk tales about Breer Rabbit, Breer Fox and other characters. Baskett tries to trick the boy into returning to his mother. When Bobby agrees and returns home, he invites Baskett to his birthday party and they strike up a close friendship. Controversy surrounded the film. The National Association for the Advancement of the Colored People condemned the idyllic depiction of the Reconstruction Period and the stereotyping of blacks as happy entertainers.

Stars in My Crown (1950), MGM. Dir. Jacques Tourneur; Sc. Margaret Fitts; Cast includes: Joel McCrea, Ellen Drew, Dean Stockwell, Alan Hale, Lewis Stone.

Jacques Tourneur's drama is based on the novel by Joe David Brown. Joel McCrea portrays a preacher who moves into a Southern town with a Bible in one hand and a pistol in the other. The town faces a typhoid epidemic and Ku Klux Klan terror and the good preacher helps the community resolve these threats. Along the way, he manages to help a doctor new to the town.

Strange One, The (1957), Col. Dir. Jack Garfein; Sc. Calder Willingham; Cast includes: Ben Gazarra, Pat Hingle, Mark Richman, Arthur Storch, Larry Gates.

Jack Garfein's drama is based on Calder Willingham's play and novel, *End as a Man.* Ben Gazarra portrays an arrogant, mean-spirited student leader at a Southern military school. Gazarra and his buddies, especially Pat Hingle and James Olsen, bully the younger students. They delight in terrorizing the lower classmen. Larry Gates, the only adult in the cast, tries to eject Gazarra from the academy and Gazarra, in turn, tries to discredit Gates at every opportunity. Eventually, some of the younger student rebel against Gazarra and his bullies.

*

The author of this play, novelist and short-story writer Calder Willingham (1922-1995), was born in Atlanta, Georgia. His violent and, at times, glaring realism often disturbed reviewers. But even these critics were stirred by the energy of his writing style. His use of dialogue and his detailed scenes impressed critics for their realism and strength – especially in such works as his stage play *End as a Man* (1947).

*

Martha Coolidge picked up Willingham's *End as a Man* and developed it into the film *Rambling Rose* (1991). The venue is Georgia in the 1930s and stars Laura Dern as an oversexed free spirit. She gets a job working for a genteel family headed by Robert Duvall and Diane Ladd.

Hollywood loved Willingham's novels and he collaborated with the movie studios on other films such as *Paths of Glory* (1957), *The Vikings* (1958), *One-Eyed Jacks* (1961), *The Graduate* (1967), *Little Big Man* (1970) and *Thieves Like Us* (1974). The last film, directed by Robert Altman, describes three misfits who escape from a prison camp and comes closest to Willingham's writing style

– his evocative use of the 1930s, strong characterization and a deep understanding of rural people.

Wild in the Country (1961), TCF. Dir. Philip Dunne; Sc. Clifford Odets; Cast includes: Elvis Presley, Hope Lange, Tuesday Weld, Millie Perkins, Rafer Johnson.

Elvis Presley is a poor country lad with inherent writing skills but without direction. Philip Dunne's romantic drama is based on J. R. Salamanca's novel *The Lost Country*. Presley's life and career change drastically when he meets pretty psychiatric consultant Hope Lange. Complications arise when they spend an innocent night together and tongues begin to wag. Lange almost commits suicide as a result of the rumors, but the couple eventually separates as friends as Presley heads for college.

Wise Blood (1979), New Line. Dir. John Huston; Sc. Benedict Fitzgerald; Cast includes: Brad Dourif, Ned Beatty, Harry Dean Stanton, Daniel Shor, Amy Wright.

John Huston turned Flannery O'Connor's 1952 novel into a film in 1979. Set in the Deep South, the intriguing drama concerns young Hazel Motes (Brad Dourif), who has returned from the war to his hometown. He meets a blind preacher with a young daughter. Only later does he discover that the preacher can see and that the 15-year-old daughter is dishonest. Motes, whose own grandfather (John Huston) was a fire-and-brimstone preacher, now becomes a pawn in the hands of a dishonest, guitar-playing reverend.

Motes is soon transformed into an obsessed preacher of The Church Without Christ. The church does not recognize sin and requires no redeemer. Instead, it suggests that the individual depend upon himself. Motes is a true believer and he decides to try and discover the "elemental truth." So, in order to eliminate all outer distractions, he blinds himself. At this point, he is completely destitute and helpless, so he winds up at the mercy of a landlady who offers him room and board in return for marriage. He tries to flee, but the police return him to the landlady.

As an actor, Huston plays the grandfather-preacher in the film. Huston superbly captures the Southern gothic world of the writer while exploring small-town spiritualism and religion. "A man don't need justification," the simplistic Motes boasts at one point, "if he's got a good car."

*

American writer (Mary) Flannery O'Connor (1925-1964) was concerned with mankind's spiritual depravity and escape from redemption. Her short stories and novels earned her a unique place in 20th-century American fiction. Born in Savannah, Georgia, she was educated at the Georgia State College for Women and the State University of Iowa. O'Connor spent many years in Milledgeville, Georgia, where she raised peacocks and wrote. She died Aug. 3, 1964, of lupus, a disease that had crippled her for the last decade of her life.

O'Connor's works – basically two novels and two volumes of short stories – are an unlikely blend of Southern gothic, prophecy, and evangelistic Roman Catholicism. In addition to *Wise Blood,* O'Connor wrote the novel *The Violent Bear It Away* (1960). Her short-story collections include *A Good Man Is Hard to Find* (1955) and *Everything that Rises Must Converge* (posthumous, 1965). She is often compared to American novelist William Faulkner for her depiction of the Southern character and to Austrian writer Franz Kafka for her obsession with the grotesque. A major theme of her work is the individual's futile attempt to escape the grace of God.

*

Within Our Gates (1920), Micheaux Co. Dir. Oscar Micheaux; Sc. Oscar Micheaux; Cast includes: Evelyn Preer, Flo Clements, James D. Ruffin, Jack Chenault, William Smith, Charles D. Lucas.

Sylvia Landry (Evelyn Preer), a Southern black woman, pays a visit to her Northern cousin, Alma (Flo Clements). Oscar Micheaux's silent drama notes less racism in the North than in Sylvia's hometown of Piny Woods. Sylvia waits for Conrad, her fiancé, to arrive North. However, she is unaware that Alma herself is interested in Conrad. Alma tricks Sylvia into a compromising situation in order to embarrass her in front of Conrad who immediately abandons her. Disappointed, Sylvia returns to her home in the Deep South and helps her reverend run a school for young blacks. The reverend doesn't turn any poor student away and is therefore short of money. He has to raise $5,000 to supplement state aid or else the school will be forced to close.

Sylvia again journeys North to raise the money but is unsuccessful. During her sojourn, she drives a child for medical help but gets into an accident with a wealthy white man. Sylvia is injured and the other driver is so compassionate and distraught that he offers to bale the school out of the red. Sylvia's other passenger, a bigoted black man, urges her to turn down the offer. The white man is so incensed at this rejection that he raises his offer to $50,000. Sylvia returns happily to Piney Woods with the money and she marries a Northern doctor.

18

Law and Order

Forms of bondage other than outright slavery existed in the first half of the nineteenth century in the South, New Mexico and Arizona. In the South, both whites and blacks worked as indentured servants while Mexicans and Indians worked as peons in New Mexico and Arizona. The 13th Amendment to the U.S. Constitution that was adopted after the war prohibited involuntary servitude except as punishment. However, several Southern states passed their own laws which permitted prisoners to be leased to independent contractors. This gave rise to the dreaded chain gangs. Convicts had their legs shackled to each other and were forced to work in the fields and mines and to build roads. In 1910 the U.S. Supreme Court declared state laws permitting such practices unconstitutional.

*

Hollywood, as early as 1910, was quick to exploit the theme of the chain gang in a series of dramas and comedies. In particular, movie directors liked to picture chained prisoners breaking rocks under a hot sun. Some of these prisoners – in imitation of older movie productions showing slaves picking cotton – even sang while they worked! With the advent of sound, these prisoners began to sing soul and work songs in chorus while racist guard looked on. Some films simplistically focused on the melodramatics of the plot while others suggested social and racial themes. Many scenes focused on the abuses of the system and the brutality of the guards and evoked sympathy for the "victimized" shackled prisoners.

Hollywood released several low-budget chain-gang films. Jerry Gross's *Girl on a Chain Gang* (1965) was simply an obscure exploitation drama dealing with civil rights as well as life on a Southern chain gang. Christopher George, as a federal agent, arranges for the escape of six convicts from a chain gang in Burt Topper's weak action crime drama *The Devil's 8* (1969), based on a story by Larry Gordon. The agent proposes to use them to help him smash a moonshine ring controlled by Ralph Meeker. George trains his ex-cons to simultaneously drive and toss bombs at designated targets. In Lee Frost's action drama *Chain Gang Women* (1972), a killer escapes from a chain gang and takes with him a shackled fellow prisoner. They engage in series of rapes and robberies and a husband of one of their victims eventually pursues and kills them. *Sullivan's Travels* (1941), *Desire in the Dust* (1960), *Take the Money and Run* (1969), *Sweet Sugar* (1972) and *Mean Dog Blues* (1978) are similar chain gang films. Other major studio prison dramas focused on the prison farm, a different kind of penal institution. *Hell's Highway* (1932), *Road Gang* (1936), *Dust Be My Destiny* (1939) and *Carbine Williams* (1952) depict the prison farm.

*

In the movies, crime paid, so Hollywood began producing detective dramas, suspense thrillers, melodramas and mysteries. The heyday for these generally escapist features was the sound era of the early thirties and forties, when many detectives, both amateur and professional, were plucked from the pages of books and pulp magazines and radio drama and transplanted to the screen. Some detectives, like Charlie Chan and Sherlock Holmes, survived through several decades. Settings varied greatly – from racetracks and nightclubs to haunted houses and eerie swamps. In Southern mysteries, the venue was usually the outdoors and/or crumbling mansions.

*

Betrayed Women (1955), AA. Dir. Edward L. Cahn; Sc. Steve Fisher; Cast includes: Carole Mathews, Beverly Michaels, Peggy Knudsen, Tom Drake, Sara Haden, John Dierkes.

Dramas about incarcerated women have always fascinated movie producers and film audiences. Edward L. Cahn's sadistic drama is set in a women's prison somewhere in the South. Its title is more fascinating than the story line, which weaves together the usual clichés of the prison drama. The plot includes the familiar prison break, the use of hostages and rivalries among the inmates. The governor has assigned young lawyer Tom Drake to investigate appalling conditions at the prison. Prisoners Beverly Michaels and Carole Mathews, although mortal enemies, team up in a prison break and it is Drake's misfortune to become their hostage. Finally, Mathews is slain and Michaels surrenders. The film is a call for prison reform.

Blackmail (1939), MGM. Dir. H. C. Potter; Sc. David Hertz, William Ludwig; Cast includes: Edward G. Robinson, Gene Lockhart, Ruth Hussey, Esther Dale.

This drama is another exposé of the brutal chain-gang system. In *Blackmail*, Edward G. Robinson is arrested and imprisoned for a crime he did not commit. Sentenced to serve his time on a Southern chain gang, he escapes and begins a new life. He marries, becomes a devoted family man and starts a business fighting oil well fires. Gene Lockhart arrives in town and confides to Robinson that he was the guilty party. After a run-in with Robinson, Lockhart turns Robinson in to authorities who return him to the chain gang. Now, conditions are worse than ever. To exacerbate matters, Robinson learns that Lockhart has grabbed his business and his wife and child are poverty-stricken. He escapes once again, purposely starts an oil-well fire in order to lure Lockhart. Lockhart responds to the fire and Robinson forces him to confess in front of witnesses. Robinson is exonerated, extinguishes the raging fire and returns to his family.

Body Heat (1981), WB. Dir. Lawrence Kasdan; Sc. Lawrence Kasdan; Cast includes: William Hurt, Kathleen Turner, Richard Crenna, Ted Danson.

William Hurt portrays a weak lawyer who becomes entangled in a web spun by femme fatale Kathleen Turner. This classy film noir is set in a steamy Florida city. Hot-blooded and sensual Turner lures Hurt into murdering her rich husband (Richard Crenna). The production includes all the noir cliches – deco titles, a heat wave, nostalgic songs, seductive dialogue and ineffective ceiling fans. The plot is similar to that of *Double Indemnity* (1944) – it's the woman who plans to murder her husband and she lures an unwitting, simple man to commit the deed. The films differ in that Kasdan, in *Body Heat*, uses steamy double entendres that are more in tune with contemporary dramas.

Broken Chains (1916), World. Dir. Robert Thornby; Sc. E. M. Ingleton; Cast includes: John Taney, Carlyle Blackwell, Herbert Barrington, Stanhope Wheatcroft.

Robert Thornby's silent drama is set in the South during a period of racial tension. Captain Harry Ford (Carlyle Blackwell) and a troop of cavalry are assigned to hunt moonshiners. Simultaneously, some blacks steal a ballot box from a polling station and demand payment for its return. One of the white officials refuses to pay the ransom, so a black kills him and frames Captain Ford. The trooper is sentenced to life on a chain gang, but he manages to escape. A young Southern woman who loves the captain helps prove his innocence.

Bucktown (1975), AIP. Dir. Arthur Marks; Sc. Bob Ellison; Cast includes: Fred Williamson, Pam Grier, Thalmus Rasulala, Tony King, Bernie Hamilton, Art Lund.

This black exploitation film imitates the revenge drama *The Phenix City Story* (1955). In *Bucktown*, Fred Williamson journeys to a Southern town in order to seek revenge for his brother's murder. His brother was killed when he refused to pay protection money to the local white policemen. Williamson takes control of his dead sibling's tavern and begins to woo his widow. But when the white cops almost kill him, Williamson calls in a gang of tough black hoodlums who not only kill off the crooked cops but also decide to take over the entire town. Enter Williamson with a tank, which he uses to knock off the new predators. Pam Grier, as the murdered brother's widow, provides the romantic interest for ex-football player Williamson.

Cape Fear (1962), U. Dir. J. Lee Thompson; Sc. James R. Webb; Cast includes: Gregory Peck, Robert Mitchum, Polly Bergen, Lori Martin, Martin Balsam.

Robert Mitchum, as a sadistic ex-convict, seeks revenge on small-town Georgia lawyer Gregory Peck and his wife and daughter. This terrifying drama is based on John D. MacDonald's novel *The Executioners*. Peck had testified against Mitchum eight years earlier. Mitchum is a psychopath who enjoys hurting and sexually violating his female victims. Peck and his family suffer as Mitchum threatens them. Finally, Mitchum is lured into the Georgia swamps for a highly suspenseful climax.

Martin Scorsese directed a color remake of the film in 1991, with Robert DeNiro in Mitchum's role and Nick Nolte taking Gregory Peck's part. Jessica Lange plays Nolte's wife. In this later version the sadistic DeNiro toys with his victim and smirks:

> You're scared. But that's O.K. I want you to savor that fear. The South was born in fear. Fear of the Indian, fear of the slave, fear of the damn Union. The South has a fine tradition of savoring fear.

*

The Okefenokee Swamp served as the venue for a number of horror films – including *Cape Fear*. The swamp is typical of the subtropics and is located in southeast Georgia and northeast Florida. It covers a total area of about 684 square miles and drains through the Sewannee River to the Gulf of Mexico and through the Saint Marys River to the Atlantic Ocean. A saucer-like depression lined with low ridges, the swamp contains more than 20 islands, freshwater lakes and about 93 square miles of prairie. Its floor is made up of up to 15 feet of partially decomposed plant matter, or peat. Vegetation includes cypress forests, water lilies, and Spanish moss. Animals include alligators, deer, wildcats, opossums and raccoons. Several films used the swamp for their setting, including Jean Renoir's atmospheric drama *Swamp Water* (1941) and Hubert Cornfield's grim *Lure of the Swamp* (1957).

*

Carbine Williams (1952), MGM. Dir. Richard Thorpe; Sc. Art Cohn; Cast includes: James Stewart, Jean Hagen, Wendell Corey, Carl Benton Reid.

In this engaging biographical drama, James Stewart portrays the title character Marshe Williams. Williams runs a still and, during a raid by the "feds," an accomplice kills one of the federal agents. Williams is sentenced to 30 years in a North Carolina prison farm. To occupy his time, Williams begins to design a new weapon – not for escape but to satisfy his curiosity about firearms. His new rifle sports a short stroke piston. When he's caught with it, he pleads with the warden to allow him to continue, since the U.S. Army might be interested in it. Williams finally creates the M-1 carbine, which help revolutionize modern warfare and becomes the standard rifle for U.S. servicemen during World War II. For his efforts on behalf of the United States army, Williams is released after serving only eight years.

Chain Gang (1950), Col. Dir. Lew Landers; Sc. Howard J. Green; Cast includes: Douglas Kennedy, Marjorie Lord, Emory Parnell, William Phillips.

Newspaper reporter Douglas Kennedy goes under cover to expose the brutality and exploitation of chain gang prisoners in this humdrum action drama. For all his noble efforts, Kennedy is almost gunned down by a hail of bullets when the corrupt camp authorities discover his real identity. The film includes a plot cliché in which the father of the female lead (Marjorie Lord) is the chief villain.

Chain Gang Killings, The (1985), VCL. Dir. Clive Harding; Cast includes: Ian Yule, Ken Gampu.

Two hate-filled, shackled convicts escape from a brutal chain gang in this action drama, which is reminiscent of *The Defiant Ones*, with Sidney Poitier and Tony Curtis. One prisoner happens to be black and the other white. They undergo a series of rather uninteresting escapades. Violence for its own sake seems to be the chief focus of this film. Like *The Defiant Ones*, this film promotes the message of brotherhood when the two escapees realize they must put aside their prejudices and help each other if they are to survive.

Cool Hand Luke (1967), WB. Dir. Stuart Rosenberg; Sc. Donn Pierce; Cast includes: Paul Newman, George Kennedy, Strother Martin, J. D. Cannon.

Stuart Rosenberg's drama treats the subject of Southern prison farms with deftness and sensitivity. The authorities, as in most Hollywood films, are the bad guys. The warden and the guards are cruel and insensitive while the prisoners are the victims. Drifter Luke Jackson (Paul Newman) receives a two-year sentence for cutting the heads off parking meters while drunk. Assigned to a Southern chain gang, he soon gains the respect of his fellow convicts when he endures a brutal beating by brawny fellow prisoner George Kennedy but refuses to quit. Luke is a man who just won't give in. The prison authorities put him in a special lockup to prevent his escape. However, when he learns that his mother is dying he breaks out twice. But each time he is caught and severely punished. "It's for your own good, Luke," the captain says. "I wish you'd stop bein' so good to me, cap'n," Luke quips.

But when he finally succumbs to his captors and begs to be left alone, he loses face with his fellow prisoners. His obeisance, however, is only a sham, for he remains defiant and escapes once again. He takes refuge in a church and armed guards soon surround the building. Luke appears at a window and mimics the captain's pet phrase ("What we have here is a failure to communicate"). Suddenly he is shot to death by a lone rifle burst. A symbol of resistance, Luke provokes the authorities into destroying him. Luke ends up a legend among his fellow prisoners, who assume the role of his disciples.

County Fair, The (1932), Mon. Dir. Louis King; Sc. Harvey Harris Gates; Cast includes: Hobart Bosworth, Marion Shilling, Ralph Ince, William Collier Jr.

Hobart Bosworth, a Kentucky colonel, and William Collier Jr., a former jockey, confront racketeers in Louis King's crime-sports drama. The villains drug a horse to help them win a race, in this weak film highlighted by a black revival meeting. The film was remade, with the same title, and directed in 1937 by Howard Bretherton. The featured players were John Arledge and Mary Lou Lender. The same studio made a third version – same title again – in 1950, this time featuring Rory Calhoun and Jane Nigh as the leads, with William Beaudine as director.

Dust Be My Destiny (1939), WB. Dir. Lewis Seiler; Sc. Robert Rossen; Cast includes: John Garfield, Priscilla Lane, Alan Hale, Frank McHugh, Billy Halop, Bobby Jordan.

Fate deals innocent drifter John Garfield a bad hand, which almost ruins his life. This dark episodic drama is based on the novel by Jerome Odlum. Picked up for a crime he did not commit, the luckless Garfield is sentenced to a county work farm in the South where he meets and falls in love with Priscilla Lane, the cruel foreman's stepdaughter. They run off together after Garfield fights the foreman. The two lovers marry, but Garfield is soon hunted for the stepfather's murder. Following a long pursuit, Lane turns her husband in to stand trial. At first embittered by her actions, Garfield forgives her when he is acquitted, and they are reunited.

Detour, a 1945 cult film, featured Tom Neal in a similar, ill-fated but more tragic role than Garfield's. When Neal remarks about life that "whichever way you turn, fate sticks out a foot to trip you," one could almost hear Garfield in the earlier dark drama saying the same thing.

Fled (1996), MGM. Dir. Kevin Hooks; Sc. William A. Whitmore II; Cast includes: Laurence Fishburne, Stephen Baldwin, Will Patton, Robert John Burke, Robert Hooks.

In this action drama, Laurence Fishburne and Stephen Baldwin portray convicts who, while chained together, bolt from a road gang. We soon learn that Fishburne is working undercover for the attorney general and Baldwin is a computer hack who has swindled a large company out of millions of dollars. Baldwin is unwittingly holding a disk containing a major drug lord's database. So now, both the law and criminals are searching for Baldwin as the fugitives head for Atlanta to meet Baldwin's contact. Will Patton, a Southern detective, suspects the escape from the road gang has been planned and asks his superior to permit him to continue his investigation. His supervisor reluctantly agrees, but warns him, "Friend or no friend I can't back you up on this."

Following some conventional car chases, shootouts and murders, Fishburne discovers that he has been betrayed by his federal contact. The agent has gone bad and has joined the Cuban mob which wants the computer disk. When members of the gang finally capture Baldwin, he asks, "You're Chinese?" "I'm Cuban," the leader corrects him. "But I have an affinity for all cultures. Part of my Mongol upbringing on the streets of New York." "New York," Baldwin then replies, "That explains your hostility." Fishburne and Patton come to the rescue, kill the villains and expose the corrupt agent. Patton finally gets the computer disk.

Fletch Lives (1989), U. Dir. Michael Ritchie; Sc. Leon Capetanos; Cast includes: Chevy Chase, Hal Holbrook, Julianne Phillips, Cleavon Little, R. Lee Ermey.

In this sequel to *Fletch* (1985), Chevy Chase returns to portray the title character, a Los Angeles reporter who inherits his aunt's Louisiana estate. When he arrives, he finds a run-down property and a dead real-estate broker. Chase is arrested and falsely accused of the crime. "You feel like making a statement?" a suspicious sheriff asks him. "A statement?" Chase repeats. "'Ask not what your country can do for you; ask what you can do for your country.'" Other one-liners don't help to salvage a completely frivolous film. For example, when Chase lands on a gangster's limousine, the hoodlum instructs the driver: "If it's a cop, kill him; if it's a reporter, cripple him." An attorney informs Chase that he owes $4,387 in back alimony and, if he doesn't pay, he will end up in jail. "You're right," Chase quips. "I've been foolishly squandering my salary on food and heat." In another scene, acquaintance Cleavon Little asks Chase, who has been investigating a big-time television evangelist, "Are you religious?" "I believe in a God that doesn't need heavy financing," the reporter replies.

Gingerbread Man, The (1998), PolyGram. Dir. Robert Altman; Sc. Al Hayes; Cast includes: Kenneth Branagh, Embeth Davidtz, Robert Duvall, Robert Downey Jr.

Kenneth Branagh portrays Rick Magruder, a divorced, hotshot Savannah lawyer who enjoys public attention, in this suspenseful drama In a rainstorm one night at a party in his honor he meets Mallory Doss (Embeth Davidtz), a waitress at his firm's party. The party is in celebration of Rick's courtroom victory at the expense of a veteran policeman. Davidtz needs a ride home, so Branagh takes her home through the storm, to her run-down place. Davidtz soon removes her soaked clothing and seduces Branagh. Soon enough, he soon finds himself involved in her problems – the biggest of which is her father (Robert Duvall), a demented woodsman living with a bizarre cult. Other characters include a casual private detective (Robert Downey Jr.), Davidtz's irritable ex-husband (Tom Berenger) and Branagh's flirtatious assistant (Daryl Hannah).

The dialogue is often raw and biting. When Branagh interviews ex-husband Berenger about his wife, he says bitterly, "I wouldn't spare a drop of piss on her if she was burnin' to death." "Yeah," the lawyer retorts, "we're aware of your urinary problems, sir." In another scene, the heavily sedated private eye Downey cracks to Davidtz, "No offense, ma'am, but it's always appeared to me your Dad's a few beers shy of a six-pack." In still another scene in the lawyer's office, Branagh's assistant Hannah repels an obnoxious flirt. "I'm simply curious," she asks, "you just keep propositioning people until somebody says yes?"

As the story becomes more violent, it includes a kidnapping, betrayal and murder. The natural hurricane that moves toward Savannah reflects the inner turmoil of the plot.

Screenwriter John Grisham prefers to paint his lawyers as dark and gloomy. He describes Savannah so vividly that the city seems to assume human characteristics.

Green Mile, The (1999), WB. Dir. Frank Darabont; Sc. Frank Darabont; Cast includes: Tom Hanks, Michael Clarke Duncan, David Morse, James Crowell, Michael Jeter, Sam Rockwell.

Tom Hanks, as Paul Edgecomb, supervises a Southern penitentiary's death row, known as E Block, or the "Green Mile," because of the worn linoleum floor. This drama is based on the novel by Stephen King. A new inmate, John Coffey (Michael Clarke Duncan), a large, seven-foot-tall, black man arrives and the film describes the subsequent changes in both the inmates and the guards. Scheduled for execution because of his conviction for brutally killing two small girls, he nevertheless appears calm, gentle and cooperative. He also reveals to Edgecomb that he is afraid of the dark. Edgecomb and the guards soon discover that Coffey seems to possess magical healing powers. They believe somehow that God has blessed Coffey with these powers, so they arrange to try to help the prison warden's wife, who is dying from brain cancer. Coffee draws and sucks in the evil and the ills of the sick and then exhales these problems.

Edgecomb thinks there is more to this inmate and finally discovers he is innocent of the charges – that another prisoner (Sam Rockwell) committed the horrible double murder. "I've done some things in my life I've never been proud of," he confides to his wife before carrying out the execution, "but this is the first time I ever felt the real danger of Hell." But in his cell, Coffey accepts his sentence. "On the day of my judgment," he explains to Coffey, "when I stand before God and He asks me why I killed one of His true miracles, what am I going to say – it was my job?" Coffey, burdened by his sleepless nights and terrifying nightmares, resigns himself to his fate and welcomes it. "I want it to be done with," he pleads quietly. "I'm tired. I'm tired of people being ugly to each other. I'm tired of all the pain I feel in the world. There's too much of it. Do you understand?" As he goes peacefully to the electric chair, the guards of E Block tearfully carry out the execution.

Hard Choices (1984), Screenland. Dir. Rick King; Sc. Rick King; Cast includes: Gary McCleery, Margaret Klenck, John Seitz, John Sayles, John Snyder.

Rick King's crime drama takes place in the backwoods of Tennessee, where Gary McCleery portrays Bobby, a fifteen-year-old with good prospects for making something out of his life. His older brothers, however, are involved in drugs and robberies. When they decide to rob a drugstore to pay for drugs, they take Bobby along. A police officer is killed and the district attorney decides to try Bobby and his brothers as adults for the murder. Although the local sheriff has some sympathy for the young boy, Bobby is treated brutally in jail. Margaret Klenck portrays the social worker who deals with juvenile offenders. When she hears about his case, she travels to the small town and gets to know Bobby and becomes convinced that he was an unwilling participant in the murder. Klenck believes Bobby's story that he was simply an innocent bystander. Although she appears to be a conventional adult bureaucrat, she soon shows her compassionate side and works within the system but is not part of it.

Hell's Highway (1932), RKO. Dir. Rowland Brown; Sc. Samuel Ornitz; Cast includes: Richard Dix, Tom Brown, Louise Carter, Rochelle Hudson, C. Henry Gordon.

The main focus of Rowland Brown's morbid drama is in a Southern prison camp, where African-Americans are the majority of the convicts. A local contractor has hired the prisoners to build a new road and, in order for him to make a profit, the convicts must work twice as hard. The guards use the dreaded "sweat box," a corrugated iron box which barely holds a man as a threat against slower workers. One man who faints is strangled to death from a leather collar around his neck. This death is the final straw for the convicts who lead a revolt against their miserable conditions. Eventually the contractor loses out.

I Am a Fugitive From a Chain Gang (1932), WB. Dir. Mervyn LeRoy; Sc. Sheridan Gibney, Brown Holmes; Cast includes: Paul Muni, Glenda Farrell, Helen Vinson, Preston Foster, Edward J. McNamara, Sheila Terry, Allen Jenkins.

More of a social drama than a crime film, director Mervyn LeRoy's powerful and memorable tale tells the story of James Allen's terrible life. The grim work, based on the novel by Robert E. Burns, remains in the moviegoer's thoughts long after the final scenes have left the screen. Allen, played expertly by Paul Muni, experiences his most degrading and brutal conditions as a member of a Southern chain gang. He escapes and, by dint of hard work, he rises in the engineering field. The authorities are obsessed by Allen and continue to pursue him. When the officials break their promise of a nominal sentence in return for his voluntary surrender, he escapes once more and fades into obscurity. On a secretive nocturnal visit to his one-time girlfriend, she asks how he has been surviving. The edgy fugitive replies, "I steal," as he fades into the blackness of the night.

Invasion U.S.A. (1985), Cannon. Dir. Joseph Zito; Sc. James Bruner, Chuck Norris; Cast includes: Chuck Norris, Richard Lynch, Melissa Prophet, Alexander Zale, Alex Colon.

A crazed Russian agent leads a small military force in an assault on Florida in this action drama. Rostov, the Soviet spy (Richard Lynch), fears only one man who may interfere with the success of his invasion – Matt Hunter, a U.S. intelligence super-agent. So he assigns some of his top underlings to annihilate Hunter. Chuck Norris, as the agent, is currently retired and living with his wife in Florida's Everglades. His former chief informs Hunter about his old enemy, Rostov, and asks him to return to duty but Hunter rejects the request. When Rostov's men blow up his house and murder his old Indian friend, Hunter swings into action. In an effort to capture Rostov, he sets up a trap. The two rivals finally confront each other and engage in a fight to the death.

Leadbelly (1976), Par. Dir. Gordon Parks; Sc. Ernest Kinoy; Cast includes: Roger E. Mosley, Paul Benjamin, John Henry Faulk, Loretta Greene, Lynn Hamilton.

In Gordon Parks's biographical drama, Roger E. Mosley portrays the title character, a blues singer and accomplished guitar player. The film explores highlights from his life on the road and his experiences as a convict on the Texas and Louisiana chain gangs. The sometimes brutal and often realistic drama features several songs, including "Rock Island Line" and "Goodnight Irene," but most of the selections are far from the typical light Hollywood music that audiences have been accustomed to over the years.

*

The story line parallels the life of Leadbelly (Huddie Ledbetter) (1888-1949), who was born and raised in Louisiana. He roamed the southeast in his younger years and, during one of his sojourns, learned to play the blues from Blind Lemon Jefferson. He had a violent temper and, in 1930, was sentenced for 30 years to Angola Prison in Louisiana for two murders. While in Angola, Leadbelly entertained the guards and other prisoners with his renditions of popular songs, blues and folk ballads.

Alan Lomax, the famous musicologist, discovered Leadbelly during one of his trips to Angola. At the time, the musicologist was recording black folk music and was so impressed with Leadbelly's musical talents that he petitioned Louisiana Governor O. K. Allen to pardon the prisoner for no other reason than for his musical ability and his knowledge of black folk music. Surprisingly enough, the governor pardoned Leadbelly into Lomax's custody.

Leadbelly worked for Lomax for one year, but then, in 1935, moved to New York City where he met a group of left-wing folk singers, including Woodie

Guthrie and Pete Seeger. They became close friends and eventually Leadbelly left his roots in the blues and developed into a folk singer. He wrote some of the most famous left-wing songs of the day, such as "Bourgeois Blues" and the "Scottsboro Boys," which carried strong political messages. One year after Leadbelly's death in 1949, Pete Seeger and the Weavers recorded his song, "Goodnight Irene," and it immediately rocketed to number one on the charts.

*

Lure of the Swamp (1957), TCF. Dir. Hubert Cornfield; Sc. William George; Cast includes: Marshall Thompson, Willard Parker, Joan Vohs, Jack Elam.

A bank robber hides $20,000 in a swamp and is then killed. In this grim drama based on the novel by Gil Brewer, his partner returns to search for the loot. He tries to hire a local swamp resident to help him in the search. Meanwhile, others arrive – an insurance investigator and a blonde magazine photographer. The blonde is actually the widow of the dead robber and perishes in quicksand, along with the money. Brewer perishes as well, in this tale of greed.

Mean Season, The (1985), Orion. Dir. Philip Boros; Sc. Leon Piedmont; Cast includes: Kurt Russell, Mariel Hemingway, Richard Jordan, Richard Masur, Andy Garcia.

A mad serial killer develops a telephone relationship with Miami newspaper reporter Kurt Russell. This harrowing thriller is based on the novel *In the Heat of the Summer* by John Katzenbach. Richard Jordan, as the killer, calls Russell to congratulate him on his story about the murder of a young woman, and promises further exclusives in a projected series of killings. Russell gains national recognition on magazine covers and he makes guest appearances on television talk shows. Both murders and stories continue as Russell is torn between his moral obligations and his ambition.

Jordan grows jealous of the reporter's popularity and he kidnaps Mariel Hemingway, Russell's girlfriend. Following several complications, a struggle ensues in which the reporter kills Jordan. Russell is disgusted with his own articles, but his editor reminds him, "We're not manufacturers, we just retail. News gets made somewhere else, we just sell it." The film raises questions about journalistic ethics as it wonders about who is exploiting whom in this perverse cat-and-mouse game.

*

Miami served as background for other crime films as well. One of the most popular – and most violent – was Brian DePalma's *Scarface* (1983), an updated version of the 1932 classic, with Paul Muni. This newer version traces a Cuban refugee in Miami, played by Al Pacino, who becomes a cocaine drug lord. Paul Michael Glasser's *Band in the Hand* (1986) portrays a group of teenage toughs who are transformed into vigilantes in order to rid Miami of drug dealers. In Stephen Seemayer's low-budget mystery *Miami Vendetta* (1987), Los Angeles detective Maarten Goslin travels to Miami where he tracks down drug dealers who killed his best friend. Alec Baldwin is the psychopathic killer in George Armitage's mystery *MiamiBlues* (1990). Baldwin picks up Jason Leigh, a gullible prostitute, and poses as a policeman.

*

Midnight in the Garden of Good and Evil (1997), WB. Dir. Clint Eastwood; Sc. John Lee Hancock; Cast includes: Kevin Spacey, John Cusack, Jack Thompson, Irma P. Hall, Jude Law.

John Cusack is a writer who journeys to Savannah, Georgia where he is mesmerized by the scenery, the eccentric talkative characters, the quaint architecture and the history of the city. Clint Eastwood's slow-paced drama is based on the successful novel by John Berendt. Cusack meets a gay antique dealer (Kevin Spacey), whose friendly, cavalier ways and lifestyle fascinate the writer. Suddenly a young hustler is found dead and Spacey falls under suspicion. "Savin' face in the light of unpleasant circumstances," his lawyer announces, "is the Savannah way." One of the more outrageous characters is the transvestite who calls herself the Lady Chablis and who taunts the writer. Several scenes display some of the more characteristic features of Savannah – its Spanish moss, its unique graveyards and its special town squares.

New Orleans Uncensored (1955), Col. Dir. William Castle; Sc. Orville H. Hampton, Lewis Meltzer; Cast include: Arthur Franz, Beverly Garland, Helene Stanton, Michael Ansara.

U.S. Navy veteran Arthur Franz exposes union racketeering and corruption on the New Orleans waterfront. This fairly interesting drama was filmed chiefly in that city. Franz is new to his job as dockworker and he observes the activities – including smuggling – of crooked union boss Michael Ansara. After his friend is murdered, Franz goes to the authorities and volunteers to help gather evidence against the racketeers. He sets a trap that eventually ensnares the gang. This film was only one of several city exposé films released during the 1950s.

*

New Orleans has served as the locale for a variety of genre films, including dramas. For example, in Arthur Lubin's *Mysterious Crossing* (1937), set in New Orleans, reporter James Dunn becomes involved in a murder while he is on a ferry crossing the Mississippi. Vivien Leigh, as Blanche Du Bois, a fading Southern belle, joins her sister Stella (Kim Hunter) and her husband Stanley in New Orleans in Elia Kazan's *A Streetcar Named Desire* (1951). By the time Stuart Rosenberg's social drama *WUSA* (1970) appeared, audiences were seeing a much-changed New Orleans as well as a radically different America on the screen.

*

No Mercy (1986), Tri-Star. Dir. Richard Pearce; Sc. Jim Carabatsos, Beth Henley, Tom Rickman; Cast includes: Richard Gere, Kim Basinger, Jeroen Krabbe, George Dzunza, William Atherton.

Once again, New Orleans serves as the venue for a Hollywood film, this time Richard Pearce's tough drama. Richard Gere, as a maverick Chicago police officer, poses as a hit man for a New Orleans couple visiting Chicago. Gere wants to get them for killing his partner. He finds Kim Basinger, the female half of the couple, in New Orleans. He handcuffs her and drags her through the Louisiana bayous. After putting her through hell, Gere believes that Bassinger is a victim herself. As a young woman, she was sold to Jeroen Krabbe, a drug dealer and slave trader. Gere and Basinger survive a series of murderous attempts on their lives and an implausible final shootout in a local hotel.

Road Gang (1936), WB. Dir. Louis King; Sc. Dalton Trumbo; Cast includes: Donald Woods, Carlyle Moore Jr., Kay Linaker, Harry Cording, Ed Chandler, Marc Lawrence.

Once again, Hollywood glorifies the prisoners and vilifies the prison guards. Louis King's grim drama is set in a Southern prison camp and uses several graphic sequences to show the sadistic treatment of prisoners by their brutal guards. A local crusading newspaper editor exposes a political clique that not only allows these abuses to exist, but contributes to them. The plot centers on two youths, played by Donald Woods and Carlyle Moore Jr., who suffer severe beatings at the hands of their vicious prison guards. Warner Brothers Studios turned out a number of socially relevant features throughout the 1930s. Some of these films included dramas like *White Bondage* (1937), which dealt with the exploitation of poor sharecroppers, and *The Black Legion*, also 1937, with Humphrey Bogart, which exposes a Ku Klux Klan-type of organization.

Smokey and the Bandit (1977), Rastar. Dir. Hal Needham; Sc. James Lee Barrett, Alan Mandel, Charles Shyer; Cast includes: Burt Reynolds, Sally Field, Jackie Gleason, Jerry Reed, Mike Henry, Paul Williams.

Southern driver Burt Reynolds transports beer from Texas to Atlanta in Hal Needham's boisterous comedy. Meanwhile, perplexed and frustrated sheriff Jackie Gleason drives in hot pursuit. Stunts, chases and car wrecks dominate most of the predictable action. "Don't you ever take your hat off?" runaway bride Sally Field asks bootlegger Reynolds. "I take my hat off for one thing and one thing only," he replies. "You've got a nice profile," she says, complimenting him, "especially from the side."

Meanwhile, Sheriff Gleason cannot believe his dim-witted son could possibly come from his genes. "First thing I'm going to do when I get home," the fuming sheriff yells, "is punch your mama in the mouth!" The combination of plot and stars in this film so appealed to audiences that it sprouted several sequels.

Sporting Blood (1931), MGM. Dir. Charles Brabin; Sc. Willard Mack, Wanda Tuchock; Cast includes: Clark Gable, Ernest Torrence, Madge Evans, Lew Cody, Marie Prevost, Harry Holman.

A racehorse is moved around from one owner to another and is abused and exploited along the way. This above-average drama is based on the novel *Horseflesh* by Frederick Hazlitt Brennan. Horse breeder Ernest Torrence sells his steed Tommy Boy to J. Farrell MacDonald, who sells it again. The horse ends up with gambler Clark Gable in payment for a bad debt. Gable uses drugs on the horse in order to slow him down and so lose a race, an action that brings condemnation from his employees, Madge Evans and Lew Cody. Eventually Tommy Boy is returned to Torrence, who resists gangster threats to make the horse lose the Kentucky Derby. Evans, although in love with Gable, eventually leaves him and marries Cody.

Swamp Water (1941), TCF. Dir. Jean Renoir; Sc. Dudley Nichols; Cast includes: Walter Brennan, Walter Huston, Anne Baxter, Dana Andrews.

Dana Andrews portrays a trapper who finds accused murderer Walter Brennan hiding out in Georgia's Okefenokee Swamp. The two men strike up a friendship. When Brennan explains how he was railroaded, he wins the trust of his young friend. Andrews soon becomes romantically involved with Brennan's daughter, Anne Baxter. They set up a profitable trapping business as Brennan snares the animals and Andrews sells their pelts. Virginia Gilmore, a young woman who likes Andrews, grows jealous of his relationship with Baxter, and informs the authorities of Brennan's whereabouts. Questioned by lawmen, Andrews refuses to reveal where the fugitive is. Instead, he solves the crime by proving that testimony at Brennan's trial was perjured to protect the guilty killers. Brennan is cleared of all charges and returns to civilization. Brennan repeated his role in the 1952 remake, *Lure of the Wilderness.*

Sweet Sugar (1972), Dimension. Dir. Michel Levesque; Sc. Don Spencer; Cast includes: Phyllis Elizabeth Davis, Ella Edwards, Pamela Collins.

Women prisoners on a sugar plantation revolt against their brutal overseers and escape into the swamps. This sexy action drama deteriorates into just another "women in bondage" exploitation film. Before the young women leave, the audience is treated to seeing one man skewered and another burned at the stake. A third has one of his hands chopped off. However, to make things more palatable to the audience, all three men were portrayed as villains. The cast includes Phyllis Elizabeth Davis, Ella Edwards and Pamela Collins.

Tennessee Nights (1989), Academy Video. Dir. Nicolas Gessner; Sc. Larry Koenig; Cast includes: Julian Sands, Denise Crosby, Ned Beatty, Johnny Cash.

Julian Sands gets caught up in a web of intrigue during an innocent fishing trip in the hills of Tennessee. Following his meeting with the sexually alluring Denise Crosby, he is pursued by unidentified stalkers. He seeks help from the law but he is arrested and accused of killing Crosby. Sands is incarcerated in a cell with hostile, violent criminals. Ned Beatty, Ed Lauter and Rod Steiger have other parts in this nightmarish tale. Singer Johnny Cash plays himself.

Johnny Cash (1932-), the son of a dirt-poor cotton farmer, was born in Kingsland, Arkansas. He never forgot the flooding of the Mississippi River in 1937 near his boyhood home and, in later years, he immortalized it in his song "Five Feet High and Rising." Director E. A. Dupont's minor drama *On Such a Night* (1937) dramatized the flooding. The film portrays the mighty Mississippi River overflow its banks and threaten a prison and a farmhouse.

Cash moved to Memphis in 1954, where he started playing guitar while singing on radio station KWEM. Sun Records gave him a contract and, in 1955, recorded his two songs "Hey Porter" and "Folsom Prison Blues." Cash's next offering, "I Walk the Line," sold over one million records the following year. He was jailed twice for substance abuse and his health subsequently declined. Fortunately, these setbacks were temporary and Cash overcame his drug dependency and went on to record over 150 major songs. He appeared in *Door-to-Door Maniac* (1961), *Festival* (1967), *A Gunfight* (1971) and *The Gospel Road* (1973). Cash also made numerous guest appearances on television.

*

Thieves Like Us (1974), UA. Dir. Robert Altman; Sc. Calder Willingham; Cast includes: Keith Carradine, Shelley Duvall, John Schuck, Bert Remsen, Louise Fletcher.

An absorbing remake of *They Live by Night*, Robert Altman's crime drama is based on the novel by Edward Anderson. It's set in the 1930s and tells the story of a group of incompetent and unlucky lawbreakers. Keith Carradine, as Bowie, escapes from a Mississippi jail with older inmates Bert Remsen and John Schuck, who plays a psychotic criminal. They soon return to their only trade – robbing banks. Bowie's girlfriend, Keechie (Shelly Duvall) joins the gang and they all go on a rampage. After a few bank holdups, Bowie plans to retire in Mexico, together with Keechie. The police begin to close in on the gang and kill Remsen. Schuck is caught and the lovers continue alone. Following a series of complications, Bowie returns to his hideout, where the cops are waiting. As they hold down his screaming, pregnant girl friend, Bowie is gunned down by other lawmen. Duvall gives birth to their child and moves on to search for a new life. The title refers to the trio's philosophy that all people – including bankers and businessmen – are thieves to some degree.

Walking Tall (1973), Cinerama. Dir. Phil Karlson; Sc. Mort Briskin; Cast includes: Joe Don Baker, Elizabeth Hartman, Gene Evans, Noah Beery Jr.

The explosive drama is a highly fictionalized account of Buford Pusser's career as a Tennessee sheriff. Don Baker has the lead role. The mythology begins once Pusser swings a stout hickory club at the heads of mobsters who operate a stripclub in his hometown. One of the casinos cheats Pusser's friend and Pusser tries to recoup his money. For his troubles, he is beaten, stabbed and left for dead. He recovers and begins swinging his club and taking the law into his own hands. After being arrested, he defends himself in court by claiming a natural right of self-defense. When Pusser rips open his shirt to display his knife wounds, he is immediately acquitted. He is elected sheriff and cleans up the town – although at a high cost to his family.

The film appeals to our belief in simple justice – total, swift and crude. It operates on a level that is emotionally charged and virtually compels us to cheer for each blow he strikes against criminals. Audiences tend to agree with Pusser's extreme and violent justice. Some incidents in this film biography may not be accurate, but the drama is generally faithful to the biography of Buford Pusser.

*

In real life, Pusser was beaten up in 1957 in a brawl in a casino over some money he lost. About three years later, when the casino owner was robbed and beaten, Pusser and two buddies were charged with robbery. But they were acquitted because of a strong alibi. Pusser entered police work in 1962 and succeeded his father, who retired as chief of police in Adamsville. He then ran for sheriff in 1964, when the incumbent sheriff was killed in an auto accident. Pusser won the post and appointed his own father as his first new deputy. He racked up a large number of arrests as a result of his raids on moonshiners and, when he ran for office again in 1972, he was defeated. His own wife was killed during his tenure in office and he himself was beaten up several times. Townspeople felt that these beatings were in reprisal for his brutal treatment of suspected criminals. Pusser promoted his own style of law enforcement and he was lauded in a number of magazine articles, a television piece and a series of popular action dramas.

*

Whistling in Dixie (1942), Dir. S. Sylvan Simon; Sc. Nat Perrin; Cast includes:
Red Skelton, Ann Rutherford, George Bancroft, Guy Kibbee, Diana Lewis.

Red Skelton is the lead sleuth on the radio show "The Wolf." In this comedy, he is persuaded by his girlfriend (Ann Rutherford) to accompany her on her trip to Georgia. A Southern sorority sister wants Skelton to help find some hidden treasure. Meanwhile, some local inhabitants want the treasure for themselves and are willing to do anything to gain possession of the coveted wealth. Skelton's antics are quite funny. As victims disappear and suspicious characters come and go, Skelton keeps on investigating an old Civil War fortress.

19

Show Business: Way Down South in Dixie

The cinema is entertainment and, as such, musicals and musical biographies have always been at the heart of it. Unfortunately, not all were successful or overly popular with movie audiences or critics. Nevertheless, even the weakest low-budget productions offered audiences an opportunity to see and hear the talents of many obscure entertainers and talents that once graced the stages, radio stations and screens of America. Many of these films serve as museum pieces, with their quaint circus routines, slow-moving showboats and nostalgic theatrical and vaudeville acts. Some of the early films of Al Jolson, who was once billed as "the world's greatest entertainer," remind us of the old minstrel shows, where whites often appeared in blackface. The Ritz Brothers capture the slapstick of the old vaudeville days. Films like *Grand Ole Opry* (1940) show us the once-popular hillbilly acts, such as those offered by the famous Weaver family. Other musicals like *New Orleans* (1947) give us a chance to see and hear jazz giants like Louis Armstrong, Billie Holiday, Kid Ory and Woody Herman and his orchestra. These works and personalities emphasize the rich contributions of the South to the world of music and entertainment.

Music has always been an integral part of the history of the South. The phrase "folk music" is usually applied to songs and ballads that have originated within a specific geographic area and have been passed down from one generation to the next. Because the music is handed down orally, the same folk song can be sung differently by different performing artists. Nevertheless, the variations can generally be recognized as different representations of the same material.

Unlike "classical music," folk music is the product of working-class people and not the output of an intellectual elite. The dirt-poor, rural farmers and hunters of Appalachia developed Southern white folk music and, from them, it trickled down to the rest of the southeast.

The minstrel show probably evolved from two types of entertainment popular in America before 1830 – the impersonation of blacks by white actors between acts and by black musicians who sang with banjo accompaniment in city streets. The "father of American minstrelsy" Thomas Dartmouth "Daddy" Rice (1808-60) developed a song-and-dance routine between 1828 and 1831 in which he impersonated an old black slave, dubbed Jim Crow. The term was later appropriated to describe discriminatory laws in the South.

After the American Civil War, black entertainers – often also in blackface makeup – became more prominent. The most famous of the black minstrel composers was James Bland (1854-1911). His show offered the most popular music in the 19th century and its banjo music contributed to ragtime and the evolution of tap dance. From 1850 to 1870 at least ten theaters in New York City alone were devoted to minstrelsy. After 1870 its popularity faded rapidly.

Country and western music is actually a misnomer, for it was initially developed and nurtured as "hillbilly music" in the southeast and some parts of the southwest and not the West. Folk music and Elizabethan songs of the earlier Irish, Scottish and English immigrants as well as African-American blues were key influences on country and western music.

The recording industry initially targeted "hillbilly music" for Southern agrarian white audiences. One of these hillbilly bands, the Carter Family, purposely used unsophisticated singing techniques and Appalachian instruments to play old folk ballads and sentimental songs. During the fifties, the "hillbilly" bands borrowed from rock and roll, added amplified music and made their presentations as snazzy as possible. The record companies, in an effort to capture a wider audience, renamed the genre "country and western" and they were very successful. Skillfully handled, country and western music moved from local cable stations to nationally syndicated television.

Ragtime, an American musical genre, mainly for piano, reached its peak between 1897 and World War I. Its roots were in minstrel-show plantation songs, cakewalks, banjo playing and African-American folk music.

Spirituals, which are deeply emotional, often melancholy, religious folk songs were originally thought to stem spontaneously from African-American slaves. They were considered to be the only original folk music of the U.S. Spirituals are often heard in romantic or nostalgic films about the South, particularly those set in plantation life in the days of slavery. King Vidor's all-black drama *Hallelujah* (1929) contains scenes of revival meetings, river baptisms and several spiritual numbers.

Al Jolson, mostly in blackface, portrays a black jockey who overcomes several hurdles before he wins the Kentucky Derby in Alan Crosland's musical comedy *Big Boy* (1930). Besides the songs "Liza Lee" and "Down South," Jolson leads a group of black children in a series of spirituals, including "Go Down,

Moses." Bernard Vorhaus's drama *Way Down South* (1939) includes several spirituals sung by blacks and other songs rendered by young Bobby Breen.

Gospel music, an American musical form that developed in Protestant churches of the South, is performed today by Americans of all backgrounds. However, African-American gospel music is more significant, with its roots in field and work songs. African-American gospel music is more intense and joyous than its generic form. Gospel and jazz were considered incompatible in African-American society until both forms gained general acceptance by the mid-twentieth century. In time, both have influenced "soul" and rock music.

For African-Americans living in the post-Civil War era, emancipation did not live up to its promise, and the blues reflected their depression and suffering. Blues songs usually included recurrent groans and snorts that tapered off at the end. Blues singers described their personal melancholy and agonies – usually in three-line stanzas. The groans and snorts and the unusual notes were definitely outside the mainstream of American music and have been traced back to their West African origins. As the genre developed, blues music was recorded and disseminated throughout the U.S. In the 1920s, black blues singers and guitar players migrated from the South to Chicago, Detroit and Indianapolis where they recorded bestsellers.

Although blues was a distinctively black medium, jazz seems more biracial. There were white and black jazz bands and soloists. White and black jazz musicians, however, often approached and played the same music quite differently. In 1926, Red Nichols, a white musician, composed and played "Black Bottom Stomp." Following World War I, jazz expanded from New Orleans to the rest of the country. Louis Armstrong (trumpet), Peewee Russell (clarinet), Benny Goodman (clarinet) as well as Bix Beiderbecke (cornet) appropriated the jazz sound for Chicago. From there, the distinctive sound of jazz extended to New York City, where the big bands played it in theaters and ballrooms.

Rock 'n' Roll had its roots in rhythm and blues, hillbilly music and gospel. Some of the groups, like the Ink Spots, sang rock during the week and gospel in their churches on Sundays. Other singing groups featured "shouting singers" who emphasized the beat by screaming and used techniques directly inherited from Southern Baptist ministers. Screamin' Jay Hawkins and Little Richard were two of the leading "screamers."

Rock 'n' roll ran into a lot of flack from older, more conservative people – and, of course, parents. When the volume was turned up and the electric guitar and drums were added, the adversaries of rock 'n' roll also escalated their opposition. They claimed that rock 'n' roll was a corrupting influence, that it was innately immoral in that it included lewd material and, in addition, it would rot children's minds.

Some Hollywood studios tried to exploit the rising popularity of rock 'n' roll and began producing their own rock films aimed at the youth market. They used middle-aged contract players and employed such techniques as wide screen, Technicolor and costly sets. For example, 20th Century-Fox's zany rock 'n' roll comedy *How to Be Very, Very Popular* (1955) featured Betty Grable (the famous pin-up girl of World War II), Sheree North, Robert Cummings, Charles Coburn, Orson Bean and Fred Clark. They were all veteran players from a decade earlier, with virtually little drawing power from current teenagers. The studio poured their resources into the production, added color and Cinemascope, but failed to use younger, contemporary rock stars of the period. Perhaps worst of all, the film was adapted from a 1933 play by Howard Lindsay titled *She Loves Me Not*. Needless to say, the film was a flop.

*

Bird (1988), WB. Dir. Clint Eastwood; Sc. Joel Oliansky; Cast includes: Forest Whittaker, Diane Venora, Michael Zelniker.

A warm biography about the legendary saxophonist Charlie Parker, the drama focuses on his drug addiction and self-destructive life. Forest Whittaker plays the talented musician who revolutionized jazz in the 1940s. Parker's own soundtracks enhance the production, along with the performances.

*

Jazz musician Charlie Parker (1920-1955), whose real name was Charles Christopher Jr., was also known as "Bird" or "Yardbird." He was born in the slums of Kansas City, Kansas. A leading exponent of bebop, he exerted great influence on later saxophonists, especially during the 1940s and 1950s. Although he was an unhappy vagabond and a drug addict, Parker nevertheless was able to write the music for Louis Malle's French drama *Murmur of the Heart* (1972) and contributed to the lyrics and music of *'Round Midnight* (1986).

*

Blonde From Brooklyn (1945), Col. Dir. Del Lord; Sc. Erna Lazarus; Cast includes: Robert Stanton, Lynn Merrick, Thurston Hall, Mary Treen.

Army veteran Robert Stanton, a song-and-dance man and wannabe crooner, teams up with jukebox singer Lynn Merrick. Del Lord's entertaining and lighthearted musical romance pokes fun at Southern traditions such as the old plantation and the "Deep South." Stanton and Merrick pose as Southerners, meet a Southern colonel (Thurston Hall) and then appear on his radio show. Merrick claims she is a Southern heiress, but when the real heiress appears, the couple runs. Stanton and Merrick finally go legitimate as a vocal duo and succeed on their own.

Buddy Holly Story, The (1978), Col. Dir. Steve Rash; Sc. John Robert Gitler; Cast includes: Gary Busey, Don Stroud, Charles Martin Smith, William Jordan.

This realistic and very entertaining autobiography covers several highlights in the rock star's career, which was suddenly cut short by a tragic plane crash in 1959. The film includes scenes from his early days in Lubbock, Texas where he chiefly played be-bop, as well as his later performances with The Crickets, his back-up band. *The Buddy Hollly Story* builds up to the point where Holly achieves national recognition. Gary Pusey, in his portrayal of the title character, captures Holly's drive and desire for musical perfection. The film touches upon his conflicts with his drummer, Jesse, and his bassist, Ray Bob. Other sequences include his relationship with his Puerto Rican bride, played by Maria Richwine.

*

Buddy Holly (1936-1959) was born Charles Hardin Holley in Lubbock Texas, but his father decided to shorten his given name to "Buddy." While still in high school, he organized a hillbilly band and even got his own weekly radio program. Perhaps the defining moment in Holly's life occurred when Elvis came to town in 1955 and Holly appeared on the same bill at the Cotton Club. He was so overwhelmed by Presley, that he decided to change the focus of his band from hillbilly to rock.

When Norman Petty set up a modern recording studio in Clovis, New Mexico, Holly went to record some of his songs that were destined to become major hits. Holly's band, which until then had no standard members, was organized into a regular group and cranked out one major hit after another, including, in 1958, three songs that hit the Top 100 listing in *Billboard* – "That'll Be the Day," "Oh, Boy!" and "Peggy Sue."

During the years 1958 and 1959, The Crickets went on national tour. The manager of the Apollo Theater in Harlem in New York City confused Holly and The Crickets with a black singing group, Dean Barlow and The Crickets, and mistakenly booked them. Buddy and his band played their own compositions and, for the first two days, the unimpressed black audience gave them a cold reception. The next day The Crickets decided to try for a "black sound" and opened with "Bo Diddley." That new approach woke up the members of the audience and brought them to their feet cheering. Unfortunately, his career was cut short when he was killed in a plane crash on February 3, 1959.

He appeared in a number of films, including *Cool Cats – Twenty-five Years of Rock 'N' Roll Style* (1983), *Rock 'n' Roll Heaven* (1984) and *The History of Rock 'N' Roll, Vol. 2* (1995). They all contain archive footage.

*

Can This Be Dixie? (1936), TCF. Dir. George Marshall; Sc. Lamar Trotti; Cast includes: Jane Withers, Slim Summerville, Helen Wood, Claude Gillingwater, Donald Cook.

Father and daughter (Slim Summerville and Jane Withers) lose their medicine show, which happens to be on the property of a bankrupt Kentucky colonel. This musical comedy is a satire of the South. To save the show, Jane Withers and a group of workers stage an amateur production in an old Southern home. Songs like "Uncle Tom's Cabin Is a Cabaret Now" do not help the production.

Coal Miner's Daughter (1980), U. Dir. Michael Apted; Sc. Tom Rickman; Cast includes: Sissy Spacek, Tommy Lee Jones, Leon Helm, Phyllis Boyens.

Michael Apted's musical biography was written by George Vecsey and was based on Lynn's autobiography. Sissy Spacek plays Nashville's reigning queen,

Loretta Lynn. The film begins with a young Lynn, living with her parents in a rundown shack in Butcher Holler, in hillbilly country. At age nineteen, she marries (to Tommy Lee Jones) and soon becomes a mother several times over. Her husband, an ex-soldier, rejects an offer of employment from a local moonshiner. "If you keep on in the mountains," the man warns, "you got three choices – coalminin', moonshinin' or movin' on down the line." Jones opts to return to the mines and marries Spacek. He gets her a guitar because she likes singing country songs, and she begins playing publicly in a sleazy bar, where she receives an enthusiastic reception. Before long she rises in the field of country music and appears numerous times on the "Grand Ole Opry" radio show. She becomes a close friend of Patsy Cline, portrayed by Beverly D'Angelo. Both Spacek and D'Angelo deserve credit for doing their own singing.

*

Loretta Lynn (1935-) was the daughter of a coal miner in Butchers Hollow, Kentucky. She was born during the Great Depression and experienced poverty and labor strife firsthand. "Coal Miner's Daughter" was actually her autobiography and it became a hit record. She made appearances on several television shows, acted in some, and her songs were featured in Apted's musical biography, for which Sissy Spacek won an Oscar.

*

Country and western singer Ernest Tubb (1914-1984), who plays himself in *Coal Miner's Daughter*, was so poor that he couldn't afford to buy his own guitar until the age of 20. Tubb was born in Crisp, Texas, and tried to emulate the singing style of his childhood hero, Jimmie Rodgers. His breakthrough came with the 1942 release of his song "Walking the Floor Over You," and he soon became a regular guest on the "Grand Ole Opry." Tubb became so successful that he started his own radio program on WSM, the Midnight Jamboree, which served as a platform for some of the newer talents in country and western. Tubb appeared in two other films: *Riding West* (1944) and *Hollywood Barn Dance* (1947).

*

Patsy Cline (1932-1963), born Virginia Patterson Hensley in Winchester, Virginia, sang in local clubs around Nashville in the early 1950s. She attained national prominence only after she appeared on the "Arthur Godfrey Talent Show" in 1957. The "Grand Ole Opry" soon featured Cline and her recordings "Crazy," "Imagine That" and "So Wrong" became hits. Although she died in an air crash in 1963, her records continue to be best sellers and she has influenced the singing styles of such country and western singers as Reba McEntire and Loretta Lynn.

*

Country Music Holiday (1958), Par. Dir. Alvin Ganzer; Sc. H. B. Cross; Cast includes: Ferlin Husky, Zsa Zsa Gabor, Rocky Graziano, Faron Young.

Small-town singer Ferlin Husky tries to break into big-time television in this cornball musical. Jesse White has a half ownership in Husky's career, and

Zsa Zsa Gabor owns the other half. Following several setbacks, Husky survives the pitfalls of big-city show business. Some of the tunes include "Somewhere There's Sunshine," "Terrific Together," "Just One More Chance" and "When It Rains It Pours."

Crossroads (1986), Col. Dir. Walter Hill; Sc. Thomas Baum, John Fusco; Cast includes: Ralph Macchio, Joe Seneca, Jami Gertz, Joe Morton, Robert Judd.

In Walter Hill's drama, white teenage Juilliard student Ralph Macchio tries to locate a lost song by legendary bluesman Robert Johnson. Macchio, who is studying the classical guitar, is warned by his music teacher, "You can't serve two masters" and tried to discourage his student from studying the blues. "Excellence in primitive music," the teacher cautions, "is cultural. You have to be born to it."

Macchio doesn't listen and he proceeds to track down the harmonica player and singer Willie Brown (Joe Seneca), who was Johnson's friend. The only problem for Macchio is that Brown is now 80 and confined to a prison nursing home in Harlem. When he asks the grizzled old man about the missing song, Brown dupes the young musician into sneaking him out of the home and taking him to a remote crossroads in Mississippi, where he sold his soul to the Devil. Macchio dreams of following in Johnson's steps as a blues guitarist and reluctantly agrees to take Johnson out.

Like a guardian angel, the old man begins teaching his young companion some of life's lessons. Blues, he explains, is about good men facing bad times. Meanwhile, Macchio undergoes a series of adventures on the road to the Delta country. He finally reaches the crossroads in Mississippi where the Devil (Robert Judd) appears to claim Brown's soul. To save the old man, Macchio agrees to a musical battle of guitars with the Devil's top musician. If he loses, he will turn over his own soul to the Devil. If he wins, Brown is released. Macchio wins the match and the two friends head for Chicago. Ry Cooder provided the blues numbers, and the legendary Sonny Terry contributed his fine harmonica work to the production.

*

The real Robert Johnson (1912-1938) was born in Mississippi. He was a gifted songwriter, guitarist and singer and all of his recordings were made in Texas during the years 1936 and 1937. His most popular songs, "Crossroads," "Hellhound on My Trail" and "Terraplane Blues," were all delta blues and his unusual guitar style was a precursor of the urban blues. Although Johnson was real, Brown, the old man in the film, was fictitious.

*

Dixie (1943), Par. Dir. A. Edward Sutherland; Sc. Karl Tunberg, Darrell Ware; Cast includes: Bing Crosby, Dorothy Lamour, Billy de Wolfe, Marjorie Reynolds, Lynne Overman.

A. E. Sutherland's pre-Civil War musical is a semi-biographical story of minstrel man and songwriter Daniel Decatur Emmett. Bing Crosby plays the lead character. The film includes scenes of New Orleans riverboats, minstrel routines and black spirituals.

Face in the Crowd, A (1957), WB. Dir. Elia Kazan; Sc. Budd Schulberg; Cast includes: Andy Griffith, Patricia Neal, Anthony Franciosa, Walter Matthau, Lee Remick.

Lonesome Rhodes (Andy Griffith) portrays an ignorant hillbilly guitar player who moves from an Arkansas jail to the country's most lovable, popular and prominent television personality. Elia Kazan's poignant drama is based on Budd Schulberg's story "The Arkansas Traveler." Rhodes abuses all those around him – especially those who helped him at the beginning. Patricia Neal, who discovered him in jail, is one of his victims. At the end he ridicules and rants against his fans and the public. Someone switches on his microphone and his wild insults are carried across the nation – to his ultimate destruction. "Illegal?" someone comments concerning Rhodes's techniques. "Honey, nothing's illegal if they don't catch you!"

Grand Ole Opry (1940), Rep. Dir. Frank McDonald; Sc. Stuart and Dorrell McGowan; Cast includes: Alan Lane, the Weaver Family, Henry Kolker.

This hillbilly comedy offers plenty of music, singing and routine hillbilly comedy. The story relates how rural hicks outsmart city sharpies and crooked politicians. This mild production features the Weaver family – Leon, Frank and June Weaver. The music and songs of the Weavers, Roy Acuff's Smoky Mountain Boys and other entertainers overshadow the inane plot.

*

Roy Acuff (1903-1992) was born in Maynardville, Tennessee and formed the Tennessee Crackerjacks in 1933. They soon recorded "The Great Speckle Bird" and "Wabash Cannonball" for Columbia Records. The band changed its name to the Smoky Mountain Boys and, beginning in 1938, started to make regular appearances on the "Grand Ole Opry". In 1962, Acuff became the first living performer to be selected as a member of the Country Music Hall of Fame. In many ways, the history of the "Grand Ole Opry" and Roy Acuff became intertwined and Acuff continued to sing on the radio show through 1990, one year before his death.

Acuff appeared on television and acted in several films, including Hi, Neighbor (1942), O, My Darling Clementine (1943), Sing, Neighbor, Sing (1944), Night Train to Memphis (1946), Chick Carter, Detective (1946), Smoky Mountain Melody (1949) and Home in San Antone (1949).

Great Balls of Fire! (1989), Rank/Orion. Dir. Jim McBride; Sc. Jack Baran, Jim McBride; Cast includes: Dennis Quaid, Winona Ryder, John Doe, Joe Bob Briggs.

This entertaining but flawed musical biography of rock 'n' roll singer Jerry Lee Lewis stars Dennis Quaid as the 1950s rock entertainer. Lewis was entirely unpredictable as well as self-destructive. Perhaps his most controversial act was his marriage to his 16-year-old cousin –his third wife. Quaid's amusing performance helps the production, which is enhanced by the real voice of Lewis.

*

Jerry Lee Lewis (1935-), like Elvis, was torn between his religious fundamentalism and his wild side. Lewis was born into his father's traveling entertainment troupe. He learned his vocation as a piano player on the back of his father's pick-up truck while, just as determinedly, he followed his avocation of women, alcohol and gambling off the truck. His "Great Balls of Fire" was an out-and-out appeal to raw adolescent appetites.

Lewis appeared in several films and usually played himself. He starred in *Jamboree* (1957), *High School Confidential!* (1958), *American Hot Wax* (1978), *Chuck Berry Hail! Hail! Rock 'n' Roll* (1985) and *History of Rock 'N' Roll*, Vols. 2 and 3 (both 1995).

*

Honeysuckle Rose (1980), WB. Dir. Jerry Schatzberg; Sc. Carol Sobienski, William D. Wittliff, John Binder; Cast includes: Willie Nelson, Dyan Cannon, Amy Irving, Slim Pickens, Joey Floyd.

Willie Nelson portrays a congenial country singer who divides his life with his wife and son at home with his professional life on the road. This pleasant entertaining musical is a loose remake of the 1936 Swedish drama *Intermezzo* which was itself re-issued in the U.S. in 1939 by Gregory Ratoff and starred Leslie Howard and Ingrid Bergman. The film mirrors Nelson's own life and touches upon the singer's bouts with liquor, his love of the open road and his attraction to other women. Though it's hard to see, the singer really loves his family.

*

Willie Nelson (1933-) started in show business as a master of ceremonies in country and western shows in Fort Worth, Texas. He played bass in Ray Price's band, which soon featured Nelson's "Night Life" as its feature song. Nelson became disillusioned with Nashville and, in 1971, returned to Texas. There, he and Waylon Jennings developed the Texas "outlaw" style of country and western. In 1976, the two singers produced "Wanted: The Outlaws," which became the model song of the outlaw style of singing. Nelson's great appeal is undoubtedly due to his ability to successfully combine elements of hillbilly and pop music.

Nelson has been active in both television and theatrical films as both producer and actor. He appeared in *The Electric Horseman* (1979) as the sardonic sidekick of fading rodeo star Robert Redford, who is reduced to making commercials and appearing in nightclubs. Nelson plays an aging fugitive outlaw in Fred Schipisi's *Barbarosa* (1982), befriends a farmhand and teaches him how to survive. In Alan Rudolph's *Songwriter* (1984), Nelson and Kris Kristofferson portray brothers – both country and western singers – who go their separate ways. In Barry Levinson's political satire *Wag the Dog* (1997), Nelson portrays a country singer and songwriter who is called in by professional manipulators and image-makers. They ask Nelson to help bolster the image of the President who faces a domestic scandal. Hollywood producer Dustin Hoffman conjures up an imaginary war in order to improve the President's rating. Nelson is assigned to write a song that will become the "spontaneous" anthem for the imaginary war.

Nelson appeared in *Thief* (1981), *Hell's Angels Forever* (1983), *Red-Headed Stranger* (1986), *Dust to Dust* (1994), *Big Country* (1994), *Starlight* (1996), *Gone Fishin'* (1997), *Anthem* (1997), *Half Baked* (1998), *Hi-Lo Country* (1998) and *Dill Scallion* (1999).

*

Honkytonk Man (1982), WB. Dir. Clint Eastwood; Sc. Clancy Carlile; Cast includes: Clint Eastwood, Kyle Eastwood, John McIntire, Alexa Kenin, Verna Bloom.

Clint Eastwood, an aging, alcoholic country and western singer, visits his sister and her family in their Southern home. They accept his shortcomings while admiring his free and roving spirit. His 14-year-old nephew (Kyle Eastwood, his real-life son) accompanies Eastwood to Nashville where he has been chosen to audition for the "Grand Ole Opry." The journey traces his nephew's road to maturity as Eastwood continues to degenerate.

Jolson Story, The (1946), Col. Dir. Joseph H. Lewis; Sc. Harry Chandler, Andrew Solt; Cast includes: Larry Parks, Evelyn Keyes, William Demarest, Scotty Beckett.

Larry Parks portrays the legendary blackface entertainer Al Jolson, in Joseph H. Lewis' masterful and highly entertaining fictional musical biography. Parks lip-synchs the singer's songs and captures Molson's personality, physical characteristics as well as his arrogance. The film traces the singer's rise as a member of Lew Dockstader's famous minstrel shows to Broadway and recording headliner. Scotty Beckett portrays the young teenage Jolson growing up as the son of a religious Jewish cantor in turn-of-the-century Washington, D.C. A sequel, *Jolson Sings Again*, was released in 1949.

Kentucky Moonshine (1938), TCF. Dir. David Butler; Sc. Art Arthur, M. M. Musselman; Cast includes: The Ritz Brothers, Tony Martin, Marjorie Weaver, Slim Summerville, John Carradine.

In this comedy, radio personalities Tony Martin and the Ritz Brothers try to improve their ratings. Martin journeys to Kentucky to do hillbilly music and discovers the brothers, who actually are New Yorkers posing as hillbillies. They are trying to appear on his radio show. Some believe this film is probably the Ritz Brothers' best comedy.

Lady Grey (1980), Maverick. Dir. Worth Keeter; Sc. Tom McIntyre; Cast includes: Ginger Alden, David Allen Coe, Paul Ott, Herman Bloodworth.

Ginger Laden is the aspiring country singer who struggles though hard times. A sleazy manager spots her and entices her away from her family with promises of great things to come. He soon knocks her unconscious and rapes her. As if this isn't enough, he then turns her sister into a prostitute and has her service some of his low-life cronies. Laden meets David Allen CEO, a successful country music star, who helps her out and she eventually makes it. However, at the peak of her career, she realizes that she can't ever be happy. This cliché-ridden cautionary drama is set in North Carolina. In real life, Laden gained fame as Elvis Presley's last girlfriend.

Louisiana (1947), Mon. Dir. Phil Karlson; Sc. Jack De Witt; Cast includes: Jimmie Davis, Margaret Lindsay, John Gallaudet, Freddie Stewart, Dottye Brown, Russell Hicks.

Phil Karlson's biographical drama sketches the life of country singer Jimmie Davis. The film covers his rise from poor farmer to popular hillbilly singer and, finally, to the governor's mansion. Focusing on his simplicity and honesty, the film features his most popular hits, including "You Are My Sunshine" and "Nobody's Darling But Mine."

Loving You (1957), Par. Dir. Hal Kanter; Sc. Herbert Baker, Hal Kanter; Cast includes: Elvis Presley, Lizabeth Scott, Wendell Corey, Dolores Hart, James Gleason.

Elvis Presley portrays a country boy singer in Hal Canter's easygoing musical. Publicity agent Elizabeth Scott discovers him and convinces her husband, bandleader Wendell Cory, to sign him up. The awkward youth turns into a magnetic entertainer wherever he goes – to the delight of his audiences.

*

Elvis Presley (1935-1977) walked into Sam Phillips's studio in 1954 in Memphis with the hope of cutting a record for his mother's birthday. He sang like a black man but was white. He looked like a tough guy but he had a "heart of gold." He idolized his mother and liked gospel but was also crazy about "Rock 'n' Roll" and a wild time. In short, Sam Phillips found his man.

Elvis's dual personality reflected the same schizophrenia in the Southern psyche and probably helped fuel his popularity. He was born in Tupelo, Mississippi, and while growing up, liked to mimic the great blues singers and their inflections and accents. At the same time, he began singing in the First Assembly of God church in Tupelo.

By 1960, he had racked up 19 consecutive gold records for such hits as "All Shook Up," "Don't Be Cruel," "Love Me Tender" and, perhaps the most notable of all of his recordings, "You Ain't Nothin' But a Hound Dog." Four of these songs were made into major Hollywood films – *Love Me Tender* (1956), *Jailhouse Rock* (1957), *Loving You* (1957) and *King Creole* (1958). Elvis starred in all of them and the soundtracks from his recordings were used in the films. Although Presley made a number of movies, including three sets in Hawaii, only a handful dealt with Southern themes or settings. In Robert Webb's *Love Me Tender* (1956), three brothers in a gang of Confederate soldiers rob a Union payroll before they discover the Civil War is over. They hide the money and return home to their farm. One brother, Elvis, marries Debra Page and his brother's former girlfriend starts trouble between them.

In Michael Cortex's drama *King Creole* (1958), Elvis rises from laborer in a honky-tonk to a star singer on the main drag in New Orleans. The film was based on the novel *A Stone for Danny Fisher* by Harold Robbins.

Elvis is an underprivileged youngster living in a rural area in Philip Dunne's romantic drama *Wild in the Country* (1961). He has writing talent but no guidance. Fortunately, his life and career change drastically under the tutelage of pretty psychiatric consultant Hope Lange. The film was based on J. R. Salamanca's novel *The Lost Country.*

In Gordon Douglas's musical *Follow That Dream* (1962), Presley portrays a member of a roving family of hillbillies who claim squatters' rights on an abandoned Florida dwelling. In another hillbilly movie, Gene Nelson's *Kisen' Cousins* (1964), the U.S. government wants the locals' property for a missile base. The clan refuses to budge, so the air force sends in Presley, one of its officers, and a relative of the obstinate clan. The entertaining musical *Frankie and Johnny* (1966), set in the 19th century, is based on the famous folk song. The characters include Mississippi riverboat entertainers Johnny (Elvis Presley) and Frankie (Donna Douglas). Johnny is a gambler who makes friends with another woman. His jealous girlfriend shoots him, but the wound is not fatal.

*

Mammy (1930), WB. Dir. Michael Curtiz; Sc. L. G. Rigby; Cast includes: Al Jolson, Lois Moran, Louise Dresser, Lowell Sherman, Hobart Bosworth.

Al Jolson portrays a member of a minstrel show in this musical that features several songs by Irving Berlin and a complete minstrel ensemble. The film is based on *Mr. Bones,* Berlin's play, and features such songs as "To My Mammy," "Let Me Sing and I'm Happy" and "Yes, We Have No Bananas." The minstrel show segment was filmed in color.

Minstrel Man (1944), PRC. Dir. Joseph H. Lewis; Sc. Irwin Franklin, Pierre Gendron; Cast includes: Benny Fields, Gladys George, Alan Dinehart, Roscoe Karns, Judy Clark.

Joseph H. Lewis' entertaining musical drama *Minstrel Man* is a play within a film. In the play, personable and talented singer Benny Fields portrays a minstrel who has advanced from vaudeville to Broadway. On opening night his wife dies after giving birth to their daughter. He walks out on the play, refuses to see the baby and abandons his friends. He journeys to Europe, where he stays for five years. Following a number of setbacks, he is reported missing at sea and, at that point, Fields decides to remain undercover. As luck would have it, his former agent spots him in a San Francisco dive and coaxes him to return to New York. He finally joins his talented grown-up daughter who is appearing in an updated version of his old show *Minstrel Man*. Fields appears on stage throughout the film in blackface.

Music Goes 'Round, The (1936), Col. Dir. Victor Schertzinger; Sc. Sidney Buchman, Jo Swerling; Cast includes: Harry Richman, Rochelle Hudson, Douglas Dumbrille, Lionel Stander.

Harry Richman, the star of a Broadway musical comedy, goes on vacation and meets a troupe of down-and-out traveling showboat entertainers. He discovers that the performers have very little talent, but decides to take them to Broadway anyway. He expects the troupe to make so many gaffes as to be unintentionally funny. When actress Rochelle realizes the hoax, she upbraids the hysterical audience, walks off stage, and punches Richman in the jaw. But all ends well when he quits the show and follows her to the South to apologize.

Nashville (1975), Par. Dir. Robert Altman; Sc. Joan Tewkesbury; Cast includes: David Arkin, Barbara Baxley, Karen Black, Ned Beatty, Ronee Blakely, Keith Carradine, Geraldine Chaplin.

Director Robert Alumna's satirical and biting musical drama is a fascinating kaleidoscopic view of American life as seen through more than a dozen characters. The personalities are all fleshed out during a political rally in Nashville and the plot avoids many of the clichés of other musicals. One character is a country and western singer (Ronnie Bleakly) who is about to have a nervous breakdown. Another is an aspiring but untalented singer (Gwen Welles) who is forced to strip at a stag party because she wants a chance to sing. A third is a pitiful wife (Lily Tomlin) of an unfeeling political manipulator (Ned Beauty). She has a one-night stand with an ambitious rock star (Keith Carradine) who sings the hit song "I'm Easy."

Nashville Rebel (1966), AI. Dir. Jay J. Sheridan; Sc. Ira Kerns, Jay J. Sheridan; Cast includes: Waylon Jennings, Tex Ritter, Sonny James, Faron Young, Loretta Lynn, Henny Youngman.

A showcase chiefly for country and western entertainers, Jay J. Sheridan's hoedown offers a slight plot. An unscrupulous lawyer promotes an unknown Waylon Jennings into a star. Following a disagreement, the lawyer tries to destroy Jennings. The film is set chiefly in Nashville at the "Grand Ole Opry" radio show and it introduces a host of singers and singing groups. Tex Rita gives a rendering of "Hillbilly Heaven" and Porter Wagoner and his group perform "Country Music's Gone to Town."

*

In the 1920s, Nashville, became a center of country and western music. The "Grand Ole Opry" radio broadcasts from Nashville started in 1925. Hollywood films about Nashville usually revolved about its music industry, especially its country and western performers.

Jean Yarbrough's comedy *Hillbillys in a Haunted House* (1967) describes two country and western singers who travel to Nashville and become entangled with criminals along the way. City slickers in Eddie Crandall's musical *From Nashville With Music* (1969) end up in the country's music capital and pass through a series of brainless adventures. Director Robert Altman's *Nashville* (1975) touches tangentially on the city's music industry. Burt Reynolds is a Southern con man in John G. Avildsen's road film *W. W. and the Dixie Dancekings* (1975). Reynolds takes over a small country and western act in Nashville. His ultimate goal is to get the group into the "Grand Ole Opry." Peter Bogdanovich's drama *The Thing Called Love* (1993) explores the dark side of the American dream with his look at four aspiring country stars lost in Nashville. River Phoenix plays a groovy songwriter.

New Orleans (1947), Levey. Dir. Arthur Lubin; Sc. Elliot Paul, Dick Irving Hyland; Cast includes: Louis Armstrong, Arturo de Cordova, Dorothy Patrick, Billie Holiday.

Some very talented performers could not help the weak plot of this musical about a wealthy young soprano (Dorothy Patrick) who is seduced by jazz. Louis Armstrong, Billie Holiday, Kid Ory, Woody Herman and his orchestra, and others appear and are a delight to see and hear.

*

American jazz musician, Daniel Louis "Satchmo" Armstrong (1907-1971), one of the most influential figures in the history of jazz, was born in New Orleans, Louisiana, and didn't receive much of a formal education. He learned to play various instruments, including the bugle, clarinet and cornet while taking trumpet lessons from the noted jazz artist Joe ("King") Oliver. Armstrong made his professional debut in 1917 as a trumpeter, with the band of Kid Ory (1886-1973) in New Orleans. Within the next few years he won recognition as one of the foremost jazz trumpet players of all time and as an outstanding jazz vocalist.

Armstrong appeared in several motion pictures. His earliest screen appearance was notably in a Betty Boop cartoon, *I'll Be Glad When You're Dead You Rascal You* (1932). Because of the racial barriers of the period, he was required to make his appearance through the servants' entrance. He appeared as a stable boy in *Going Places* (1938) and introduced "Jeepers Creepers," a popular ditty. He then appeared with Bing Crosby in the musical drama *Pennies From Heaven* (1936).

Vincente Minnelli's musical *Cabin in the Sky* (1943) presented a black fable with forces of good and evil battling for the soul of Eddie "Rochester" Anderson. The cast included Lena Horne, Ethel Waters, Armstrong and Duke Ellington. Charles Barton's musical *Jam Session* (1944) featured Ann Miller as an aspiring entertainer who tries to break into Hollywood. Various other talents, like Armstrong, Ellington and Charlie Barnett performed specialty numbers.

Charles Walters's *High Society* (1956), a musical remake of *The Philadelphia Story,* starred Bing Crosby, Frank Sinatra and Grace Kelly, with Armstrong contributing his unique talent. Danny Kaye (Nichols) sings duets with Armstrong in Melville Shavelson's musical biography about jazz trumpeter Red Nichols, *The Five Pennies* (1959). Armstrong appeared with Barbra Streisand in 1969 in the musical film *Hello, Dolly!*

*

Billie Holiday (1915-1959), another featured entertainer in *New Orleans* (1947), was one of the greatest jazz-blues singers of all time. Also known as Lady Day, she was born Eleanora Fagan in Baltimore, Maryland. Throughout the 1940s and 1950s Holiday attracted crowds in clubs around the U.S. Unfortunately, she became a heroin addict and her voice increasingly showed the effects of her long-term addiction. She died in Metropolitan Hospital, New York City, while under arrest for possession of illegal drugs. She rarely sang traditional blues. Instead, her reputation rests on her gift for transforming popular songs into emotionally profound pieces. Her autobiography, *Lady Sings the Blues* (1956), inspired a 1972 movie of the same name.

Holiday appeared as a blues singer in several films. She played in *Symphony in Black* (1935), in the concert film *"Sugar Chile" Robinson, Billie Holiday, Count Basie and His Sextet* (1950) and in *Sound of Jazz* (1957). She made an appearance singing vintage excerpts in *Duke Ellington & His Orchestra: 1929-1952* (1986), *Count Basie and Friends* (1986) and *Lady Day: The Many Faces of Billie Holiday* (1991).

*

Payday (1973), Cinerama. Dir. Daryl Duke; Sc. Don Carpenter; Cast includes: Rip Torn, Ahna Capri, Jeff Morris, Cliff Emmich, Henry O. Arnold.

Rip Torn portrays an unpleasant third-rate country and western singer. This drama exposes the dark side of the music scene. *Payday* seems to suggest that drugs, payoffs and sex are all part of the music scene. The film, shot entirely in Alabama, covers about two days in Torn's life on the road as he moves from one small town to another. His meaningless one-night stands and moments of violence seem to characterize his entire life. Some critics suggest the film is loosely based on the life of Hank Williams Sr.

Porgy and Bess (1959), Col. Dir. Otto Preminger; Sc. N. Richard Nash, George Gershwin, DuBose Heyward, Dorothy Heyward; Cast includes: Sidney Poitier, Dorothy Dandridge, Sammy Davis, Pearl Bailey, Brock Peters.

Sidney Poitier portrays the crippled Porgy, who loves Bess (Dorothy Dandridge), a popular young woman among the local men of Catfish Row. The film is based on the novel by DuBose Heyward and the play by DuBose and Dorothy Heyward. Crown (Brock Peters), a local stevedore, is also attracted to Bess, as is Sportin' Life (Sammy Davis Jr.). Although Sportin' Life wants to eventually take Bess out of her environment, in the interim, he's providing her with heroin. Crown kills a man during a game of dice and flees from the law. Porgy, meanwhile, takes in Bess. When Crown returns, he demands that Bess leave Porgy. A struggle ensues and Porgy kills Crown. While Porgy hides out, Sportin' Life convinces Bess to follow him to New York. Upon his return, Porgy learns that Bess has run off with Sportin' Life and prepares to follow her.

The production suffered a number of setbacks. Following a studio fire, Otto Preminger replaced veteran director Rouben Mamoulian. Although Poitier had second thoughts about the project and considered it racist, he consented to remain. Several cast members threatened to walk out as a protest against Preminger's insensitive treatment of some of the actors.

The film won an Academy Award for Best Musical Score and three nominations for Best Sound, Best Color Cinematography and Best Costume Design (Color). A home video version of the Gershwin play appeared in 1993, directed by stage director Trevor Nunn and starring Willard White, Cynthia Haymon and Gregg Baker.

Pure Country (1992), WB. Dir. Christopher Cain; Sc. Rex McGee; Cast includes: George Strait, Lesley Ann Warren, Isabel Glasser, Kyle Chandler.

Country superstar George Strait plays Dusty Wyatt Chandler, a singing star who drops out of the show-business spotlight to rediscover his roots. As part of his effort to reconnect with his family, he returns to his hometown and his eccentric grandmother (Molly McClure). He soon falls in love with Isabel Glasser, a tomboy who tries to save the family ranch by winning a Las Vegas rodeo competition. Plot complications arise when his manager tracks him down and tries to convince him to come back to show business for his next appearance – in Las Vegas.

Rhinestone (1984), TCF. Dir. Bob Clark; Sc. Phil Alden Robinson; Cast includes: Sylvester Stallone, Dolly Parton, Richard Farnsworth, Ron Leibman.

In this oddball comedy, Dolly Parton portrays a successful country singer who bets that she can turn anyone into a successful country singer in two weeks. Out of the blue, she selects Sylvester Stallone, a loud, boisterous New York City cabbie, as her subject. She takes him home to Tennessee, where her father takes one look at him and names him "Hopalong Meatball." Her father's comment only inspires Parton to try harder. Stallone tries singing but he initially sounds like a barnyard animal.

*

Born in the Appalachian backcountry of Tennessee, Dolly Parton (1946-) saw country music as her avenue of escape from poverty and, to that end, she decided to make herself look as glamorous as possible. Dolly described her mother's reaction to her new appearance:

> The first time my Mama saw me all done up with blond bleached hair all piled up, and my lips, cheeks, and nails as red as I could get them, she screamed to the Lord, 'Why are you

> testing me this way?' And she told me the Devil must have made me do it. 'Heck no,' I told Mama. 'Let's give credit where it's due. I did this all myself.'

Parton was such a hit as a country and western singer that Hollywood decided to appropriate her for the movies. In that new media, in 1980, she portrayed the working girl Dora Lee in the big moneymaker comedy *9 to 5*. Parton followed this with her role as Miss Mona, a madam, in *The Best Little Whorehouse in Texas* (1982) and as a beautician in *Steel Magnolias* (1989). In between some of her other films – *Straight Talk* (1992), *The Beverly Hillbillies* (1993) and *Heartsong* (1995) – she appeared on television.

Songwriter (1984), Tri-Star. Dir. Alan Rudolph; Sc. Bud Shrake; Cast includes: Willie Nelson, Kris Kristofferson, Melinda Dillon, Rip Torn.

Willie Nelson and Kris Kristofferson portray two country singers in Alan Rudolph's musical drama. Although they initially are a team, they eventually split up and try to make it individually. Nelson develops into the saint of country music, loved by the public while Kristofferson remains an outlaw personality with a soft and kind heart. His cavalier lifestyle marks him as a good-natured sort, but not tough enough to make it in the business.

South of Dixie (1944), U. Dir. Jean Yarbrough; Sc. Clyde Bruckman; Cast includes: Anne Gwynne, David Bruce, Jerome Cowan, Ella Mae Morse, Joe Sawyer.

A famous writer of Southern ballads, David Bruce is actually a Northerner. He is forced to move south when his partner decides to "out" him in a biography. Anne Gwynne accompanies him and they both fall in love. However, Southern belle Ella Mae Morse, the daughter of a Southern colonel, becomes interested in Bruce and the story develops from there. Songs include "I'm A-Headin' South," "When It's Darkness on the Delta" and "Weep No More My Lady."

St. Louis Blues (1958), Par. Dir. Allen Reisner; Sc. Robert Smith, Ted Sherdeman; Cast includes: Nat King Cole, Eartha Kitt, Pearl Bailey, Juano Hernandez, Cab Calloway, Ella Fitzgerald, Mahalia Jackson.

Allen Reisner's fictional musical biography of the famed composer of classic blues W. C. Handy is generally disappointing. However, it boasts an all-star cast of entertainers, including Nat King Cole (in the title role), Eartha Kitt, Pearl Bailey, Cab Calloway, Ella Fitzgerald and Mahalia Jackson. Handy, of course, wrote the title number. According to this fictitious plot, young Handy clashes with his father (Juano Hernandez), a strict minister, who insists that his musically gifted son is playing "the devil's music." Handy nevertheless continues to compose the music he knows and likes best. He meets New Orleans singer Eartha Kitt, who encourages him to continue with his music.

Kitt is frustrated at the reverend's narrow-minded rejection of his son's music and rebukes him. "Well," she remarks sardonically, "a busy man like you – you can form an opinion without wasting time bothering about facts." A crisis arises when Handy suddenly becomes blind. His condition is determined as psychosomatic – most likely a result of his father's opposition – but he soon regains his sight and wins wide recognition. The reverend eventually comes to a concert where his son is honored and he finally accepts his music.

*

William Christopher Handy (1873-1958) was a composer, cornetist and bandmaster and was born in Florence, Alabama. He appeared as early as 1893 in the World's Columbian Exposition in Chicago. His first published song was "Memphis Blues" (1912) and some of his other popular songs include "St. Louis Blues" (1914), "Beale Street Blues" (1917) and "Loveless Love" (1921). His music was also featured in Victor Schertzinger's musical, *Birth of the Blues* (1941), with Bing Crosby, Mary Martin and Eddie "Rochester" Anderson.

*

Jazz singer Ella Fitzgerald (1918-1996) was born in Newport News, Virginia, and raised in a New York City orphanage. She gained recognition for her exceptional musical talent and her skill in scat singing (singing meaningless syllables while using the voice as an instrument). Fitzgerald appeared in 1958 with jazz composer Duke Ellington at Carnegie Hall. She also toured Europe frequently with the Oscar Peterson Trio. Among her later concert appearances was a performance at the 1985 Kool Jazz Festival at Carnegie Hall. "Oh, But I Do" and "You Showed Me the Way" were some of her own compositions. She appeared in several films, including *Ride 'Em Cowboy* (1942), *Pete Kelly's Blues* (1955), *St. Louis Blues* (1958), *Let No Man Write My Epitaph* (1960), *Voyage to Next* (1974) and *Listen Up: The Lives of Quincy Jones* (1991).

*

Sullivan's Travels (1941), Par. Dir. Preston Sturges; Sc. Preston Sturges; Cast includes: Joel McCrea, Veronica Lake, Porter Hall, Arthur Hoyt.

Preston Sturges' film is a combination comedy and drama. Joel McCrea, as a successful Hollywood director, feels that his hits – such as *Ants in Your Plants of 1939* – aren't really meaningful. In order to produce a really relevant film, he decides to personally research his next project, another film tentatively called *O Brother, Where Art Thou?* He gets dressed as a tramp and goes out to investigate the lives of poor people. He is robbed, loses his identification as well as his memory and finds himself in a Southern state. McCrea is missing, so this man without identification and without memory is accused of murdering himself. He is sentenced to a chain gang, but, while serving his sentence, he starts to regain his memories.

One night, the prisoners are taken to an old church where they sit with African-American parishioners and watch an old Mickey Mouse cartoon. As

McCrea witnesses those around him, surrounded by misery and poverty, he sees the downtrodden members of the audience uninhibitedly enjoying Mickey's antics. He starts laughing almost uncontrollably and suddenly realizes the importance of comedy and its virtues – especially to the downtrodden. McCrea is finally able to convince the authorities of his real identity and returns to his studio. He can now make relevant comedies and eventually marries beautiful Veronica Lake, whom he met during one of his journeys as a tramp.

Swanee River (1940), TCF. Dir. Sidney Lanfield; Sc. John T. Foote, Phillip Dunne; Cast includes: Don Ameche, Andrea Leeds, Al Jolson, Felix Bressart, Chick Chandler.

Don Ameche portrays Stephen Foster, the famous composer of American folk songs, in this musical biography. The film doesn't gloss over Foster's failings. It shows Foster struggling to write music despite his heavy drinking problems. Foster visits Louisville and is inspired to write the folk song "Oh, Susannah." Impoverished at the time, he befriends E. P. Christy of the popular minstrel show, who buys his song and makes him famous. The two talents establish a long-lasting relationship. Foster moves to New York but continues to drink and he neglects his wife and child. In between his drinking bouts, he writes "Swanee River," "Camptown Races," "Old Black Joe," "Here Comes the Heavin' Line," "Ring the Banjo" and "Jeanie with the Light Brown Hair."

He finally succumbs to a heart attack. Jolson, who rode to fame on many of Foster's compositions, heard, during one of his own performances, of the songwriter's death and, in an impromptu gesture, sang "Swanee" to a tearful audience.

*

Composer Stephen Collins Foster (1826-1864) was the first professional songwriter in the United States and his songs are among the most popular ever written. His first hit was "Oh, Susannah." Between 1850 and 1860 Foster wrote many of his best songs, including "Camptown Races" (1850) and "Jeanie with the Light Brown Hair" (1854). Foster's songs are known for their touching melodies and simple harmonies. His musical work is made up of 285 songs, hymns, arrangements and instrumental works. Many of his songs are still popular today, and some of them have passed into the oral tradition of folk song.

In reality, Foster's life was more depressing than his life on screen. Besides neglecting his family, he spent virtually all of his royalties on drink and died a pauper at age 37 in the charity ward in New York City's Bellevue Hospital. Contrary to the film, the last song he wrote in real life was "Beautiful Dreamer," which is not in the production. Hollywood produced three film biographies based on Foster's life, each varying in quality. The earliest, Joseph Santley's *Harmony Lane* (1935), featured Douglass Montgomery as the songwriter. The film opens as a black congregation sings spirituals. Foster listens intently at the rear of the chapel. The story then traces his journey to Chicago, his failed marriage, his trip to New York and a scene with William Frawley playing Christy, the famous minstrel who sings "Swanee River." Don Ameche portrayed Stephen Foster in *Swanee River*, the second film biography. Finally, Allan Dwan's musical biography of Foster, *I Dream of Jeannie* (1952), the third work, offers more nostalgia than substance. Bill Shirley, as the songwriter, sings "Oh, Susannah," "Old Dog Tray" and "Camptown Races," and Ray Middleton, as Edwin P. Christy, the minstrel man, renders "My Old Kentucky Home," "The Old Folks at Home," "Ring, Ring, De Banjo" and several other songs. All three films emphasize Foster's ties with the South, blacks and the world of minstrels.

*

W. W. and the Dixie Dancekings (1975), TCF. Dir. John G. Avildsen; Sc. Thomas Rickman; Cast includes: Burt Reynolds, Art Carney, Conny Van Dyke, Jerry Reed, Ned Beatty.

Personable Burt Reynolds brings his likable charm to this comedy drama. He portrays a happy-go-lucky con artist who drives a 1955 Oldsmobile and makes his living robbing banks and gasoline stations. While running from the law, he meets a struggling country music band, the Dixie Dancekings, who are seeking their first big break. Reynolds convinces them that he is a Nashville agent and they all start out for the famous Music City. Art Carney plays a preacher-lawman hired by oil-company executives to track down and capture Reynolds, the mysterious crook who has been plaguing their filling stations. Meanwhile, Reynolds becomes fond of the band members and helps them make it in Nashville. This entertaining film touches upon some of the more cynical aspects of the country music business while it also highlights some more positive themes, such as loyalty to friends.

Youth Will Be Served (1940), TCF. Dir. Otto Brower; Sc. Wanda Tuchock; Cast includes: Jane Withers, Jane Darwell, Robert Conway, Elyse Knox.

Jane Withers portrays a Southern teenager who is sent to a National Youth Association camp after her father is jailed for manufacturing illegal liquor. When a wealthy landowner makes an offer to purchase the property, Withers organizes the campers to produce a talent show in order to soften the tycoon's heart. In the meantime, her father escapes from prison and manages to capture two thieves who have stolen the financier's payroll. Faced by the double-barreled goodness of father and daughter, the tycoon relents and the camp remains.

20

The Civil War

An analysis of Hollywood's treatment of the Civil War (1861-1865) gives us a greater insight into the movie industry's larger perception of Southern history as a whole. Beginning with D. W. Griffith in the early teens and continuing through the early 1940s, Hollywood idealized the Southern way of life, which included such disparate aspects as slavery, Southern manners and, above all, the Southern conduct of the Civil War. Slaves generally appeared content, serving benevolent masters and genteel mistresses. Southern officers were usually portrayed as honorable, well-mannered gentlemen while their Northern counterparts were generally depicted as roughnecks who often lacked any of the social graces.

Hollywood could not resist portraying a slovenly General Grant accepting the surrender from an immaculately clad General Lee at Appomattox. The contrast in appearances between the generals could not have been sharper. Lee, tall, handsome, immaculately groomed, a flashing sword at his side, came astride his white charger to meet the victor. Grant appeared in his "working clothes," his boots dappled with mud, a private's coat, with his stars tacked on thrown over a rumpled shirt and bearing no sword. Nevertheless, by some strange quirk of fate, the plain man from nowhere had humbled a glamorous representative of a fading aristocracy.

Southern officers, in contrast to their Northern counterparts, were usually portrayed sympathetically as professional soldiers who were defending their own land against the invaders.

Generally, Hollywood pointed no accusing finger at either side, although its earlier benevolent treatment of slavery raised questions about its grasp of reality. The "faithful black slave," already a staple on stage and on the early silent screen, played a prominent role in *Dan* (1914). The title character, a servant-slave, helps his young master, a Confederate officer, escape his Union captors. Dan remains behind in his master's place and is executed the next morning.

American film studios produced well over 100 Civil War-related films. The Confederate officers generally were gallant and fought bravely for an ill-fated cause. Slavery and states' rights fueled the conflict. Some films covered specific aspects of the war. *Friendly Persuasion* (1956) recounted the Quakers' opposition to the conflict on religious grounds. *The Raid* (1954) and *The Horse Soldiers* (1959) described two of several behind-the-lines assaults. *Tap Roots* (1948) was based on an actual Southern insurrection while *Rebel City* (1953) dealt with the controversial Copperheads.

During the first three decades of the twentieth century, Hollywood treated Abraham Lincoln (1809-1865) with particular caution. The studios were afraid of portraying him heroically for fear of losing their Southern audiences. On the other hand, they couldn't alienate the rest of the country by depicting him in a bad light. The compromise hammered out by the studios was to represent Lincoln as a tragic figure with the full burden of the war upon his shoulders. He was portrayed in numerous silent and sound films and several biographical dramas. Virtually all have portrayed him with compassion and sympathy.

With Lee in Virginia (1913) was the first of a number of silent Lincoln films. *The Heart of Lincoln* (1915) recounted an incident in which he intervenes to save the life of a young man accused of spying. *Defense or Tribute?* (1916) was a World War I documentary which invoked the image of Lincoln. *The Crisis* (1916) recreated the siege of Vicksburg. *The Lincoln Cycle* (1917) dramatized his prewar years while *Abraham Lincoln* (1924) was a biographical drama.

Characterizations of Lincoln continued into the sound era and included such dramas and biographies as Griffith's *Abraham Lincoln* (1930), which gave a generally even-handed picture of the North and South and treated Generals Grant and Lee impartially. *Are We Civilized?* (1934), an antiwar drama, invoked historical precedents (through the use of excerpts from old features and newsreels) to show the folly of war. *Hearts in Bondage* (1936) included the famous battle between the *Merrimac* and the *Monitor*. While Europe prepared for war at the close of the decade, Hollywood provided a patriotic short titled *Lincoln in the White House* (1939).

Actor Frank McGlynn practically made a career of impersonating him on screen. The most effective interpretations were given by Walter Huston in D. W. Griffith's *Abraham Lincoln* (1930), Henry Fonda in John Ford's *Young Mr. Lincoln* (1939) and Raymond Massey in John Cromwell's *Abe Lincoln in Illinois* (1940).

Lincoln's assassination by John Wilkes Booth, a crazed actor and Southern sympathizer, in Ford's Theatre (April 14, 1865) in Washington, D.C., was the subject of a number of films. D.W. Griffith's classic Civil War epic *The Birth of a Nation* (1915) and John Ford's *The Prisoner of Shark Island* (1936) both included the assassination scene.

Grant has been portrayed in numerous films, but unfortunately more care has been spent on the accuracy of his physical appearance than on his character. *The Blue and the Gray or the Days of 61* (1908), *Stirring Days in Old Virginia* (1909), *With Lee in Virginia* (1913) and *The Battle Cry of Peace* (1915) include vignettes of Grant as general. Grant is usually portrayed in a secondary role. However, he is always characterized as the Union's symbol of determination. With the advent of sound, the picture of Grant began to assume three dimensions. Grant appeared in such features as *Only the Brave* (1930), *Sitting Bull* (1954), *Drum Beat* (1954) and *The Horse Soldiers* (1959). Griffith, in *Abraham Lincoln* (1930), portrayed another facet to Grant's character by showing him agonizing over the long war and its toll in lives and destruction.

*

The Union's leading cavalry general, Philip H. Sheridan (1831-1888), was portrayed in several films as a vicious commander. *Sheridan's Ride* (1908), *In the Shenandoah Valley* (1908), *Sheridan's Ride* (1912) and *Shenandoah* (1913) all cover his scorched-earth policies during the summer of 1864. Although hated by the South, he was as popular with his troops as was General Grant, his military superior. Sheridan's major contribution was his decisive defeat of General Jubal Early in a series of battles for control of Virginia's Shenandoah Valley during the summer of 1864. His victory denied the South the use of the long, broad valley as an invasion route into the North. Sheridan followed Sherman's tactics in burning the valley and thus eliminating the area's agricultural importance to the Confederacy.

*

Like his counterpart General Grant, Lee has been portrayed in numerous silent and sound films as a minor character. Nevertheless, he is shown chiefly as a commanding and sympathetic figure in such silent films as *The Blue and the Gray or the Days of 61* (1908), *Stirring Days in Old Virginia* (1909), *The Road to Richmond* (1910) and *With Lee in Virginia* (1913). He is seen directing his troops during battle in D. W. Griffith's Civil War classic *The Birth of a Nation* (1915).

While the advent of sound movies produced a more sympathetic picture of Grant, the same technological breakthrough signaled fewer and fewer Lee films. Among the few sound films portraying Lee were *Only the Brave* (1930) and *Seven Angry Men* (1955). One noteworthy and poignant portrait of Lee appeared in Griffith's *Abraham Lincoln* (1930), which depicted him as a crushed but noble soul on the eve of his surrender.

*

Morally righteous, stern and demanding, Thomas J. "Stonewall" Jackson (1824-1863) brought an almost religious fervor to his participation in the American Civil War. General Jackson was, unquestionably, Lee's best officer among Southern generals. Jackson allegedly got his nickname during the First Battle of Bull Run (Manassas Junction) on July 21, 1861. At one point in the fight a Southern officer, seeing his lines crumbling under a Union attack, pointed to Jackson and his Virginia troops holding firm on a crest. "There is Jackson standing like a stone wall. Rally behind the Virginians!" exclaimed the officer. The sobriquet became part of the Jackson legend.

Jackson took part in a number of important battles during the Civil War. He developed a reputation for coolness under fire and successful use of tactical surprise. Besides First Bull Run, Jackson saw action in the Shenandoah Valley (March-June 1862) where he consistently humbled larger enemy concentrations, and in battles at Second Bull Run, Antietam (the war's bloodiest battle), Fredericksburg and Chancellorsville.

He died following his decisive victory at Chancellorsville. While in front of his lines organizing the pursuit of the enemy, Jackson received a mortal wound accidentally inflicted by one of his own men. Without doubt, the loss of Jackson hurt Lee's pursuit of the war. *Under Southern Stars*, a 1937 film short, depicts Jackson on the evening before his fatal charge at Chancellorsville.

Most of the Jackson films are early silents – *To the Aid of Stonewall Jackson* (1911), *With Stonewall Jackson*, also 1911, and *The Bugler of Battery B* (1912). Although generally crude in production values, these short dramas tend to be more historically accurate than later Civil War films that are based on nondescript battles and fictional characters.

*

The South's most successful and daring cavalry commander and one of the Civil War's most famous military leaders, James E. B. "Jeb" Stuart (1833-1864) electrified the nation on more than one occasion by his end-runs around Union forces. Stuart distinguished himself in the war's early stages. He saw action at both Battles of Bull Run, Fredericksburg and Chancellorsville. However, the dashing, bearded cavalry chief, because of his tendency to go off on raids, may have contributed heavily to the defeat of Confederate forces at the all-important Battle of Gettysburg (July 1-3, 1863). Prior to the battle Stuart was absent for several days on a mission of his own creation. This deprived Lee of the "eyes" and mobility he badly needed to fight the Union troops sent to stop the Confederate advance. Stuart's attempt to rejoin Lee at Gettysburg was checked by Union cavalry several miles from the main battle scene. *General Meade's Fighting Days* (1909), *The Battle of Gettysburg* (1913, 1936) and *Between Two Fires* (1914) cover this important engagement. Stuart is portrayed in an obscure 1912 silent Civil War film, *The Battle of Pottsburg Ridge*; a spy drama, *Operator 13* (1934); and a large-scale pre-Civil War Western, *Santa Fe Trail* (1940), with Errol Flynn as a dashing and heroic Stuart battling the abolitionist John Brown.

He died on May 12, 1864, as a result of wounds suffered at the Battle of Yellow Tavern after his unit had been lured away from Lee's main army and defeated by Union General Phil Sheridan.

*

Sometimes, films showed Southern forces pictured terrorizing civilians. However, in all of these cases, the troops were irregular forces. These troops were not under control of the Southern aristocratic military. They operated independently and it was not unusual for them to commit robberies and murders along with tactical military operations.

*

Hollywood grappled with the problem of prisoners of war during the Civil War by concentrating upon the catastrophic personal aspects of the situation and thus created a solution that satisfied all sections of the country. In 1909, for example, D.W. Griffith's short, one-reel drama *In Old Kentucky* underscored one of the tragedies of that war when a Confederate soldier is captured by his own brother who is fighting with the Union. Another one-reeler, *The Road to Richmond* (1910), told of a Union soldier who saves the life a Southern girl and who is then captured by the Confederates. The girl intercedes for the prisoner, and General Lee releases him. Southern gentility and honor prevailed. Three years later a similar plot unfolded when a daughter of the South falls in love with a Union officer, in Thomas Ince's *The Sinews of War* (1913). When he is captured, the girl's brother helps him escape. In turn, the Northerner later saves the girl's life.

The pro-Southern bias in the movie industry of the 1920s and '30s was evident in handling the issue of the notorious Southern prisoner-of-war camp Andersonville. This prison, located on the outskirts of the town with the same name in southwest Georgia, was the site of one of the Civil War's most shocking tragedies. Almost 13,000 inmates died in the prison and its hospital during its two years of existence (1864-1865). The North made great propaganda use of the situation. Its commander, Captain Henry Wirz, was hanged on November 10, 1865, soon after the end of hostilities, following a trial before a military tribunal. The area today is the site of a Federal cemetery and park memorializing the tragedy.

Hollywood, with its image of the aristocratic Southern officer, barely touched the issue, for to mention Andersonville was to open up the entire question of the culpability of the Southern officer class in the horrible environment at the camp. The earliest film concerning the prisoner-of-war camp was a superficial silent one-reeler, *Escape From Andersonville* (1909), which hardly mentioned its terrible conditions. Decades later, MacKinlay Kantor's novel *Andersonville* presented a more realistic version of what really occurred at that camp and it was adapted into a television production in 1966. In 1970 a television production titled *The Andersonville Trial* was presented.

*

Dark Command, The (1940), Rep. Dir. Raoul Walsh; Sc. Grover Jones, Lionel Houser, F. Hugh Herbert; Cast includes: Claire Trevor, John Wayne, Walter Pidgeon, Roy Rogers, George "Gabby" Hayes.

Raoul Walsh's action drama, set before and during the Civil War, stars John Wayne as a stalwart Texan who assumes the role of marshal in strife-torn Kansas. Tension mounts among the citizens who are split between Northern and Southern sympathizers. However, when guerrillas mercilessly raid the state, Wayne is able to unite the decent folk against their common enemy. Abundant action keeps the film moving in this better-than-average Southern/Western. The film is accurate in at least one area – the historical assault on and burning of Lawrence, Kansas, by the marauders. Walter Pidgeon plays the leader of the marauders while Claire Trevor provides the romantic interest. Pidgeon and his group of bandits closely resemble the real-life group of raiders assembled around William Quantrill.

*

Quantrill (1837-1865) was but one of a number of Southern Confederate renegades. The son of a Northern school teacher, Quantrill, for some unknown reason, decided to aid the South in the vicious guerrilla war that raged on the Kansas-Missouri border. In the aftermath of one of these raids, several wives and sisters of members of his band provided food and shelter for the raiders. Federal officials subsequently detained them for assisting the enemy. Unfortunately, the building where they were being held collapsed and a number of the women died. Quantrill and his group decided to wreak vengeance many times over for their personal losses.

He and 450 of his followers crossed the Missouri border into Kansas one summer night in 1863. The band first captured and killed ten farmers suspected of Northern sympathies. They then headed to Lawrence, an area noted for its rabid espousal of the anti-slavery cause. They struck the town at dawn on August 21, 1863. Within the next few hours they killed 183 men and boys and torched 185 buildings before fleeing from pursuing Federal cavalry to their sanctuary in the Missouri woods. *Quantrill's Raiders* (1958), is the only film to completely cover the story of the marauders. It recreates the actual bloody raid but fictionalizes the ending by killing the guerrilla leader right there. Historically, Quantrill survived the assault.

Despite increased Union attempts to capture the group, the band continued its destructive raids over the two years following the Lawrence massacre. The imprisonment of their women, which led to the tragic building collapse and some of their deaths, was merely one of several attempts to separate the band from supporters who gave them aid.

William Dieterle's *Red Mountain* (1951) and William Witney's *Arizona Raiders* (1965) are fictitious tales of Quantrill's exploits. Henry Levin's *The Desperados* (1969) has a Quantrill-like guerrilla leader raiding Northern settlements. Jack Palance plays a very-believable Quantrill.

Quantrill brought together a gang of killers, such as the James and Younger brothers, who would later become famous as outlaws. Together, they murdered innocent victims on a number of occasions. *Jesse James Under the Black Flag* (1921), *Jesse James* (1927) and *Kansas Raiders* (1950) all indicate that James joined Quantrill. Many of the outlaws joined the raiders not for any ideological reasons but rather for the opportunity to rape and plunder under the false pretenses of fighting for a political cause. In August 1862, Quantrill captured Independence, Missouri, an event that earned him an officer's commission from a grateful Confederacy.

Drums in the Deep South (1951), RKO. Dir. William Cameron Menzies; Sc. Philip Yordan, Sidney Harmon; Cast includes: James Craig, Barbara Payton, Guy Madison, Barton MacLane.

The film opens in Georgia in 1861 on the eve of the war. Time passes in brief battle vignettes until the major plot of the story unfolds, in 1864. A handful of Confederate soldiers seek to delay General Sherman's march on Atlanta. James Craig portrays a Southern major in charge of a group of 20 Confederate volunteers who are entrenched atop a mountain precipice. They shell the Union general's supply train and repel all attempts to dislodge them.

A Yankee officer (Guy Madison), Craig's former friend, is faced with a personal dilemma when he is ordered to blow up the mountain. Barbara Payton, as the wife of a Southern officer, renews her relationship with Craig, her former lover, and spies for him. When Madison mines the entire mountain, she goes to Craig to convince him to surrender, but she is accidentally killed. Craig orders his men to leave, but he remains, holding Payton in his arms, as the mountain is blown to bits.

Aside from the stress on the two officers, the film offers little insight into other aspects of the war. The final screen statement seeks to bring about national unity: "Out of the chaos of brother against brother, came a new realization of our common destiny."

General, The (1927), UA. Dir. Buster Keaton, Clyde Bruckman; Sc. Al Boasberg, Charles Smith; Cast includes: Buster Keaton, Marion Mack, Glen Cavender, Jim Farley, Frederick Vroom, Charles Smith.

Buster Keaton's famous Civil War comedy focuses on a bizarre plot to capture a train called *The General.* The plot is based on an actual incident, known as the Andrews Raid that occurred during the Civil War. In the real event, Union soldiers, dressed as civilians, stole *The General*, a rebel locomotive. In Keaton's version, he plays Johnnie Gray, a railroad worker, who tries to impress his girl (Marion Mack) by enlisting in the army. The army brass rejects him because he's more useful as an engineer. His sweetheart thinks him a coward and snubs him. However, when he learns that his train has been stolen, he springs into action. Following several hilarious incidents, our Southern hero saves his sweetheart who is held captive by the enemy, foils a Union surprise attack and captures a high-ranking Union officer.

The film has been noted for its authentic backgrounds and its photography. Keaton's superb timing of his sight gags deserves praise as well, especially in two sequences. In one, a cannon placed on a railway car begins to focus on Keaton until the mouth of the weapon stares him straight in the face. The train turns just in time and the cannonball barely misses him. The second sequence shows his train approaching railroad ties strewn across the tracks. He dislodges the ties by dropping some ties of his own on top. Keaton's split-second timing is a marvel to behold.

Many critics consider *The General* Keaton's best work as well as one of the best films about the Civil War. The film is based on William Pittenger's *The Great Locomotive Chase* and contains the longest chase sequence in the history of film comedy. The Kalem studio's earlier film *Railroad Raiders of 62* (1911) presented a short but generally accurate account of the incident. Later on, Walt Disney used some of Keaton's original photography in his own film, *The Great Locomotive Chase* (1956), a fictionalized but colorful version of the incident. When asked why the war scenes in his film looked more authentic than they did in *Gone With the Wind*, Keaton replied: "They went to a novel, we went to history."

*

Perhaps seeking some balance for their favorable treatment of Southern raiders such as Quantrill, Hollywood sympathetically portrayed a group of Northern volunteers, under James J. Andrews. These volunteers, however, were quite different from Quantrill's raiders. Andrews' men were well disciplined and they had specific military – not civilian – objectives.

A squad of 22 Union soldiers under James J. Andrews volunteered to penetrate Confederate lines and cut rail communication between Marietta, Georgia, and Chattanooga, Tennessee. On April 22nd, 1862, the troops seized a train pulled by a locomotive named *The General* and headed West to destroy bridges and other communication links on the line. Confederate forces discovered the plan and, in another locomotive named *Texas*, chased the Northerners for a distance of about 90 miles. The Southerners captured the hijackers after *The General* ran out of fuel. Andrews and seven of his men were executed as spies. The remaining men, after surviving internment in prisoner of war camps, were the first ones ever to be awarded the Congressional Medal of Honor – the nation's highest military award for bravery

*

Horse Soldiers, The (1959), UA. Dir. John Ford; Sc. Lee Mahin, Martin Rackin; Cast includes: John Wayne, William Holden, Constance Towers, Althea Gibson, Hoot Gibson.

In April of 1863, General Grant assigned Colonel Benjamin Grierson to invade 300 miles into Confederate territory in order to demolish the rail link between Newton Station and Vicksburg. Grierson and his three cavalry regiments, a force of 1,700 men, succeeded in their mission; they rode 600 miles in a little more than two weeks and returned safely to Union lines

John Ford's *The Horse Soldiers* is based on Grierson's exploits. John Wayne, a battle-hardened Union colonel, leads his cavalry on a raid behind enemy lines. When Constance Towers, a Southern belle, overhears Wayne's plans for the raid, she is taken along as a prisoner. Towers provides the romantic interest for both Wayne and William Holden, who plays a humane army surgeon. By the end of the film Towers and Wayne fall in love. Director John Ford's penchant for humor shows in several places. On one occasion, an elderly headmaster of a Southern military academy proudly but foolishly leads his eager young boys in a march against the Union cavalry. Wayne doesn't want to slaughter the young boys, so he sounds the retreat. At another point, Holden makes sarcastic observations about Wayne's bent for fighting and killing.

Two major battle sequences add to the excitement of this outdoor action drama. In an early portion, Wayne's troops surprise a trainload of rebel soldiers who come to rescue a town under siege by his cavalry. In the ensuing battle, the brave but foolhardy Southerners are slaughtered in their head-on attack. The film ends with another engagement between Wayne's troops and the enemy. When a column of Southern soldiers approaches Wayne from the rear and an enemy force confronts him in front, he leads a desperate but heroic charge across a wooden bridge and wipes out the rebel troops. Holden, who acts as Wayne's foil, volunteers to remain behind to care for the wounded as the advancing Confederate column approaches. Meanwhile, Wayne blows up the bridge and leads his troops to safety.

Aside from some bloody scenes of wounded troopers and one amputation operation, Ford embellishes the action with his romantic views of war, heroism and glory – distributing these elements equally between the North and the South. The brave Southern citizens of Newton Station make an abortive stand against the invaders. Long shots of Wayne and his troops riding along the horizon in silhouette are quite effective. His men, at times, appear overly chivalrous toward their adversaries and we seem to be more in Ford country than in the thick of the Civil War.

Last Outpost, The (1951), Par. Dir. Lewis R. Foster; Sc. Geoffrey Homes, George W. Yates, Winston Miller; Cast includes: Ronald Reagan, Rhonda Fleming, Bruce Bennett, Bill Williams.

A curious blend of cavalry-vs-Indian Civil War action films emerged in the 1950s. These dramas show Confederate and Union troops putting aside their differences and uniting in order to fight their common adversary, the Indians. Lewis R. Foster's (1951) entry carries brotherly concern beyond politics by showing two brothers on opposing sides during the Civil War temporarily joining forces to fight the Apache. These films barely stop short of sending a racist message – that whites must stand together against other races.

Morgan's Last Raid (1929), MGM. Dir. Nick Grinde; Sc. Bradley King, Harry Braxton; Cast includes: Tim McCoy, Dorothy Sebastian, Wheeler Oakman, Allan Garcia, Hank Mann.

Nick Grinde's drama, *Morgan's Last Raid,* is loosely based on the life of John Hunt Morgan. Tim McCoy portrays a Southern captain who decides not to take up arms against Tennessee, his home state, when it secedes from the Union. Dorothy Sebastian, as the young woman he loves, accuses him of being a traitor. Later, he joins John Morgan and his raiders, a unit of the Confederates. During one of their raids, McCoy rescues Sebastian who, of course, forgives him. The film was one of four Westerns McCoy made for MGM before he moved on to other studios where he became a popular cowboy star.

*

John Hunt Morgan (1825-1864), although a commissioned Confederate general, acted independently of the high command and became famous for his raids during the Civil War. Operating chiefly behind Union lines, he and his raiders captured a Northern garrison in Huntsville, Alabama, in 1862 and was promoted to brigadier general. He was captured by the Union on one of his forays later that year but managed to escape. Transferred to a different command, he was killed in action in Greenville, Tennessee.

His daring exploits into enemy territory made exciting screen material. *The Chest of Fortune*, released in 1914 by Kalem, was the first to appear. It portrayed Morgan and his raiders as cold-blooded murderers who butcher a Northern officer and his family. Other action melodramas included *Morgan's Raiders* (1918) and *The Little Shepherd of Kingdom Come* (1920).

Red Badge of Courage, The (1951), MGM. Dir. John Huston; Sc. John Huston; Cast includes: Audie Murphy, Bill Mauldin, John Dierkes, Royal Dano.

The film is based on Stephen Crane's Civil War novel about the psychological impact of war on a young recruit. John Huston is the director and Audie Murphy is the young soldier. At the beginning, Murphy gripes openly among his comrades about the useless drilling and the endless marching and is impatient for the first battle. Inwardly, however, he is worried about his reaction in actual battle – will he show fear and run? During the first enemy attack, he becomes part of the whole; he fires his rifle into the advancing Confederates and watches them fall back. A moment of pride engulfs him; he has been tested and has come through. Suddenly, however, the enemy mounts a cavalry charge. This time he breaks ranks and runs, witnessing the deaths of his comrades. When he rejoins his unit, his initial fear turns to rage against the enemy. Almost unconsciously, he picks up a flag and leads his regiment in an advance. When the din of battle subsides, his buddies praise his courage as they march off. The youth is satisfied with himself. A narrator, quoting from the novel, says: "He had been to touch the great death and found that, after all, it was but the great death."

The narrator quotes passages from the original book. For instance, when the youth sees all the wounded, the narrator remarks: "He wished, too, that he had a wound – a red badge of courage." John Huston directed the film without any glamour or glory and, instead, presented a grim, stark depiction of men at war. Audie Murphy, who was the most decorated hero of World War II, was cast against type. He subsequently developed a long career in films, playing leads in action, adventure and Western dramas.

Revolt at Fort Laramie (1957), UA. Dir. Lesley Selander; Sc. Robert C. Dennis; Cast includes: John Dehner, Gregg Palmer, Frances Helm, Don Gordon.

The start of the Civil War causes additional problems for a cavalry outpost already plagued by Indian unrest. John Dehner, as a Virginian major in charge of Fort Laramie, prepares to pull out those troops loyal to the Confederacy. He turns over the command to the Northern captain (Gregg Palmer) who is faced by Chief Red Cloud's demand of $50,000 in gold. Once outside the fort, the hostile Indians attack the major and his Southerners. The Northern captain gallops out of the fort and leads his troops to the rescue their Southern comrades.

Revolt at Fort Laramie is another entry in a handful of films in which troops, split in their allegiances between North and South, ultimately join forces to fight the Indians. In Hollywood, it seems that as bitter as the sectional hatred was, the Indians represented the greater foe. In all of these features, there is a subliminal racist message when Northern and Southern troops unite against the Indians.

Ride with the Devil (1999), USA Films. Dir. Ang Lee; Sc. James Schamus; Cast includes: Skeet Ulrich, Tobey Maguire Roedel, Jewel Kilcher, Jeffrey Wright, Simon Baker.

Ang Lee's stirring Civil War drama concentrates on an obscure incident in this tragic war. The film really explores the nature of evil and how normally good people sometimes choose to "ride with the devil." While large armies were fighting in the South, a dirty conflict arose along the Missouri-Kansas border in 1862 between the pro-Union jayhawkers and the Confederate-sympathizing bushwhackers. Both groups, composed chiefly of young men barely old enough to join the army, resembled gangs rather than uniformed and organized troops. Lust and money rather than ideology usually motivated them. They subsequently randomly robbed and murdered anyone who stood in their path.

Jake Roedel (Tobey Maguire) breaks with his immigrant pro-Northern father and joins the Confederate bushwhackers simply to be with most of his boyhood pals. Daniel Holt (Jeffrey Wright), a freed slave, also joins the bushwhackers out of loyalty to his benefactor and friend, George Clyde (Simon Baker). The psychologically disturbed and racist Pitt Mackeson (Rhys Meyers) respects no one, regardless of their loyalty, if they are not part of his small world. Soon Black John (James Caviezel) joins them and begins to take charge.

The film generally avoids the familiar romanticism and epic sentimentality (except for the last scene) often found in Civil War dramas. Jake Roedel is tested for loyalty and courage and a major portion of the plot suggests Jake's coming of age. The director moves between stylized old-fashioned dialogue and poetic settings (such as the winter scenes during a lull in the fighting) and extremely realistic battles. In these battle scenes, a sense of nihilism and moral chaos is suggested when homes are burned and numerous people are killed. One particularly bloody encounter takes place at an abolitionist stronghold when the defenders are gruesomely slaughtered. The bloody sequences only emphasize the senseless carnage in this conflict.

Rocky Mountain (1950), WB. Dir. William Keighley; Sc. Winston Miller, Alan LeMay; Cast includes: Errol Flynn, Patrice Wymore, Scott Forbes, Guinn Williams.

In William Keighley's outdoor drama, a band of Confederate soldiers, led by their stalwart officer (Errol Flynn), meet at a Western rendezvous with a gang of California outlaws. They want to help the Confederacy gain control of the territory. The Confederates and the outlaws face hostile Indians, a vast desert and patrols of Union soldiers. As they wait for the rendezvous, Flynn and his men rescue a stagecoach from a group of hostile Indians. The passenger, a Northern woman (Patrice Wymore), has journeyed West to marry her Union lover. A Union patrol is sent to meet Wymore and accompany her to the fort. However, Flynn decides to use her as bait to capture the Union soldiers. Soon, the small Union force is threatened by a larger number of hostile Indians. Flynn, a Southern gentleman to the end, leads his men to divert the Indians and engage them in battle. They sacrifice their lives so that the woman can make it to safety.

Sam Davis, The Hero of Tennessee (1915), Connor. Sc. Lillian Nicholson Shearon.

This early silent drama captures the highlights of Samuel Davis' career during the Civil War. Following real life, Davis becomes involved with rebel spies, is caught carrying their military secrets to his own lines and is hanged by Union troops. Unlike reality, however, the film introduces a female spy. She works for the South and attracts the attention of a Union captain. She soon tricks the captain into sketching out future battle plans. The pretty spy takes the plans and turns them over to a fellow spy who, masquerading as a doctor, has penetrated Union lines. He, in turn, hands them to Sam Davis and tells him to deliver them to the Southern military staff. Davis rides off with the important map but is captured by Northern troops who then sentence him to hang. Davis goes to his death a Southern hero.

*

Samuel Davis (1844-1863) was a product of Rutherford County, Tennessee, where he had the misfortune to get caught up in the torrents of the Civil War. Tennessee had seceded from the Union and Davis, an uneducated farmer, joined the state's infantry and participated in the Battle of Stones River at the end of 1862 and the Battle of Chickamauga in September 1863, both under the leadership of General Bragg.

In the fall of 1863 Davis was sent as a scout to reconnoiter Union positions in Tennessee and Alabama. He was soon assigned as a full-time spy to Captain Henry Shaw, who ran the intelligence service for General Bragg. Davis was sent back through Union lines on several other occasions. In November 1863, Shaw and Davis set off for Pulaski, Tennessee, which was within Union lines. They split up and Davis continued north where he joined Confederate agents who provided him with plans of Union fortifications in Tennessee. After meeting with these agents, Davis was stopped by two men in Confederate Army uniforms who were actually working for the Union counterintelligence unit of General Naron. Upon producing Confederate Army identification, Davis was seized; his secret documents were discovered and he was delivered to General Naron.

Davis was given the choice of execution or revealing his Confederate contacts; the Southern agent steadfastly refused to name his co-conspirators, whereupon he was court-martialed and hanged on November 27, 1863.

Southern Yankee, A (1948), MGM. Dir. Edward Sedgwick; Sc. Harry Tugend; Cast includes: Red Skelton, Brian Donlevy, Arlene Dahl, George Coulouris, Lloyd Gough, John Ireland.

Red Skelton portrays a bungling bellhop who daydreams about catching Confederate spies for the U.S. Secret Service in Edward Sedgwick's Civil War comedy. Working in a St. Louis, Missouri, hotel, he spends more time pestering a Union colonel to hire him as a secret agent than he does at his job. The colonel, however, has more serious concerns. The South's most successful spy, known as the Gray Spider, has infiltrated the North's top command and has been stealing its military maps and plans. Skelton, while delivering a major's uniform to one of the hotel rooms, stumbles upon the officer's secret identity – the notorious Gray Spider. When the spy (George Coulouris) returns to his room, a scuffle ensues and Skelton accidentally knocks the spy unconscious and assumes his identity. He then notifies the Union colonel and the spy is arrested. The colonel then sends the reluctant Skelton, who would rather catch spies than impersonate them, behind enemy lines with false battle plans.

The comic predicaments do not come naturally from the material itself. They depend chiefly on false identities, mix-ups, chases and slapstick. There are some clever moments, including one scene in which Skelton, caught in the midst of battle, is dressed half in Yankee uniform and half in Confederate uniform. Carrying flags of both armies, he nonchalantly parades between both forces who cheer his bravery. When the wind reverses the flags, both armies begin to fire upon him. Verbal humor, for the most part, is weak, although there is one bright spot when the exasperated Union colonel tries to spell out Skelton's dual mission: to turn over the false map to a Confederate officer and give another secret paper to a fellow agent. "The paper's in the pocket of the boot with the buckle, and the map is in the packet in the pocket of the jacket," the officer explains. Naturally, this befuddles Skelton.

Tap Roots (1948), UI. Dir. George Marshall; Sc. Alan LeMay; Cast includes: Van Heflin, Susan Hayward, Boris Karloff, Julie London.

In George Marshall's drama, the Dabney clan of Mississippi's Lebanon Valley and a group of neighboring farmers have prospered on their plantations and abolished slavery in their corner of the state. Determined to secede from the rest of the state as well as from the Confederacy, they raise their own army. Ward Bond, as Dabney, the acknowledged leader of the valley, entreats his neighbors to avoid the impending civil war. When the state secedes from the

Union, the valley withdraws from the state. Newspaper publisher Van Heflin believes in the farmers' cause and falls in love with Dabney's strong-willed daughter (Susan Hayward). Family members are willing to take on the Confederate Army in order to protect their plantation and remain neutral during the conflict between North and South. Julie London plays Hayward's younger passionate sister. Boris Karloff, as an Indian, is a loyal friend to the family. The superior Southern troops decimate the brave but ill-equipped force in a pathetic battle. However, Heflin rescues the wounded Bond and they seek shelter in a cabin, where Hayward joins her father and the man she has grown to love. The farmers reorganize and finally drive the invading army from the once-peaceful valley.

The film, adapted from the novel by James Street, was based on an actual incident during the war. Southern troops crushed a seditious Mississippi community that seceded from the state and declared its independence and neutrality. The lopsided battle occurred at Lebanon Valley where the defenders were slaughtered. Marshall's drama was one of the earliest Hollywood productions to break the mold of the idealized plantation of the ante-bellum South.

Two Flags West (1950), TCF. Dir. Robert Wise; Sc. Casey Robinson; Cast includes: Joseph Cotten, Linda Darnell, Jeff Chandler, Cornel Wilde, Dale Robertson.

In Robert Wise's Western drama, Confederate prisoners of war volunteer to help Northern troops man an outpost. They drop their plan to escape and, instead, return to help their Union white brothers when the Indians attack. Another Civil War outdoor film, which has been transplanted to the West, the plot is based on fact. In 1865, the Union recruited Confederate prisoners to help guard Western army posts. Joseph Cotten portrays a Confederate colonel who volunteers to man one such outpost, together with his fellow prisoners,. He hopes to avoid the ordeal of prison life while attempting an escape. A Union officer, Cornel Wilde, is assigned to guard these men while they are transported to Jeff Chandler's fort. Chandler is a bitter officer who has been wounded and crippled in his first engagement early in the war. Linda Darnell, his widowed sister-in-law, lives with him at the fort. Chandler loves the beautiful widow, but Wilde soon also falls in love with her. Chandler murders a local Indian chief's son, so the Indians decide to retaliate and attack the fort. At this point, Cotton and his Southern officers escape, but they soon decide to return to help their Northern counterparts fight the common Indian enemy. The Indians get their revenge when they kill Chandler.

Bibliography

Addiego, Walter, "Haunting *Beloved*," *San Francisco Examiner*, Oct. 16, 1998.

Agee, James, and Walker Evans, *Let Us Now Praise Famous Men.* Boston: Houghton Mifflin, 1961.

Anderson, Nancy Scott, *The Generals: Ulysses S. Grant and Robert E. Lee.* New York: Vintage Books, 1989.

Anglesworth, Thomas G., *The Southeast: Georgia, Kentucky, Tennessee.* New York: Chelsea House, 1996.

Archer, Jules, *A House Divided: The Lives of Ulysses. S. Grant and Robert E. Lee.* New York: Scholastic, 1995.

Arnold, Jams R., *Grant Wins the War: Decision at Vicksburg.* New York: John Wiley, 1997.

Bartlett, Irving H., *John C. Calhoun: A Biography.* New York: Norton, 1993.

Bergman, Andrew, *We're in the Money: Depression America and Its Films.* New York: Harper, 1972.

Blassingame, John W (editor), *Slave Testimony: Two Centuries of Letters, Speeches, Interviews and Autobiographies.* Baton Rouge, LA: Louisiana State University, 1977.

Budd, Louis, *Our Mark Twain.* Philadelphia: University of Pennsylvania Press, 1987.

Burns, Robert Elliott, *I am a Fugitive from a Georgia Chain Gang.* Detroit: Gale Research, 1972.

Caldwell, Erskine, *The Complete Stories of Erskine Caldwell.* Boston: Little, Brown, 1941.

Carlson, Margaret, "A Terminal Case of Telling the Truth," *Time*, May 11, 1998.

Carter, Hodding, *Southern Legacy.* Baton Rouge, LA: Louisiana State University, 1950.

Catton, Bruce, *The American Heritage New History of the Civil War.* New York: Viking, 1996.

Cooper, William J., *Jefferson Davis, American.* New York: Knopf, 2000.

Corliss, Richard, "*Eve's Bayou*: Getting Down to Family Values," *Time*, Oct. 13, 1997.

Cox, Clinton, *Fiery Vision: The Life and Death of John Brown.* New York: Scholastic Press, 1997.

Crane, Stephen, *The Red Badge of Courage.* Hauppauge, NY: Barron's, 1999.

Diggins, John P., *On Hallowed Ground: Abraham Lincoln and the Foundation of American History.* New Haven: Yale University Press, 2000.

Dodd, William Edward, *The Cotton Kingdom.* New York: Glasgow Brook, 1919.

Ebert, Roger, "*The Client*," *Chicago Sun-Times*, July 20, 1994.

Faulkner, William, *Absalom, Absalom.* Thorndike, ME: G.K. Hall, 1997.

Faulkner, William, *As I Lay Dying.* New York: Vintage Books, 1985.

Faulkner, William, *Novels, 1942-1954.* New York: Library of America, 1994.

Faulkner, William, *The Sound of Fury.* New York: Norton, 1987.

Fellman, Michael, *The Making of Robert E. Lee.* New York: Random House, 2000.

Freedman, Suzanne, *Roger Taney: The Dred Scott Legacy.* Springfield, NJ: Enslow Publishers, 1995.

Gaines, Francis Pendleton, *The Southern Plantation: A Study in the Development and the Accuracy of a Tradition.* Gloucester, MS: Smith, 1962.

Gaston, Paul M., *The New South Creed: A Study in Southern Mythmaking.* New York: Alfred A. Knopf, 1970.

Griffin, Alice, *Understanding Lillian Hellman.* Columbia, SC: University of South Carolina Press, 1999.

Haskins, James, *The Scottsboro Boys.* New York: Henry Holt, 1994.

Hellman, Lillian, *Another Part of the Forest.* New York: Dramatists Play Service, 1947.

Hellman, Lillian, *The Children's Hour.* New York: Dramatists Play Service, 1953.

Hellman, Lillian, *The Collected Plays.* Boston: Little, Brown, 1972.

Hobson, Fred C., *Serpent in Eden: H. L. Mencken and the South.* Chapel Hill: University of North Carolina Press, 1974.

Holden, Steven, "*Down in the Delta*: Family Values," *The New York Times*, Dec. 25, 1998.

Jacobs, William Jay, *Lincoln.* New York: Scribner's Sons, 1991.

Kael, Pauline, *Reeling.* Boston: Little, Brown, 1976.

Kempley, Rita, "Blood in the Face," *Washington Post*, May 17, 1991.

Kirby, Jack Temple, *Media-Made Dixie: The South in the American Imagination.* Athens, GA.: The University of Georgia Press, 1986.

Kirby, Jack Temple, *Darkness at the Dawning: Race and Reform in the Progressive South.* Philadelphia: J. B. Lippincott, 1972

LaSalle, Nick, "*Chamber's* a Hollow, Tawdry Tale of Death Row," *San Francisco Chronicle*, Oct. 11, 1996.

Leadbelly, *Leadbelly, No Stranger to the Blues: The Songs of Huddie Ledbetter.* New York: TRO Folkways, 1998.

Maslin, Janet, "*Amistad*: The Pain of Captivity Made Real," *The New York Times*, Dec. 10, 1997.

McCullers, Carson, *Collected Stories.* Boston: Houghton Mifflin, 1987.

McIlwaine, Shields, *The Southern Poor White: From Lubberland to Tobacco Road.* Baton Rouge: Louisiana State University Press, 1939.

Mico, Ted, John Miller-Monzon, and David Rubel, eds., *Past Imperfect: History According to the Movies.* New York: Holt, 1995.

Nichols, Peter N., editor, *The New York Times Guide to the Best 1,000 Movies Ever Made.* New York: Random House, 1999.

O'Connor, John E., and Martin A. Jackson, eds., *American History/American Film: Interpreting the Hollywood Image.* New York: Ungar Publishing, 1979.

Osborne, John, *The Old South: Alabama, Florida, Georgia, Mississippi, South Carolina.* New York: Time-Life Books, 1968.

Perret, Geoffrey, *Ulysses S. Grant: Soldier and President.* New York: Random House, 1999.

Phillips, Ulrich Bonnell, *Life and Labor in the Old South.* Boston: Little, Brown, 1929.

Ramsaye, Terry, *A Million and One Nights: A History of the Motion Picture.* New York: Simon and Schuster, 1986.

Randall, J.G., *The Civil War and Reconstruction.* Lexington, MS: Heath, 1969.

Schickel, Richard, *D. W. Griffith: An American Life.* New York: Simon and Schuster, 1984.

Schwartz, Barry, *Abraham Lincoln and the Forge of National Memory.* Chicago: University of Chicago Press, 2000.

Shepard, Jim, "*Chinatown*: Jolting Noir With a Shot of Nihilism," *The New York Times*, Feb. 7, 1999.

Shulgasser, Barbara, "Anjelica Huston Shines As Director of *Bastard*," *San Francisco Examiner*, Apr. 25, 1997.

Stokesbury, James L., *A Short History of the Civil War.* New York: William Morrow, 1995.

Stowe, Harriet Beeecher, *Uncle Tom's Cabin.* New York: Signet Classic, 1981.

Thompson, Holland, *The New South.* New Haven, CT: Yale University Press, 1919.

Tindall, George B., *The Emergence of the New South, 1913-1945.* Baton Rouge: Louisiana State University Press, 1967.

Twain, Mark, *Adventures of Huckleberry Finn.* New York: Signet Classic, 1997.

Twain, Mark, *The Adventures of Tom Sawyer.* New York: Signet Classic, 1997.

Walker, Alice, *The Color Purple*. Boston: G.K. Hall, 1986.

Warren, Robert Penn, *A Robert Penn Warren Reader*. New York: Random House, 1987.

Washington, Booker T., *Up From Slavery*. New York: Oxford University Press, 1995.

Watters, Pat, *The South and the Nation*. New York: Pantheon Books, 1969.

Wiencek, Henry, *Plantations of the Old South*. Los Angeles: Knapp Press, 1988.

Wilkins, J. Steven, *Call of Duty: The Sterling Nobility of Robert E. Lee*. Nashville: Cumberland House Publications, 1997.

Williams, Tennessee, *Plays*. New York: Library of America, 2000.

Winders, Gertrude, *Jim Bowie: Boy with a Hunting Knife*. Indianapolis: Bobbs-Merrill, 1961.

Woodworth, Steven E., *Davis and Lee at War*. Lawrence, KS: University of Kansas Press, 1995.

Woodworth, Steven E., *Jefferson Davis and His Generals: The Failure of Confederate Command in the West*. Lawrence, KS: University Press of Kansas, 1990.

Wright, Courtni Crump, *Journey to Freedom: A Story of the Underground Railroad*. New York: Holiday House, 1994.

Title Index

About the Compilers

LARRY LANGMAN is the author of *A Guide to Silent Westerns* (Greenwood, 1992), *A Guide to American Crime Films of the Forties and Fifties* (Greenwood, 1995), and *American Film Cycles: The Silent Era* (Greenwood, 1998).

DAVID EBNER has taught mathematics and history on the university and secondary school levels and has published extensively in professional journals. His books include *The Encyclopedia of American Spy Films*.